ROAD TRIP
TO THE
FUTURE

Between the Lines Publishing
1769 Lexington Ave N, Ste 286
Roseville MN 55113
btwnthelines.com

First Published: April 2024

ISBN: (Paperback) 978-1-958901-84-7
ISBN: (Ebook) 978-1-958901-85-4

ROAD TRIP

TO THE

FUTURE

ROGER MOURAD JR.

For old friends, some lost, others found

On madness and other maladies

After the shock went through my body, the unreality of lightness descended. White light. The cab disappeared into the gray of the city, down the line. Lost among the Ubers. Then there was me, standing and staring, stunned, here on this cracked up sidewalk in Chicago. What just happened, and what the hell do I tell Lew? One thing's for certain. There's blood on my hands. Alright. Get a grip. Try to walk straight and keep from stepping on the carcasses propped up against the Old Town storefronts, with their little signs about the God-Child and dented tin bowls. I'm fucking freezing, with nothing under this coat except the insulation that adheres to the body and remains stuck in the mind. The insulation acquired from growing up in the deathly silence of white Grosse Pointe, not far from the invisible wall that divides it from black Detroit. How did it get to this point? Much time has elapsed, memory is unreliable, and given all the calamities that Lew and I have managed to create over the last few days, I oughta be satisfied I'm still standing.

"Quit bitching," Lew said a couple days ago, when we still had a purpose, however suspect. It's an old conflict of ours. I want things to be a certain way and Lew sees things as they seem to be. Or so he thinks. He'd taken action, seen the world, while I tried to hold on to an idea, that the Gods knew the way. What I will do is tell you, as best I can remember, when the madness might've begun, and how it manifested itself on this little journey that Lew and I took to rescue an old friend, which was itself a kind of madness. Chasing after someone, some ghost whose worth I was ambivalent about from the get-go. A road trip amid terrible insights and visions that appear and won't go away.

It all started last week, when I received an unexpected email from Lew about an old friend who had gone missing. It said something like, "I'm coming to Michigan, get my car tuned up, we need to go to Chicago to save Cam." Cam? I had to think for a few seconds before my brain found that name in the registry. Last I heard, from somebody I met in a bar some years back, Cam had gotten rich as a management consultant and then got in trouble with several governments about an offshore shell game thing. Supposedly. And "my car," what car was Lew talking about? I tried to e-mail him back, no reply, tried calling, he didn't pick up my calls, so I figured he's probably one of those people, like my kids, one on each coast, who text instead of talk. That ludicrous activity of tapping little characters with your thumbs and forefingers, like the fucking apes we are. One letter at a time, are you kidding me?

I left a voice message a couple of times, asking what's going on with Cam, but Lew didn't call back. Then I used my wife Ginny's phone to text him, on account of the fact that my phone, being a flip-phone, doesn't do texts. I send him a single word: CAR? And what does Lew do? He texts back almost immediately. Which meant he could've picked up my call. Still an asshole. His text said, "Cam's in some kind of trouble in Chicago. Get the LeMans tuned up, I'm flying into Saginaw via Toronto on Sunday, you'll need to pick me up." Saginaw? Didn't know it had an airport. Fuck him if he wants me to do all this shit and he can't even make the effort to talk to me. And ask nicely.

Couple days later, I was sitting at home on the floor of my wee guitar room, trying to get my Epiphone to sound like a Gibson in open G tuning for that gritty old Rolling Stones sound. My ancient Strat was laid up in the corner, out of commission. Almost as old as me. Needs a tune-up, but I'm too lazy to do it myself, and too cheap to have it done by somebody else. It's post-Christmas break, a break from driving all those miles to teach for pocket change. Time to play guitar, but no desire. Alone, in guitar ghetto.

I'm surrounded by CDs all over the floor. CDs, yeah, try not to laugh. Can't adapt to the whole download thing. Yeah, I know, you can keep millions of songs on your handheld. Or better, you can go high and get your music from a cloud, whatever that is. Stream. But real streams are here on Earth and I need things I can see and hold to make sense of the world, even though when it comes to anything involving coordination between brain and body in the exercise of a skill, I'm inherently a hack. Except for casting a fly in tight places. And parallel parking, I've always been really good at that. I'd rather fumble around through a pile of CDs like an idiot 'til I fling them when they skip or don't play. You know, when these things came out, the big marketing schtick was, not only are they smaller than LPs, they sound way better, don't scratch, and the recording is "digitally remastered." Bad jokes.

There I was, sitting on the floor, fumbling around, winging a few of those CDs against the wall, making a lot of noise. Empty bottle of Black Stallion Stout next to me, and another one tipped over on the floor. Half drunk, half spilled black liquid on refurbished hardwood.

"You need to stop this," Ginny said.

I watched the black slowly spread and stain the floor. Lick the floor, that's what Iggy Pop would do, even now, even as an old man. But I didn't have the energy, and then there's all the dust you can't see that wouldn't be good for my body, given all its maladies. I just watched that black creep toward my crotch. Like missed opportunities that take a long time to expire.

"Stop this," Ginny said again.

3

"I'm going through something." The kids hadn't come home for the holidays this year, too much work to do, they said. Whenever I ask them to explain exactly what it is they do for a living, I don't understand their answers. I'd like to think that's only because after a minute or two, I lose interest and choose not to listen carefully enough.

"You're always going through something," Ginny said. "Lighten up."

Ouch. That was possibly, no, likely true. Ohhh, Ginn, why, why do you treat me this way? Why do you treat me this way?

"It's not that simple," I said.

"You make everything too complicated."

Maybe so. But there is no simple, that's what the French philosopher Jacques Derrida said. There are, however, recurring dreams, nightmares, and visions. And bad experiences, like watching a tribute concert the other night. Maybe that's what Ginny was pissed at me about. She thought I'd like watching this show of kiddie bands I never heard of, a tribute to Led Zeppelin on Netflix. It was thoughtful of her, a gesture to cheer me up. I merely noted that some young stiff's guitar solo in "Stairway to Heaven" was lightweight. She got mad and said something like, "Why can't you get off your righteous cloud and just enjoy the show?" It was a rhetorical question.

I think Ginn pushing the tribute show was her stab at trying to compensate for insisting we leave the Alice Cooper concert a couple weeks ago, after barely three-quarters of an hour. I can't really blame her; we were in the middle of a crowd of white people with tattoos and metal piercings all over their bodies. A screaming bunch of rejects acting all American guts and glory. I noticed a couple of the black security detail exchange a glance. I wanted to say to them, the two of us, we're cultural anthropologists, just here to do field work. You know, participant observation. Ginny just wanted to get the hell out of there. She coulda been a little more flexible, she might've tolerated another half-hour until Alice got guillotined. On the way home, I tried to explain that Alice Cooper is just shtick, he doesn't want

4

you to take him seriously, all the stage props were analog. She pointed out that all those people in the crowd seemed to take it seriously.

Which is interesting.

I watched the spilt black stout reach my crotch. "I just need a drummer."

Ginny didn't respond. In her defense, she'd heard it before. It was then that I told her, I had made a very big decision.

"I'm going away for a few days."

"Where?"

She worried about me too much for my own good. Yes, my own good.

"Chicago. To see Cam." Cam's someone she'd heard of but never met, so no risk there, except of the unknown variety. I wasn't gonna tell her that Cam had gone dark. Dare I say the next thing? I did. I have this terrible problem of filling in gaps in discourse before they become uncomfortable, a problem, yes, for my own good. "With Lew."

Right then, I kid you not, my balls went cold from the great black wet. Stout shouldn't be refrigerated.

"Lew? Lew? That's great."

Which meant she didn't really like this idea. She didn't know Cam, but she had known Lew a long time ago, and hadn't exactly liked him. Thought he was a bad influence on account of he and I having lived the high life in our younger days. Which didn't give me much credit. As a matter of fact, Ginn never liked any of my old friends. Thought they were a bunch of assholes. She wasn't the first person to express that opinion. At least they're my kind of assholes. It's actually a personal point of pride. A kind of badge of courage, to have friends who are assholes. There's a certain undervalued art to it. Even Cam, who everybody back in the day liked, was an asshole after you spent enough time with him. Besides, some people think I'm an asshole. Anyhew, my old friends, these assholes, there aren't many left, just a few and they all live far away in places where I'll never go, like Melbourne and Zurich and Cardiff-by-the-Sea, the beach town north of La Jolla, that is. And I don't use Facebook or any of that other crap, too bad for me.

I can't blame Ginny for not liking Lew and the others, although her standards were a little unfair considering she didn't have many friends either. On the other hand, her friends actually live here in Ann Arbor, and she has actual relationships with them.

At that point in our dialogue, I decided to take Ginn's suggestion and make things a little lighter with an encore, for all of the quasi-appreciative folks who may be out there in the crowd.

"Yeah, Lew. As in 'Louie-Louie.' I got to go."

"Free association is dim and boring and gets you nowhere."

Ouch. Our marriage had become kinda shaky. It's not a new condition. While I was spinning in circles, Ginny had gone corporate. A psychiatric nurse once, she's now into something called strategic planning and special projects. She said she'd been targeted, whatever that means. Sounds military. Now she's on track to being a VP at this big hospital system run by a bunch of nuns, while I'm still driving all over the place, teaching at four different community colleges, making barely living wage and relying on her benefits to cover my array of medical problems. Teaching philosophy, sort of. Something I used to dig, now just a chore. I'd stopped trying to give essay exams, none of the kids can write, maybe I'm partly to blame. Or mostly to blame. Maybe I could work harder. Too burned out, so I resort to multiple choice. Easier to succeed, or guess right, and easier to grade. This is what happens if you don't finish your dissertation and remain permanently stuck in a condition called All-But-Dissertation.

Ginny and I had never actually gotten married. Unless you count going to the local magistrate's office to get it done, which in terms of procedure was not all that different from getting a permit to raise chickens in the backyard. Point being, we weren't married in a church. Lapsed Catholics, that's what the priest at each of the churches in Ann Arbor said. I don't know if it's an official Church term, but it sounds kinda mysterious, like the idea of space-time. Eventually we found a unitarian minister. Some guy who had supposedly quit, or got kicked out of, a Jesuit seminary in San Francisco. When we were planning our vows, he said he'd recite whatever we wanted, with one exception. He wouldn't say the word "god." Which totally pissed me off. We're paying him, what's the big deal? We hadn't even brought it up, the god-word. Why should he give a shit? It's not like we expected him to swear fealty to any particular otherworldly entity. What's the dude's hang-up? Why the fuck can't he say god? It's just a word, and we can't get out of words anyway. So, I said, fuck this.

Ginn was probably still a little mad at me for disrupting our neighbor daughter's holiday violin recital last Saturday. It wasn't my fault; my bladder was full of Saint Pauli Girl, I had to pee, and there are abnormalities involved. You see, most people, when they pee, they have two forces to work with. There's contraction of the bladder, and gravity. Whereas I rely on gravity and catheters because my bladder doesn't contract. The urine just kind of falls out rather than squirts. With the consequences that A, the sound of urine hitting the water is loud and B, it takes a long while to complete the process. A slow loud ripple. In this particular instance, how was I supposed to know that it was so loud it practically drowned out the violin? I hadn't been in the neighbor's house before, much less used their bathroom, so did not—could not—know the finer points about its acoustics. In a rational world, I would've had the opportunity to evaluate the situation ahead of time, conduct a test, and on the basis of its results, formulate a plan. That opportunity had not been afforded me.

Maybe they should have had carpeting. Maybe if the bathroom door had been located on the other side there wouldn't have been a problem. I'm not blaming anybody, but there were a lot of variables involved. For example, how could the home builder have neglected to consider the possibility that someone with a non-functioning bladder might use that bathroom during a recital? In the civil state of nature that we live in, there's much that occurs by chance. One thing happens, somebody reacts to it, and then you get these squiggly strings of events, because people are complex organisms. Too many unmeasurable, not to mention unanticipated, variables. Not everyone is normal.

In any event, all I could prepare was my defense for the walk home. Which would be tough, since I'd been a thoroughly disinterested law school student. How could I persuade Ginny that I had tried to do the right thing? That I had not wanted to attend the recital in the first place, that I was only being group-minded, and that during the urination I had stifled a strong sudden urge to belt out the first verse of a Bob Dylan tune? The one about the daughter of an old guy who wouldn't give him a break. "Tears of Rage." And the inner struggle that had ensued. That I was also blameless, for the reason that the homeowners had made the Saint Pauli Girl visible there in the fridge, hence available, and before their daughter's recital? I even wiped the rim of the toilet bowl with the double-ply after the urine was fully excised. Which may not seem relevant, Your Honor, but is evidence of good faith. All I needed were the right words, the best arrangement of characters in space, to effectively persuade while remaining truly self-critical, and thereby honest.

Well, Ginny didn't buy it. Ginn can be tough, but she's got her shit together. Grounded. Frankly, I suspect that we'd all be a helluva lot better off if people like her did all the judging. Mainly women, that is, broadly defined in all its fluidity. It's the hardcore men on the planet who tend to create all sorts of problems by their unchecked obsession with trying to leave the ground. A lot easier for women, at least, women with their head screwed on like Ginn, to drop the pursuit of all things strategic for all things Good. No doubt, they wouldn't be so uptight about maintaining make-believe borders of all kinds. They wouldn't tolerate all the needless suffering in the name of money and security. All the guns. All the fear. All the killing.

She was right about the dim and free association bit, though. My intellect, while high on the verbal side, is mediocre on spatial reasoning.

That combination, although maybe exceptional, isn't necessarily a good thing. I found that out from a bunch of tests after I had been in a coma. The first thing the neuropsychologist said was that there were no major problems. There was only one area where there was a deficit, my short-term memory. I had a helluva time trying to remember how to fit the blocks together with my eyes closed. Or something like that.

"The most very interesting thing is your IQ," he said. "You're in the ninety-ninth percentile for verbal comprehension, but barely average on spatial reasoning." Then he gave me a serious look. "I must tell you, having the one so high and the other so much lower is rare. It puts you on the extreme end of your segment of the population."

The "most very?" He seemed to find it intellectually stimulating, as if this was a dramatic moment in his professional life. What was I supposed to do with that? What segment do I belong to? Like a line segment? If I'm on the extreme end of the segment, does that mean I could fall off? And memory issues. Is that why I drove in circles? Did that explain my frustration with trying to put thoughts together? In elementary school I was good at spelling bees until the nuns, in their divine creativity and general boredom with life, flipped the game upside-down. Instead of giving you a word to spell, they'd recite the spelling, a letter at a time, and you had to blurt out the correct word before the kid on the other team did. I lost every time. I mean, every fucking time, for years. It was an awful feeling, not being able to put the letters that hovered out there in space back together, making all language beyond my cognitive reach. Felt like utter helplessness, like getting hit with multiple calamities at once.

But I digress. Back to Lew. I had seen him just a handful of times over the last thirty years. He was always on the move, working around the world, though we had kinda stayed in touch, mainly by my efforts. To hear from him across the digital void was practically an event, like a transformative shift. At least I thought it could be, reconnecting to try and find an old friend. So, yeah, I'll do it. I need a comrade and a tangible purpose. Didn't really fathom how we were gonna find someone in a huge metropolis, but I wanted to see Lew. Go back out on the road with him like we'd done so many times so long ago, us against the world. It could be an adventure, like Bilbo Baggins and his tall sidekick, that Strider guy.

I first met Lew in grade school. Lew Rozin. He had moved to Grosse Pointe Woods from somewhere in upstate New York when he was just a tyke. His dad, Ben, sold insurance and got transferred to southeast Michigan. Lew's real name was Lewis Rosenberg, and his father was Jewish. Ben liked to tell people that he was the only Jew in Grosse Pointe. Lew said his dad even bragged about it with neighbors. Which embarrassed Lew. In any case, Lew was the only son of a Jew I could know back then because his father probably really was the only Jew in Grosse Pointe. Lew himself was only sort of Jewish on account of the fact that his mother Mary was Catholic. Not only that, but she also insisted that Lew and his little sister Mona be raised Catholic, at least for a while. According to Lew, Ben didn't really give a shit one way or the other. This was back in the Sixties, and Lew said his dad liked to think of himself as a kind of rebel. Maybe that was his way of coping with his otherness. Ben knew Mary wasn't Jewish before he knew her name. He didn't even mind getting married in a Catholic church, although his family didn't care for all the hocus pocus. Then he left them for Michigan, which to his family was like going to an East European country after the Soviets took over. Ben also liked to tell people, "I'm from upstate." He'd just conveniently leave out the part about New York, so they'd think he was referring to northern Michigan. It gave him a sense of place, because like a lot of white men who went to northern Michigan on weekends, Ben hunted and fished.

When Lew was old enough for Catholic school, Mary fretted about him being singled out if the teachers saw "Rosenberg." Ben shrugged and suggested they just drop the "berg." Mary thought that wasn't enough. Ben had another idea.

10

"Change the S to a Z and the E to an A. 'Rozan.' Sounds French, like the sculptor."

"That's not the name of the sculptor," Mary said, "and it's no good, either." She thought "Rozan" looked and sounded like some kind of circus performer or magician. They made the E an I. "Rozin." Never mind the school would see "Rosenberg" on their kids' birth certificates. Then again, Ben didn't give a shit. Besides, Lady of the Lake was desperate to cram as many students into classrooms as they could, Catholic or not, because they needed the cash.

Lady of the Lake Elementary. The kids called it Tuna Tech. The church was on prime real estate on Lakeshore Drive, right between two mansions. You'd walk out after Sunday Mass, the sunlight would be shining on the lake, and people thought that meant the gods were pleased with their moral lives. Anyway, when we were kids at Tuna Tech, Lew was a playmate like any other. We played marbles behind the school during lunch, and tackle football in the parking lot after school. He was big and pudgy and tackled hard, and in marbles, he always seemed to have the most boulders and puries. Once, when I beat Lew for the grandest marble of all, a gold purie boulder, he grabbed it in his big fat fist and refused to give it to me. Asshole. I called him fat and tried to punch him, but he just held it high and laughed, called me a little punk. I was lucky he didn't take a swing at me. Nobody fucked with him, not even with him being Jewish. Not after he kicked the shit out of a snot-nosed Irish kid named Danny who called him Lew the Jew.

When Mona got the green dye washed out of her hair by Sister Serious on Saint Patrick's Day, she was practically burned. That was too much even for Ben. He raised a fit and Mary had to pull both Mona and Lew out of Tuna Tech and put them in Grosse Pointe Public. After that I didn't see Lew for a few years. Until high school, when my parents finally let me out, because the only boys' Catholic high school in Grosse Pointe had closed and the nearest one was a long bus ride deep into black Detroit. I transferred in ninth grade to Grosse Pointe South High. It was a shock because you could wear whatever you wanted, and it was easy to sneak a smoke in the boys' bathroom. Lew was a lot different by then. His hair was down below his shoulders, and he wasn't chubby anymore. In fact, he'd become a jock. By our junior year he was all-state in butterfly. Six foot four and lean with big shoulders shaped like a V, he was a star tight end who knocked linebackers on their asses and caught passes over their heads. That is, 'til he blew out one of his knees in the North-South game our senior year.

Here's a key historical piece about Lew that drew me to him. He listened to rock bands before they became mainstream, if they ever did. Like Queen. Not the Queen of the *Night at the Opera* album. Before that. The Queen of *Queen One* and *Queen Two*. And Roxy Music, when they were still spooky, before they became a dance band. Sparks, who nobody liked except Lew. The Stooges, who nobody we knew had even heard of except us. T. Rex. The Modern Lovers. And Lou Reed. Most of our classmates liked music they could dance to and have a party with. Like Earth Wind and Fire, Elton John, and Peter Frampton. Yuck. For Lew and me, there was nothing to dance about in Grosse P. We wanted to be on the edge. That's what music was to us. None of that lovey-dovey celebration shit. We were bored out of our minds.

Lew was able to maintain a nonchalance about this quandary. There was an independence in how he acted and what he said. Maybe some of it was feigned, but he spoke up in class a lot and asked tough questions and expressed opinions that were a little off the wall. Like, we can't really know for certain that the Earth is spherical, it could be some other shape we don't have the senses to discern. Or how do we know that all of the people in communist countries are oppressed and their leaders evil? Or even, how can we really know what really keeps living things alive? Which impressed me. Lew was different from the rest.

He hung out with a guy named Cam. Cam Miles. Cameron Beauregard Miles. Seriously, that was—is—his name. Cam also had long hair, except whereas Lew's was long and straight and brown, Cam's was shiny golden loopy curls. Like Roger Daltrey's. He had the crystal blue eyes, too. Some kids even called him Daltrey, who was big-time back then, being the lead singer of The Who and starring in a couple movies, like the one where Ann-Margret wiped baked beans all over her body and made me lose sperm cells for the first time.

I remember sitting behind Cam in Geology class before I knew him. All the loops of hair falling on my desk, crossing the line. Who the fuck is that, who is this asshole on the other side of that junk? The loops glistened, like they had permanent spray or gel on them or something. They looked plastic.

Turned out Cam was a guy who traversed boundaries, such as those between the jocks and the freaks, gearheads and geeks, even the brainy and the bewildered. You couldn't help but like him, even if you were jealous. He seemed to breeze through the AP classes that I was afraid to take, while I had to work my ass off to do well. The pretty girls loved his hair and his upbeat affect. Nothing seemed to bring Cam down. He was all-city in cross-country and one of only a couple guys who had a motorcycle, an ancient BMW. Rode it to school every day and all over Grosse P on weekends, usually with a babe on back, and him in his Dingo Boots. Cam the Cowboy. He made a bunch of money doing modeling. You'd see him in *The Detroit News* weekend advertising supplement, ads for Hughes & Hatcher and J.C. Penney, and even the fucking *J. L. Hudson Christmas Catalog*. But Cam was cool, and he was ours. Cam hung out with us, partied with us, fished with us, and shared in our boredoms. This godless Protestant kid who didn't go to church because he didn't have to.

And he played drums. It wasn't long before we formed a trio, with Lew and I taking turns on bass and six-string and all of us taking turns singing. Cam was a pretty good drummer; his beat drove the band. After a while it became apparent that Lew and Cam were in better rhythm than Cam and myself, and besides, I couldn't hold down the low bass string on a full neck with my weak little pinkie without making a buzz. I ended up on six-string by default, which was fine with me. I wasn't particularly good at that either, so we would periodically recruit another guy to play lead while I played rhythm. Then I would inevitably drive him out by interrupting his solos. Each time that happened Lew would be pissed off at me for a week or two. Cowboy didn't seem to care; he just played his drums. There was never a question of kicking me out, at least, it never came up in my presence. Besides, the big tube amps were mine, I figured they were my job security.

Cam didn't have a dad. It was just him and his mom, in a little bungalow on Pembrooke. They lived on the Grosse Pointe side of the Ford Freeway, across from the old blue-collar suburbs. Cam called his street Plumbroke on account of the fact that it was plain jane compared to much of the rest of Grosse Pointe. It wasn't clear exactly what Cam and his mom lived on. She worked part-time at a women's clothing store on the Hill, the sort of swanky Grosse Pointe shopping district. There was also Cam's modeling, but my dad wondered how they paid their mortgage and other bills. He figured that maybe Cam's father had good life insurance.

Except it wasn't clear that Cowboy's dad was dead. On most subjects Cam was generally a pretty easy-going guy. But you couldn't ask him about his dad. Once, out of the blue, he said his dad was out West. Another time he said he didn't know whether his dad was alive or not. That was it. Cam would talk a little about his mother, or rather, his mother's family. He said his mom was a descendent of people who came over on a boat like the Mayflower and that he was the last of his kind, whatever that meant. I couldn't tell if he was bragging or being sarcastic. Or making it up. The other thing about Cam, he liked to call everybody "Ace." Guys, not girls. Like, "Hey, Ace, how's it going?" Ace. Seemed kinda arcane. Sometimes it got a little irritating, like he was keeping everybody at a certain distance.

Okay, what the hell, let's go look for him. Maybe something life-altering would occur, something that would make it all worthwhile. All these burdens I've been carrying around, this madness about America that needs to be released. Maybe an encounter with a ghoul could flip a switch and break the spell. A paradigm change that could make sense of all the circles I've been driving in all my life. What the fuck, it doesn't have to be redemptive. Just not too predictable. Holiday break, I've still got a week before I gotta teach again. Chicago's a straight shot down Interstate ninety-four and it was laid out in vertical and horizontal lines. Lew said he had an address. Maybe we'd encounter adversity or danger, and rescue Cam from whatever dire wolf may be salivating at his door. Help out an old friend, yeah. Perhaps it all fits together somehow, Lew suddenly emerging from exile on a quest for Cowboy. Two old souls, old friends. And me and my blues. I want to think it's all connected, along with all the dirty laundry about America that needs a deep wash. An encounter with the past and the present. Anything could happen.

Honestly, I wouldn't agree to go on this endeavor if it had been anybody but Lew. Although come to think of it, he didn't ask. Maybe that's part of it, that he's on some kind of mission of such importance it rendered an invitation irrelevant. I'm curious about whether there's anything left on his end as far as reclaiming a relationship. He took off to work overseas ever since he got his MBA out east. As far as I knew he never married. I figured he'd gone total corporate and kinda wrote him off. So, when he emailed me out of the blue, it meant something. At least I hope it will. He hadn't been communicating exactly, not that initiating interaction had ever been a habit of Lew's. At least he'd been acknowledging my existence. Every so often, a shoebox full of CDs would arrive on my porch from some country. No note, just the CDs. None of the cases were sealed, so I figured he musta ripped the music off them. Send them to Rick, I don't need them anymore. Like he knew I'd be only semi-digital.

For my part, I kept renewing the *New York Review of Books* subscription I got for him a long time ago, sent to an address in London. As far as I knew he got them. It was easier checking off the renewal notice than trying to find out whether he still lived there. He had a stale cell number, and I gave up trying to email him because he never responded, so that was probably overripe, too. After the French philosopher Michel Foucault's lectures started to appear in English a while back, I'd send him one or two volumes a year for his birthday or at random times. Sent him Iggy Pop's biography, too. No reply to those, either.

One other thing. There's a little more to this trip than finding a ghost, or even going on the road with Lew. My maladies. After making it through my twenties more or less whole, I got hit with all kinds of shit. It started when I went septic from some undetermined bacteria while I was laid up in the ER. Put me in a coma for a while and I almost didn't make it. A few years later, I had a couple seizures, so I'm on meds for that the rest of my life. Then I managed to get meningitis. The infectious disease doc speculated that it was West Nile from a mosquito bite incurred while I was fly fishing for salmon in the rain on the Pere Marquette. Which sucked, especially since I'd taken all proper precautions, liberally applied bug repellant all over my exposed skin. Not the watered-down stuff, but the real thing, one hundred percent DEET. I did recall a swarm of them flying around while I was peeing on the side of the stream in a downpour. Hadn't occurred to me that I oughta apply DEET to my privates. You just can't foresee all possible contingencies in life. Figures, with all those Dutch Reformed right-wingers over there on the west side of Michigan, that I get West Nile while peeing on the west side of the river. To top it off, some straight-arrow asshole from the local Rod and Gun club accused me of trespassing. While I'm peeing in the pouring rain, are you kidding me? Told him to fuck off.

Moving on. There's irregular bleeding in my large intestine from colitis. I'm managing that okay for the moment, but I gotta get a new gastro doctor. The guy who did my last colonoscopy got pissed off because the chia seeds in my intestine clogged up his camera and busted it. Wasn't my fault there were chia seeds in the granola Ginny made. How was I supposed to know that the shit they made me drink to clear my colon didn't work on chia seeds? I don't even know what a chia seed looks like. Come to think of it, how could the doctor even see them in there, if they busted his camera?

I'm starting to get osteoporosis and arthritis from all the steroids I've had to take for the colitis, after the pericardial fluid around my heart pushed in one of the ventricles like Play-Doh. Plus, I've got a bad right ear from the time I walked to school in a cold winter wind and didn't put on my headband. Thought wearing it would jinx my chances with a certain girl in eighth grade art class who turned me down anyway. Ever since then, whenever it gets real cold outside, or I turn up the tunes too loud it aches.

There's a big piece of metal in place of my hip after I destroyed the original in a bad skiing accident, so somewhere deep in my left buttock it hurts when I sit very long or try to run. Some kind of shit's growing on a few toenails that I can't get rid of cuz the topical doesn't work. All I can do is use my rusty carpenter's file to grind it down every few days, and it's a bloody mess. My pants size, the difference between the number for waist and the one for length keeps narrowing. I have trouble getting it up and the drugs for that give me migraines. My lifestyle is tragically unhip. I frequently find myself telling the precious people on the public radio station to shut the fuck up, and I watch a lot more TV than I used to even though it's still almost all junk. Recently, a youngish doctor informed me that I've got a fatty liver and shouldn't drink any alcohol. I protested, "doesn't seem fair that I can't drink because of my liver and Lou Reed got to do all that drinking before his liver finally went out." The doctor didn't seem to get it. Probably never even heard of Lou Reed, or The Velvet Underground.

My legs hurt frequently for reasons nobody can figure out and I've got a herniated disk that can waylay me until I get yet another cortisone shot. Rock is dead and there will be no meaningful catharsis, yet I can't get the lyrics of certain songs out of my head. I don't know what the fuck a Millennial is, much less a Gen X or Z, or why the hip-hopsters just hip and hop instead of doing something to change the world, and I can't get anything original about the human condition from new American fiction that I didn't already get out of therapy and philosophy. None of the antidepressants do much except keep me from falling off the edge and help me sleep, with the additional aid of a BiPAP machine that sometimes makes my nose bleed. I've tried mindfulness but I couldn't get my mind to stop overflowing with moral questions. Which shouldn't be confused with living a particularly ethical life. Some would classify that contradiction as neurosis, others as personal indulgence. Okay. But there's a moral plague all around me when there should be moral indignation. Maybe moral rage.

Then there's the issue that I can't piss. Little did I know what was coming when I got sent to a bladder specialist, starting with the diagnostic procedure. First, his team of four women strapped me, naked, in a crouch between two parallel bars. Like I was a carcass in a butcher shop. Then they stuck this big hose up my unit and turned on a loud machine that filled me full of water until I felt like I would explode. Like going through some kind of Inquisition truth torture ritual, only they didn't ask me any trick questions. They didn't have to, I freaked out during the procedure anyway, from what I saw on the wall in front of me. Four large color photos of cats on hind legs with their front paws crossed over their crotches. Framed. I still don't know whether that was supposed to humor me or embellish the torture. Probably both. But in century twenty-one? It's exactly what Foucault was trying to get at. The gaze. Disciplinary technology in a nutshell. The invasion of the body in the clinic. Practices and procedures and technologies. Only Foucault never wrote much about sadism and misogyny. At least not involving cat-women and bladders. Afterward, the urologist informed me that the bladder's really simple, it's designed to do just two things, expand and contract. "Unfortunately, yours doesn't contract. Think popped balloon. There's no technology to fix it."

Beneath this accumulation of maladies there lurks, in what's left of my consciousness, the following persistent questions: A, what have I done with my life, and B, is this it?

Thus, A-B-D has taken on a meaning other than All But Dissertation. It also means, All But Dead. Though I don't feel old. I mean, I don't feel like someone who's developed a sense of authority over their personal world. I feel like I did when I was young. Not physically. In the head, in the sense of carrying around the expectation that I'm not quite legit. Probably a symptom of a pervasive predisposition to question the customary. Is it about getting old? Maybe. Maybe it's more like fighting getting old.

I've grown tired of going to this bar, it's called Alive, that has an older adult night with a live band. Not really a night, they give you two hours, seven to nine on Wednesdays. At nine they kick you out and let the kids in. Anyway, Ginny likes to dance and sometimes I tag along for a beer and the music. They always have the same band, it's composed of people my age, give or take. Call themselves Still Kicking. I go up to the balcony with a beer and look down on the dance floor, which is always packed. Mounds of gray matter bobbing up and down. There it is, what's left of my generation, the last of the Baby Boomers. Everybody's got a big smile, they're having a blast, it's a regular funhouse. As our bodies break down. The band, it's ridiculous, three guitars, two horns, a bass player, two singers, a drummer, and keyboards, all squished together on a little stage. I get that there's no pretension involved, that they're past having anything to hide. I get that they're enjoying themselves, I'm not, and that's on me. And it's not like Still Kicking can't play. But they're on the same stage where I once saw The Ramones and The Stooges and Black Uhuru. To top it off, there's the smell of weed throughout the place. Give me a break, pot's for kids who want to feel and act goofy, which is just a natural extension of being a kid. There's nothing goofy about getting older. If you want to dance and drink and smoke pot though, fine, go ahead. I'm just not ready for that party yet. The party of acceptance and pacification.

I have to drive through this private little purgatory I've been carrying around before it all turns to Hell. Which I imagine is something like the guy in Dante's *Inferno* who has to push a boulder up a hill, over and over, forever. Sisyphus. Only for me, instead of a boulder and a hill for eternity, I'll have a cheap Cabela's fly rod and be fated to make the exact same cast to snag the exact same fish, over and over. And it's a sucker. That leaps out of the water and squeals at an ear-splitting pitch, over and over. My just punishment from the gods for all the rock and roll excess. Or even worse, maybe I'll remain in that incoherent realm somewhere between desire and discouragement, the one I'm in now, only forever.

Perhaps personal decline has nothing to do with the body but is instead the aftermath of repetitive traumas to the mind. The political polarities spin endlessly across the map like two perpetual tornadoes, feasting on fears, ripping up lives. When Lew and I were young and seeking to drive against the constraints of convention, the racial and class divisions left unavoidable rocks in the road. We coped with what we didn't understand by maintaining an edge. This time, when we get on the highway to rescue a long-lost friend, after so many years apart, how will Lew and I relate? Will we, once more, fuck with each other, and regain some grit? I hope so, I need a guy I trust to give me a hard time. A punch in the gut, and a return favor.

In which Rick and Lew get on the road—and off

The road to madness started a couple of days ago. Or was it three? Four? Fuck, I don't know.

"Where exactly is Cam?" I ask Lew, who is behind the wheel as we barrel down the highway.

"Chicago."

"You told me that already. Where in Chicago?"

"I've got an address. What are you doing?"

"Just trying to find something." I was fumbling around in my pockets to make sure I have a catheter handy, don't want to tell him about this malady yet.

"What?"

"A tissue."

"Look in the glove compartment."

"It's locked."

He sticks his Marlboro Light between his thin lips, reaches over, and bangs once on the front of the glove compartment with the side of his fist. Doesn't open.

"Lew, you haven't been in this car for over thirty years. Why do you think there would be any tissue in there?"

"Because I always kept tissue there."

He bangs on it again as the car swerves into the left lane, cutting somebody off, who hits the horn and speeds by.

"Pay attention to your driving."

I had picked up Lew at Tri-City Airport at three in the afternoon. Just like him to do that, fly to a dinky airport more than halfway up the Michigan mitten. He couldn't do it the normal way and fly to Detroit Metro, which is just a hop and a skip from Ann Arbor. As I drove up to the little terminal, there he was, nobody else in sight, in a gray trench coat flapping in the wind. This tall figure with the hawk nose and now totally bald, smoking as always, tensed up a bit in the cold. His mannerism looked the same, the aloofness there, but something was different. He still had the big shoulders of a swimmer—he'd always been a big motherfucker—but it looked like the trench coat was too big for his body. Kinda like David Byrne in *Stop Making Sense*. Thin and a little pale. As I pulled up, he reached out and grabbed the door handle on the passenger side before I intended to stop, so I had to slam on the brake. He opened the door, threw his luggage case in back, and tossed the cigarette in that nonchalant way like he always had.

"Hey Dahd." Like it was nothing, like we had just seen each other last week. Dahd, that's what he had always called me, it was kind of a play on my last name, Haddad, on account of the second syllable is pronounced like "dahd." He called me that except when he was irritated at me, then it was just Rick. Which used to happen a lot. It could go back and forth in a single conversation, Dahd and Rick, Rick and Dahd.

"Lew."

Instead of getting in, he closed the door and starts to walk around the front of the car. What's he doing? He stops outside my door and opens it.

"Dahd, let me drive."

"You just got here."

"I wanna drive."

He'd asked me a long time ago to take care of this car, the LeMans. 'We might need it someday,' he said, 'take it out for a spin once in a while.' I did for a little while, then forgot about it. Who gives a shit about an old car with rust all over the edges and a cracked windshield? And all the junk in the trunk. A couple old bamboo fly rods we made, warped and guides broken or missing, they never cast well anyway. Torn navy sweatshirt with UNIVERSITY OF MICHIGAN in gold, and some red and white stains on it from who knows what. Large screwdriver and a couple curled up issues of *Playboy* from 1978. A discolored Trout Unlimited cap with a patch of what looked like rust but was probably dead mold. A cracked red bong and a tangle of bass guitar strings. A canvas tent and an army green backpack that contained some yellowed paperbacks in it: *Breakfast of Champions, Gravity's Rainbow, Catch-22, Tropic of Cancer, Nausea, Armies of the Night*. A bunch of ancient 8-track tapes scattered about, some cracked. A little wrinkled piece of paper with handwriting, the top half gone. It read, "head downstream on old sawmill pathway off into woods on right then trail on left to river." Shitty handwriting, like whoever wrote it couldn't follow a consistent pattern, or didn't care to try. My handwriting. And a small, overexposed color photo of Lew and Cam standing in front of some white pines, fly rods in hand, grinning in the sun. From the waist up, in their fishing vests. What you couldn't tell from the water damaged stock was that they wore nothing below their waists. Fishing vests, fly rods and nothing but grins in the sun. Old sawmill pathway. What the fuck, I folded it in half and slipped it in my wallet.

LeMans. A joke of a name for a car, this car, since it sure as hell didn't look like something that could go twenty-four hours in a race. A cheap version of a GTO for the older set. It was a Rosenberg family hand me down that we had put through some hard miles. A lot of hard miles. When Lew raised the idea about taking it out of storage, I said, "How am I supposed to drive the thing? It probably isn't even street legal anymore."

"It's not a big deal, the title's in the glove compartment, just get it registered, get a plate and some insurance."

"It's not in my name."

"Yes, it is." I'd forgotten that he had transferred title to me for a dollar before he left the States. "Get it thoroughly checked out and a tune-up," he said, "I'll pay for it."

I had it towed to the place he told me to take it, a shop way down Nine Mile that works on old cars. They even got the 8-track player to work, though they couldn't guarantee it would last for long because the heads were pretty worn out. Most of the tapes played okay, which kinda fired me up, although the sound sucked: *Blood on the Tracks, Country Life, Houses of the Holy, Quadrophenia. Berlin, Blind Faith, The White Album. Wish You Were Here, Exile on Main Street, Station to Station, Thick as a Brick, Lust for Life, Waiting for Columbus,* and *Electric Warrior.* We could rock on the road like we used to.

But damn, I'm glad to see Lew. He took an interest in ideas and observations about the world and so on. At least, he did. When we were young, he was always reading serious literature and smoking and, in the summer, getting a deep tan. Hawaiian Tropic. There was a kind of artistic space we inhabited together ever since we started going to films with subtitles in them, barely after we'd gotten our driver's licenses. We'd drive all over metro Detroit to see some foreign film or other. After we got to college in Ann Arbor, we had our choice of five or six films any night of the week in the lecture halls on campus. That was before VCRs and cable, when people would sit and watch serious sixteen millimeter. We'd go to a film and then to a bar, or somebody's apartment, and discuss what we saw while we did bong hits, drank beer, and smoked Marlboro Reds with filters dipped in cheap cocaine.

Maybe Lew still had curiosity about ideas and would let me work on him. I could talk to him about Foucault, which he brought up. No, actually I did. After the how you doing niceties, after we'd been driving a little while, after he failed to open the glove compartment.

"Did you get any of those Foucault books I sent you?"

"That French philosophy shit? Yeah. Did you get the CDs?"

"Yes, Lew."

"What'd you like?"

"None of them."

"What! I've probably sent you a couple hundred."

"I couldn't get into them."

"That's insane, Dahd. Did you even try?"

"I probably listened to most of them once or twice."

"You're way too picky."

"I hate to break this news to you, Lew, but the vast majority of rock music blows. Particularly after Nineteen-eighty."

"You're still so out of touch."

"I have high standards."

"It keeps you irrelevant."

"Did you read the Foucault?"

"Too dense."

"The lectures aren't that dense."

"All that shit about power and bodies. I have no context."

"In a democracy like the U.S., we're used to thinking about individual rights in law. Like freedom. Equality. Foucault argued there's another idea of the individual, outside the law."

"What is that supposed to mean?" Lew asks.

"All the different ways people act, how they think, what they care about. What they believe in, what they don't. Different ways people live. Cultural differences. Racial differences."

"What does race have to do with it?"

25

"Social forces maintain inequalities."

"People have civil rights, Rick. What's the big fuss? I mean, the police brutality, police killing blacks who commit a misdemeanor. That can't happen. Black lives matter. But the laws are there."

"That's little solace to someone who lost their teenager forever."

"Then enforce the laws. Make new ones if necessary. And get rid of the bad cops who hide behind their frickin' union. But all this stuff about reparations and so on—don't create new inequalities based on a long time ago."

"C'mon, Lew. It's a legacy of discrimination. Poverty falls disproportionately on minorities. You know that."

"I get it, but it can't just be about proportions. There are way more whites who are poor."

"They haven't been historically discriminated against."

"What difference does that make, Dahd? Poor is poor."

"Lots of white people get government aid."

Lew lit a cigarette with the car's lighter. "See, that's the problem. People wanting something for nothing. Gimme, gimme, gimme. How about, work? How about, get an education?"

"You mean college? A lot of people can't afford that."

"I had to take out big loans."

"A lot of people didn't get the grades in high school."

"Whose fault is that?"

"Schools in poor areas don't get funding compared to others."

"Yeah, but at some point, a person, a parent, has to say to their kid, 'do your schoolwork even if we don't have all the bells and whistles.' It's about dedication and effort. Stop making excuses."

"That's not fair, Lew."

"You can't pretend that all the advocacy for advantage based on what demographic group you belong to is fair. It's a power grab."

"Power grab? You're kidding me, right?"

"That's sure how it seems on the media, Dahd. All the aggressiveness, all these aggressive talking heads that the cable networks like CNN push."

"So, you get the truth from Fox?"

"No. Those people are worse."

"You don't even live in this country."

"What difference does it make where I live? I get my news like everybody else. I doubt you're spending a lot of time travelling around the U.S. getting first-hand observations."

"I get mine from the *New York Times*. PBS and NPR. I used to watch CNN but I can't take it anymore."

"Exactly. All those big news networks, they all push slanted views. What happened to straight news reporting?"

There's a sign for a gas station at the next exit. "Lew, pull off, I need to piss."

It's a Speedway. Hand-written cardboard sign in the window advertises a variety of homemade jerky: Beef, Whitetail, Elk, Turkey, Black Bear, Rabbit, Boar. I get out of the car. Cold wind cuts right through my coat and skin.

Lew rolls down the window a bit. "Get me a big Diet Pepsi. The biggest. And a pack of Marlboro Lights. And fill up the tank, why is it so low?"

Jesus, what else. Is he going to start telling me what to do already? How can he stand Diet Pepsi, I'm thinking as I stick the pump in the tank. Why is the tank so low? Maybe because it's a really old shit car that burns gas like a bonfire. Maybe it's leaking gas already.

I leave the pump running, go in the store. The young woman behind the counter's got way too much makeup around her eyes and fake yellow hair. Like those downriver Detroit women who imagine they can overcome their hard life looks that way. Big dog on the floor behind her, didn't expect to see a pit bull this far north. I associate them with Detroit, where they run wild in packs and make old people afraid to go outside without a handgun.

27

In the lavatory, one toilet and a sink. Smells like pot. Did somebody just sit here on the toilet and smoke a doob? Pretty weak. No heat in here, cheap fiberboard. What was that Lou Reed song? Something about a dumpy apartment in West Berlin with moldy walls that didn't have a private bathroom. Take out the necessary supplies from my coat: catheter, Surgi-Lube, Purell. Usually I wash my hands first, unless the sink looks bad, like this one. Don't wanna invite more bad bacteria than I'd wash off.

Okay, here's the procedure. First you go to the Purell, apply to fingertips, that's so you don't get an infection, but you often get one anyway. Rip open a package of the French coudé tip style catheter—gotta go with the French tip, anything else, you'd rather kill yourself than cath the rest of your life—whip out the Surgi-Lube and squeeze some of that on your fingers. Next, wipe that goop up and down the catheter, being mindful of your surroundings as you don't want to let the tip of the catheter touch anything. Otherwise, you'll have to toss it and start all over with another one. If that happens, and it will, and you don't have another catheter handy, well, then you're screwed. Assuming that all goes well, in the catheter goes, most of it, maybe twelve or fourteen inches, all the while taking care to aim for the toilet so the urine doesn't spill all over you and your shoes. Then you gotta just stand there because it takes a while to empty. You can whistle, or count to see how long the urine flows. If it's gonna be a real long time, you can count one-apple, two-apple, et cetera. Maybe try to set a world record. You can thank God for the French and sing "La Marseillaise."

Finally, bladder's tapped out. I've gotten so used to this routine that I sometimes forget to zip up. There's this continuous low-grade fear that one day I'll walk out of the john with my dick hanging out. In the store, the Diet Coke and Diet Pepsi in the fridge don't feel nearly cold enough, and the pop machine's only got Diet Pepsi. Fuck, I hate that. I grab a big cup, filling it with Diet Pepsi and ice. Then I fill another cup with some ice, grab a forty-ounce Diet Coke from the fridge, and take everything to the counter. To Downriver Daisy.

"Is that your gas outside?"

Of course it is, we're the only frickin' car out there, in this wasteland. "Yeah. And a pack of Marlboros. Lights."

"I have to charge you for the ice and cup. With the gas, fifty-three thirty total."

Nobody has to do anything, but she doesn't know that, how could she, hardly anybody gets it. I glance at the homemade jerky behind the plastic case. They all look the same, ground up guts and whatever else. Pretty old and wrinkly, too dried out, even for jerky.

"Which one do you like?"

"They're all pretty good," she says. "I like the boar."

"I didn't know there are wild boar in Michigan."

"It's from Texas."

"Then how is it home-made?"

"The raw meat's from Texas. We make the jerky here."

"Jesus. Just the pop and Marlboros."

Outside again, there's sleet with the wind now, hitting my face. Put the nozzle back on the pump, finally get back in the car.

"Here's your Diet Pepsi and cigs."

"This isn't the biggest size."

"I don't know how you can drink that shit."

Lew takes a sip and puts the cup between his legs. "What's wrong with Diet Pepsi?"

"It tastes like formaldehyde with a little bit of lemon."

"How would you know what formaldehyde tastes like?"

"Okay, not formaldehyde. Ajax with a little bit of lemon."

He opens the pack of Marlboros, takes one out, uses the car's cigarette lighter to light up. "What about that shit you're drinking?"

"Diet Coke is totally different from Diet Pepsi. Besides, Lew, it's your fault."

"What's my fault?"

"That I'm hooked on it. The sickly sweet."

"How's that?"

"You used to drink Diet Coke. You pushed it on me in college."

"I didn't push it on you, I never pushed anything on you," Lew says. "Even if I did, maybe you wanted to get hooked."

He's probably right, I probably did want to be hooked on something, anything. Once upon a time. Maybe now.

Back on the highway, the long flat ashen road. Dirty snow piled up high.

"Why'd you switch sides, Lew?"

"Switch sides?"

"To Diet Pepsi."

"I don't know, it was probably easier to get in some country where I was living."

"Where was that?"

Suddenly the car started bucking. "What the fuck!" Lew yells.

Again, and again. Our bodies jerk violently forward and back, again, and again. Lew manages to pull over to the shoulder. Then the LeMans stops, dead.

"I thought you said you got this car tuned up."

"I did."

We get out and look under the hood. Lew checks the oil. "It's full. Engine didn't seize."

He looks at me. "Wait a minute. You filled the tank. What kind of gas did you get?"

"What do you mean? Gas."

"What kind of gas?"

"I don't know, the one with the green handle."

"You idiot, you must've put diesel in it!"

"Oopsie."

"What were you thinking?" He looks up the empty highway. "We're gonna have to get it towed and flushed and it's Sunday. If we're lucky, the engine won't be destroyed."

"That blows."

"We gotta go online and find a tow." He reaches into his trench coat pockets. "Where'd I put my phone?" He opens the driver side door, looks around under his seat, then drags his luggage out of the back and rummages around in it. "Where's my fucking smart phone? Do you remember seeing it?"

"I didn't see it, Lew. I never saw it. What did you do with it when you threw your shit in the car? Is it on you?"

"No, I checked." He sticks his hands in his pockets again anyway. "Fuck! I must've left it on the plane. We'll have to use yours."

"It doesn't have data."

"What? What do you mean, it doesn't have data? All cell phones have data."

"Not mine."

"Let me see it."

I pull out my trusty Nokia and toss it to him.

"Rick, what are you doing with a fucking flip phone?"

"It's a phone."

"It's not a smart phone!"

"Smart enough for me. I like it."

"It's not about what you like, it's about the way it is," Lew says. "This isn't even charged!"

"Yes, it is, the light's on. We must be out of range."

"That's ridiculous. What kind of plan do you have?"

"I don't know. A cheap one."

"Fuck!" He slams the door. "C'mon."

31

"Where are you going?"

"Where do you think? We have to hoof it. Here, here's your archaic phone back, Rick. I don't know why you'd even carry it." He quickly lights another cigarette and starts walking.

"Wait a minute. Aren't we closer to the Speedway?"

He mumbles something without stopping.

"Lew!"

He turns around, takes a big drag on his Marlboro. "What!"

"Let's go back to the Speedway. It's closer."

"It's just a Speedway, not a service station."

"They might have a phone. The cashier probably has a cell."

"We've barely gotten started. I'm not going backwards. C'mon, there's an exit ramp."

He resumes walking, so I follow, grudgingly. Fucking cold. Idiot wind. Walking along the shoulder of the highway, at our age. Everything gray. Gray and gritty and fucking freezing. No more sleet, at least. To catch up with him, I gotta jog a bit despite my fucking fake hip.

"What were you thinking?" he asks.

"I guess I wasn't."

"Well, who filled it before?"

"The guys at the repair shop."

"Why would you put diesel in it?"

"It's an old car, Lew, and you're the one who stopped in front of the green pump."

"No, I didn't."

"Yes, you did."

"There were two pumps, Rick. One regular, the other diesel."

"I guessed wrong. You were distracting me, with your cigarette and soda order."

"There was no need to guess."

"It wasn't a guess. We've got a different kind of car, so I figured it took a different kind of gas. Besides, it was your idea to get a very old heap out of storage and drive it across Michigan in the dead of winter. We would've been better off with my van."

"That's not helpful."

"We wouldn't be disabled."

"You probably don't even have a real van. You probably have a minivan."

"What's the difference?"

"A minivan is for schlepping mobs of little kids to soccer games. This is more serious."

"I'm just saying." A car rushes past us, one of those black Cadillacs that look like stealth military vehicles. "Maybe we should hitchhike."

"I'm not hitchhiking," he says.

"Why not?"

"That would be embarrassing."

"Why?"

"We're too old to hitchhike." He moves ahead of me again and I trudge along, breathing in his fucking cigarette smoke, as we reach the exit ramp. My legs ache already. Maybe I am too old to hitchhike, too old to walk up an exit ramp, too old to be doing any of this. I reach in my pockets for my black knit cap and wool gloves. Fuck, left the gloves in the car. At least I have the cap, whereas Lew's got nothing but a trench coat and a bald head poking up there in the sky. How can he stand it?

At the top of the ramp, wind's blowing harder. Snow on empty cornfields, gray asphalt, nothingness. A white farmhouse a little way off, and behind it, a big red barn. Wasn't that the name of a restaurant chain once? The Red Barn.

"Let's walk over to that house," Lew says. "Maybe somebody's there."

As we get closer, the scene doesn't look very promising. Turns out the barn's in the process of collapsing on itself, so no cows or goats. The house is white yellowing clapboard and dirt smudges, as if it endured a slew of dust storms. Blinds are down and no dogs bark. Lew walks up the creaky wood porch and knocks on the door. Nothing. Doorbell doesn't work. What now? It's too cold to stand around on an abandoned porch.

"Maybe we should break in, Lew. They might have a working land line."

Lew doesn't respond. A non-response from Lew had always meant, "I will ignore you when you say something superfluous or stupid. Like that." But I was serious, kind of. Actually, I wasn't, I'd be afraid to break in. Somebody in there might be sleeping on a shotgun. Maybe Lew would do it.

"I'm serious."

"We're not breaking into somebody's house," he says.

"It's abandoned."

Lew starts walking back to the road and I follow, like Simon following Garfunkel. Even though he looks damaged, with his long strides he still walks too fast for me. Not that I've ever walked fast, not that I could now.

"Slow down."

Asshole ignores me. No cars in sight. Just desolation, in the air, in my head. Ice on the blacktop in places where the asphalt hasn't cracked, so I'm trying not to slip. Soybean and corn fields, plowed over dead for winter. Flatland. Some woods up ahead on both sides of the road. As we get closer, it becomes apparent we're nearing the edge of a full-fledged forest, covered in snow. A little further down, we reach a break in the woods. There's a winding path, maybe fifty feet wide, that cuts through the trees and then disappears from sight. The path is lower than the woods and it runs right under the road where we're standing. On the other side of the road, the path seems to break up. Headwaters. It's a river, frozen over.

Lew takes a couple steps off the road and peers below it. "We're standing on a culvert."

"So what?"

"Let's follow the river."

"How do you know we won't go through the ice?"

He steps down and tests it with his left foot, then stands on it. Does he weigh less than me now?

"It's fine."

I pull my coat sleeves down to protect my hands. "Lew, we're at one end of the river. We have no idea where it's going, except away from the road."

"We're not gonna get anywhere on this road. Nobody uses it."

"What are you talking about? We're not even a half-mile from the freeway. It makes no sense to follow the river. It's gonna get dark in a couple hours."

"We've got plenty of time 'til dark. It makes perfect sense. C'mon. Let's follow the river."

Follow the river. It's what we said when we were young, and lost. When we were young, and it wasn't winter, we waded rivers with fly rods, searching for trout. No good topographic maps back then, we had to make our own. Sometimes there were crude paths along those remote streams. Other times we'd have to force our way through all the brush and buckthorn. Better to stay in the water. We'd eventually find some kind of civilization, even if it was just a decrepit general store. But it could take a long time before we reached anything. A long, long time.

"This makes no sense, Lew, to follow a river into the woods. When we fished, we followed rivers to get out of the woods. Let's go back on the road, find somebody, and ask for a ride, or directions at least."

Lew peers around without stopping. "This looks familiar. We fished here. It's a tributary of the Rifle."

"You're on drugs. The Rifle's way north of here. We're too far south for trout."

"It's a smallmouth stream. We fished it once."

"No, we didn't."

"It's the Shiawassee."

"No, it's not. That's way south of here. I passed it on the way to the airport."

"I remember this river. There's a town not too far."

"No, Lew."

Maybe we really did fish here. Hell, we fished everywhere. But smallmouth stream? We didn't travel this far just to fish for smallmouth. Probably something Lew just made up. I always thought he exaggerated how many fish he landed. Since he was usually well downstream from where I was, he could say anything. We'd get in a river, and within an hour he was out of sight. It got to the point where I might as well have been alone. Why did I even fish with him? Although, if it wasn't for Lew, I probably wouldn't have ever even stepped in a stream in the first place. Lew had always been the one who took the lead in all things physical.

We'd been walking for a half-hour or so, silently for the most part. Mainly because it's hard to converse with somebody who's walking ten or twenty yards ahead of you. Smoking in a river, like so many times before, and me having to smell his exhale.

"Lew, slow down." I am ignored. Big clod. "Lew!"

Finally, he stops. I think he just sighed.

"Slow yourself down."

"We'll freeze out here if we go your pace."

"You're being an asshole."

We resume walking side-by-side. He'll be ahead of me again in a few minutes.

"It's like when we fished together, Lew. You always abandoned me." He bulled his way through a river, whereas I tried to finesse it. At least, that's the way I liked to think of it. I could be wrong.

"First, we're not fishing. Second, this is an emergency situation. And third, you always took too long."

"I was being patient with the river. You gotta work the pocket water."

"What do you think happens when you're doing all those casts in tight spaces? You were spooking the fish, if there were any even down there."

"That's why you had to have a light touch. There were fish there. Besides, you were the one scaring the fish, with your massive weighted streamers. You might as well've been using a big bait casting rod and a spoon with a bunch of treble hooks and nightcrawlers."

We haven't fished together in more than thirty years. On top of the river, like we are right now, the complexity of it is hidden, frozen over. It might as well be blacktop. We're going somewhere, or nowhere.

"Lew, this sucks. Let's turn around and go back to the road. All we had to do was wait for somebody to drive by."

Pow-pow, pow-pow-pow.

"What the fuck was that!" I yell. I know what it was. Gunfire.

Lew doesn't answer, he's listening, tensed up.

Pow-pow, pow-pow-pow-pow, louder, closer.

Lew drops to the ice. "Get down, Rick!" He reaches up, grabs my forearm and yanks. I slip and fall down on the ice. Ouch.

Rustling in the woods, and somebody's shout. More gunfire. Suddenly a big whitetail buck comes tearing out of the woods, about thirty feet from us, upstream. It cuts across the river in a couple leaps, slips a little on the ice, recovers, and heads directly at us. The deer springs by, almost trampling me, then veers off into the woods on the other side, breaking through the thicket behind us. More gunfire, closer, too close.

A few seconds later, more rustling. Two rotund guys come running out of the woods in bright orange, carrying rifles, and stop. They look like prison escapees.

"Didja see the big buck?" one of them asks. They're both panting, hands on knees.

"What the fuck, you could've killed us!" Lew yells as we get up.

"Didja see it?"

"No."

"Damn," the other guy says. "Coulda swore I hit it." He's still bent over, like he's gonna heave, then he looks up at us. "It's deer season. You shouldn't be out here. Especially without orange. You coulda been a deer."

I didn't exactly follow his logic. Maybe some kind of transcendental phenomenology thing. Like, if he perceived we're deer, we are deer. To him, valid knowledge.

"Wait a minute," Lew says. "It's the end of December. Deer season's in November."

"It's the second season," the first guy says.

"What second season?" Lew asks with a look of disbelief, and a little disdain.

"Too many deer. DNR's trying to control the numbers."

"Our car broke down. Is there a town around here?"

"Gladkin's only about a quarter-mile."

"Down the river?"

"No, that'd take you forever. You gotta go the way we came, through the woods. Just retrace our steps in the snow."

"Let's go, Dahd."

I follow Lew into the woods, following their tracks. Glance back, they're still standing there talking to each other, gesturing around. Then they disappear into the woods on the other side.

"Lew, did you see the blood on its side?"

"Yeah."

"Why didn't you tell them where the deer went?"

"Because deer hunting's stupid."

"Isn't it gonna die anyway?"

"Probably. They'll eventually find it."

It's not much of a path we're on, there are low lying branches, and as Lew plows through ahead of me, the branches whip against my face.

Thanks, hunters, for providing us with a way to get off the fucking river. Thanks, after almost shooting us.

"Take it easy with the branches, Lew." Like the old days, no reply. Asshole.

With the thought of getting out, and getting warm somewhere, we move through the woods pretty quick. Doesn't seem to take very long and we're finally on cracked asphalt again. Down the road a bit, there's a flashing yellow light at an intersection, and the bare outline of a few small buildings.

In a few more minutes, we're there. Old gas station on the corner with a pile of rusted car parts behind it. Gus's Gas. A couple bars and a motel. Thank God. Civilization, sort of. The gas station looks like it's got a lift and a repair well. While Lew goes inside, I walk down the road a bit further and look around. Motel's one of those decrepit little single-story ones. A row of rooms with big windows and curtains. Electric sign in the parking lot says, "The Ventura. Rooms. Clean. Cable."

A bunch of F-150s and Rams are parked out front in the dirt lot. A little grocery store across the street. More trucks and a bar. The Dead Boar. Stars and stripes on a flagpole, and a red banner above the entrance. Welcome Hunters. An oversized concrete bear statue stands on hind legs next to the door, with its front legs outstretched over its head menacingly. It's holding a little American flag in one paw. On one side of the building, there's a deer pole with a couple carcasses hanging, blood on the ice beneath. And a scrawny dog licking it up. Coulda been us hanging there.

Lew's back, looks upbeat, that's good.

"What'd you find out?"

"They can tow the car and all our stuff when somebody gets in with the truck later today, and there'll be a mechanic who can flush it first thing in the morning."

"Shit, you mean, we have to stay here overnight?"

"C'mon, let's go get a room."

"Not in that fleabag."

He sighs. "Quit bitching."

The Ventura had only one room left, so we took it. A little room with a double bed and a fold-out sofa in front of the window. A nightstand with a lamp is squeezed in between the bed and the far wall, and a small TV on top of a small table in the corner by the bathroom door. Barely room to walk. Fake pressed wood paneling. Suspicious-looking green shag carpet, well worn, must be ten, twenty years old. Electric baseboard heat panels. I hate baseboard heat, never warm enough. And the whole room smells like a long history of smokers have stayed here.

"Lew, how are we gonna get the sofa-bed out?"

"We just have to move the nightstand and shove the bed against the wall."

He flops down on the bed, which creaks. Guess he just claimed it. Asshole. "I'm burned out," he says. "I need a nap."

"A nap, after all this?"

"I still have jet lag. Don't forget, I flew into Michigan from fucking Frankfort via Toronto. Then all this walking in the freezing cold, thanks to your bungling. And I'm over sixty years old. Of course, I need a nap."

"If you take a nap now, you'll be up 'til two in the morning."

"I just need a short one."

"What am I supposed to do?"

"Take a nap."

"I'm not a napper."

"Wake me up in an hour."

I poke my head in the bathroom. "Where's the light switch?"

"It's out here."

"That makes no sense." I flip it on and inspect the layout. Tiny. Cracked linoleum floor, and the toilet's got one of those papers wrapped around that's supposed to mean it's been cleaned. Small sink and no counter, but I can use the back of the toilet for my catheter shit. As I pee, I think about how long it's taking and how noisy it is, and wait for Lew to say something.

He's already asleep. How can he do that, after us almost getting shot? Not to mention trampled. I gotta just sit here, I guess, and do what I do, which is ruminate about the genesis of madness and all things gone wrong. Which might have begun the morning that the priest we called Father Grim went up and down the single corridor of my elementary school, one classroom at a time, and yelled at all the kids because somebody had scratched a little something on the wall in the boys' locker room and wouldn't confess. You could hear Grim's voice yelling from every classroom because he left the doors open, so you knew he was getting closer, in his black garb. He looked scary in all that black. Kinda like Johnny Cash.

Or maybe madness first emerged when Sister Serious stuck Mona's head under hot water. Maybe it was madness the first time I heard the n-word on the school playground, which was the only bad word except for shit and fuck, and the only Negroes you'd see were the cleaning ladies.

Then again, madness may have first made its presence known years later, when Lew took a bullet for me and almost died. Or it coulda been in embryo. It coulda even been from that shit the doctors used to push on young mothers in the Sixties to give their babies instead of breastmilk. That was before they realized that breastmilk was probably way better for white babies and pushed the fake shit to those so-called free markets offshore. To give to colored peoples' babies because, being of color, far beyond the other side of the border and not knowing the only language that mattered in the world, they were less human. But what alternatives were there? Are there? You gotta keep moving, pushing the product over all obstacles to generate revenues at maximum possible twenty-four-seven, or else the world as we know it will end and we will truly be in a war of all against all, like the English philosopher Thomas Hobbes had warned four hundred years ago. That's what some people want you to believe, anyway.

41

Whenever and wherever the madness started, people think it's all emotion but there's plenty of calculation involved. To be specific, geometric figures. A big one in southeast Michigan was the line between the drug- and gun-infested ghettos where only blacks lived and the green grass where whites lived. With their guns and drugs. The line between Detroit and Grosse Pointe. Alter Road. That border may as well have been the Berlin Wall. It was so sharp yet never spoken of that sooner or later, it cut through your consciousness with a crack and you were alone with it, as though a supernatural entity placed you under some kind of spell that set you apart from everything else. Some kind of haunting, of the mind.

Growing up in Grosse P, the idea you're living in madness, you'd think that would be the furthest thing from everybody's mind. At least nobody on the white side, busy with their golf clubs and sailboats, ever talked about it. Too busy preserving the stillness. Grosse Pointe had its own geometric figure, a flat plane that organized the houses from modest to medium to large and finally, the mansions on the water. The problem was what all of this did to a kid's head. Where could you go, what could you do, to get out of it? The readymade blueprint fell over you like wet newspaper and stuck there, so you ended up with a fissure in your head, and something always leaking.

You could watch the buses that came down from Detroit to Grosse Pointe early each morning to drop off the cleaning women and pick up white men for their jobs downtown. The black and white polarities were a way of life, regular and redundant. The fact that you were immersed on one side meant you couldn't possibly comprehend either side, not really, except from what you could gather in isolated empirical fragments. Which wasn't really knowledge. You didn't know there were still lots of whites living in Detroit because you didn't see them.

You were taught in school by the nuns about suffering and being good to each other and making personal sacrifice. You got all these stories about the Child of God who says, be good to each other even if you're different, you're all the same in the eyes of the gods. Like in the famous parable of *The Sneetches*. But nobody talked about the line, that invisible wall that's still there. You knew it didn't square with the message of the schoolteacher nuns. The therapist, who was a kind of Protestant, said it's not your problem. White flight.

Needless to say, those days are over, the olden days. The days of *Spy vs. Spy* and the *Creature from the Black Lagoon*, of *Dark Shadows* and Dippity Doo. Those were good things, for some reason. Hippies and bippies. Coppertone, the Cowsills, and shiny gold peace medallions from a store called The Bottomless Pit, or from the other one called The Nude. Those Sky Blue pops from Popsicle Pete. Matchbox cars, made of metal in some faraway land called Great Britain that we kicked the shit out of twice and then rescued from the evil Germans a couple times after that. Ninety-nine cents apiece, in a neat little cardboard box. Indestructible. Those little cars were mass-manufactured but in a kid's hand each one was unique. It had extension in the Cartesian, philosophical sense, it had essence because it took up space. The vehicle emerged, this shiny new thing, you brought it into being in the world by taking it out of the box with your own little hands. Call it a child's developmental stage to absorb into the next higher state like the Swiss psychologist Jean Piaget theorized, if you want. But who's to say that a child's apprehension, without the clutter of words, isn't a direct experience of the Real that you lose as you mature, and your brain gets clogged up with all kinds of make-believe bullshit?

When you got a little older, it was slot cars. The Ford J. Ran on an electric track. Back then, you could get a pack of five Topps baseball cards for a nickel. Plus, you got a big piece of Bazooka gum and that smell of pink all over the cards. You had the simple thrill of opening the pack to discover what Major Leaguers you got, you didn't want to know ahead of time, it would spoil the only surprise in life. You imagined JFK was a saint because he was young and strong and your world was wholly Catholic, and you think you remember watching his funeral live on the black and white even

43

though you were only five. Just like you remember seeing The Beatles the very first time they were on the *Ed Sullivan* show. Did you really see it, live? You could only be imagining you saw those events when they actually happened. Maybe all you really saw were the reruns a few years later, after the dust settled. Like after Kennedy turned out to be something less than a saint, weakened by perpetual pain, in the reruns of presidential lives.

There were those other Beetles, they were everywhere, parading up and down Mack Avenue, too many to count. Almost every other vehicle was a Bug of a different color. It was like a continuous celebration of fun and innocence. But we were a Ford family, for better or worse. Mainly worse. Planned obsolescence, controlled madness. The car accidents were bloodier and more deadly back then because the metal was thicker and nobody wore seat belts, if they even had them. Now we're on track to get cars that are gonna drive us from point A to point B. All zeroes and ones flying around. How would Descartes account for the digital?

Thus, the circles we spin around in. *Go Dog Go*. That division between the black and the white, it's like being on an edge between two squares, an edge that seems so easy to step across, like simply walking across the street. Simple for a kid, anyway. Foucault was right when he said there was no madness before civilization. But he said that a while back, back in the days of Creepy Crawlers and Snoopy and the Easy-Bake Oven. No more *Laugh-In*. Or Uncle Joe, he's a movin' kinda slow. Not even a Friendly Ghost. Now it's all danger, *Naked and Afraid*, evil zombies, and *Hunger Games* at high rates of speed. And wife-swapping and paying kids to compete like adults. Which begs the question of whether competition is a mature adult activity. I mean, what do you get out of it, besides momentary surges nobody can maintain without alcohol and other drugs? All this intensity, of digits and drones whizzing by, people throwing them at each other, millions of them in an instant, right between the eyes. Never mind the myriad ways that lucrative "technological advances" come to permeate consciousness and communication and take on the status of truths. While we get brainwashed into believing these impositions are inevitable. So, we have to live with them, and remain docile and productive for the greater good.

No more Friendly Ghost, who was, after all, white. Not even the Holy Ghost, they got rid of it for something less halloweenish, more ambiguous, less ghastly. Replaced by a spirit of some kind, a spirit lacking shape. Where was one to go, for Holy Spirit? There was the tall gregarious chain-smoking Irish American priest who came to us with his unfiltered Camels, and all the smoke and incense seemed to transform everyone in the parish. Father Dooley was incendiary and enigmatic. He talked openly about inequality. People got fired up. Then he left us for the real action in the inner city and we were stuck with the old pissed-off pastor.

I suppose these little glimpses of memory could be classified as random sense-impressions of an overly sensitive kid, revealed to others only when the quantum particles in a particular time-space continuum got disturbed. Like when the therapist, who lived on a big piece of land in a big house in Grosse P, seemed to bristle once, for just the slightest moment. Right before he asked why I suggested that the white people in the suburbs ought to go live in Detroit with the black people. He bristled; it was a visceral reaction. Maybe the bristle was in response to a ridiculously naive suggestion. Maybe it meant something else. We like to believe that people think and act and react for one reason at a time, so we can pretend that we truly know. A single right answer, and all the other ones wrong. Maybe believing that creates a new national problem. A problem of single-mindedness.

Rick and Lew get in trouble

Wake up, Lew. Talk to me. I don't nap, only think, can't help it. Thoughts of the past, when we were young, and they told us anything was possible because it's America. Now, no more. Finally, he rolls over and opens his eyes.

"What are you doing?" he asks.

"Waiting for you to wake up."

"Hand me my cigarettes."

"Where are they?"

"I don't know, where did I put them?" He sits up, looks around. "Look in the bathroom."

Yep, his smokes are there with his lighter. What am I, his house servant? Huh, there's a bottle of meds that aren't mine. Some drug I've never heard of.

"Here you go. What's the drug for?"

"Drug, what drug?"

"The one on the sink."

He lights up, takes a big drag, exhales. "Nothing."

"What happened to you, Lew?"

"What do you mean?"

"You've become right-wing."

"I'm not right-wing."

"You sure sounded like it earlier."

"I'm reasonable."

"You didn't sound reasonable. You sounded right-wing."

"I consider myself middle of the road."

"How can you say that, when you go knocking people seeking equality?"

"I didn't say that. I'm all for treating people equally. I'm for individual freedom. That's pretty damn mainstream."

"Foucault argued that freedom is the means by which people are mobilized to act in certain ways."

"How's that?"

"He argued that knowledge about individuals is associated with efforts to control human behavior."

"Like what?"

"He looked at how people were categorized as criminals, or insane, or sick, or homosexuals, for example. How that happened, how did these categories emerge. Like, how is someone deemed a criminal?"

"Easy," Lew says. "You commit a crime, you're a criminal."

"You committed an act that's classified as a crime. But saying you're a criminal, what makes that happen? What in the development of modern societies needed to be addressed?"

"Fighting crime. Catch bad guys."

"Categorizing somebody as a criminal, marks that person as different, as someone other than normal, as a danger to society. It labels them as deviant and bad. You get stereotypes. Like, if a black kid goes into a store wearing a hoodie, he poses a danger."

Lew takes another drag and coughs. "That's just a normal reaction."

"You mean, a racist reaction. Or at least, race based."

47

"No, a human reaction. It's the kid in the hoodie who's reinforcing stereotypes."

"What, that if you're young, and black, you're a criminal?"

"That's not what I meant."

"Needless to say, Lew, the vast majority of blacks don't commit crimes."

"I'm not saying he can't wear a hoodie. And I definitely don't think somebody can go assault a kid just because he's wearing a hoodie. But it raises suspicions."

"Do white people react the same way if the kid in the hoodie is white?"

"Yeah."

"Bullshit."

"Alright, Rick, here's an example. Suppose you're lounging by a pool in a white neighborhood, and you see a couple black people enter. Aren't you going to take notice, maybe even stare, before catching yourself? Does that make you a racist?"

"Nobody's saying that."

"Same thing if two guys walk in holding hands. Most people would take note of that."

"Is that all you think racism is?"

"Of course not. I'm sure there are plenty of out-and-out racists. You gave an example about stereotyping, and I gave one."

"Your example sucks, Lew. It doesn't remotely capture racism."

"Don't you think I know that? Yours doesn't either!"

"Why are you getting all bent out of shape?"

He coughs again. "Because I just woke up, and you're pissing me off with the accusations."

"I'm not making accusations."

"Yes, you are."

"All the discomfort that people of different races have with each other, that's why we have to be a more diversely integrated society."

48

"How are you gonna do that, Rick? Force people to live together?"

"No, but people need to know the different ways people express themselves. So they don't stay stuck on their impulse to be afraid, and avoid."

"It's not gonna happen when you have policies that favor one group over another. That does the opposite. It causes resentment."

"So does discrimination."

"Right," Lew says. "But I think a lot of what gets called 'racist' is more of a reaction to favoritism. Like when someone gets a job over someone else who's maybe more qualified based on race."

"What do you call whites favoring whites?"

"That shouldn't happen either."

"But it does."

"Look, Rick, in this country, the bottom line has always been about protecting individual freedom. When you favor one group over another, then it's not about the individual anymore."

"Put it this way. There's a history of individuals in the majority group who discriminate against other individuals based on what they look like."

Lew sighs. "Let's go get some food at that bar across the street."

"We were talking about something important, and now you want to go eat at a place called the Dead Boar?"

"Yeah. The Dead Boar."

"Alright, I guess I can eat."

A few minutes later, we cross the road for the bar. I stop in front of the big bear statue with front legs over my head. One paw holds a little U.S. flag. The other paw's missing. Looks like it broke off.

"Hey, Lew, where's the dead boar?"

"You're standing in front of it."

"No, this is a bear. Not a boar."

Lew's already opened the door and stepped inside. I glance over at the deer pole. A third carcass has been added and the dog's gone. No new blood on the tracks. The dog must've lapped it all up.

I expect the Dead Boar will be a dark dump with nobody in it, but it's bright and more of a restaurant than a bar, all shiny knotty wood, and plenty of customers. Surprising thing, maybe half of them are black. Some bad southern rock music playing, yuck. There are dining tables on the left side and a long bar on the right. On the dining side, round tables are ringed by booths along the walls, which are lined with mounted deer heads and little gold-plated plaques beneath them. About three-quarters of the tables are filled with families and couples. Above them, maybe fifteen long strings of white Christmas lights hang from the center of the ceiling in big loops all the way to where the ceiling meets the walls, kinda like spokes in a wheel.

Down the middle of the room, there's a row of small booths open on the bar side. The bar's pretty crowded, mostly men. Up high at each end of the bar, massive flat screen TVs are showing NFL playoff games. And up there, in between the TVs, right next to a big U.S. flag, there's a dead boar. Just head and fur and claws, facing the floor. Nailed on a board, looking down, defeated. Like the God-Child, for goodness' sake.

I follow Lew past a Seat Yourself sign and we settle down at one of the booths across from the bar. Everybody at the bar has that exaggerated shit eating grin that goes with having had a couple drinks or more. A waitress approaches with a basket of tortilla chips, salsa, and a couple menus. She's got the fake blonde hair look. "Welcome to the Dead Boar," she says. "I'm Carrie. We feature Mexican food. Can I get you two gentlemen anything to drink?"

"I'll have a Miller," Lew says.

"How about you, sir?"

"Do you have any local stout on tap?"

"Stout?"

"Yeah, you know. Dark beer. Black. The heavy stuff."

"The only beer we have like that is Guinness, in a bottle."

"Guinness has fish guts in it. How about bourbon? Do you have George Dickel?"

"I'll have to check. Be right back."

I grab a chip and glance through the menu. Standard stuff.

"Why did you say that?" Lew says as he dips a chip in the salsa.

"What?"

"About Guinness being made out of fish guts."

I reach for another chip. "Somebody in New Orleans told me that once. This old guy in the Latin Quarter, he insisted that Guinness was made with fish guts."

"That's ludicrous."

"The Guinness on this side of the Atlantic isn't really Guinness, it's made in Canada. Not Ireland."

"There's no beer on the planet made with fish guts. Except maybe in Scandinavia or Iceland. What does that even mean, beer with fish guts?"

"That's what this old guy told me. Actually, he was yelling it loudly outside of a bar. Then he threw up in the street. Too off the wall to make up. Besides, Canada has lots of fish."

"What?"

"Fish. Canada has lots of fish, just like Iceland and Norway. They may very well use fish guts in the beer."

Carrie returns. "I'm sorry, sir, we don't carry Jim Dickel. But we do have Jim Beam, Wild Turkey, and Jack Daniels."

"It's George Dickel. Why is it that every frickin' bar I ever go to outside of Ann Arbor has never heard of George Dickel?"

"I don't know, sir."

"We used to drink it in college."

"Dahd, just order a Jack Daniels."

"Jack Daniels blows. How about Old Granddad?"

"I don't think so," she says. "We have Southern Comfort."

"Shit. I'll have a Corona. And a shot of Wild Turkey."

"Sure thing. Do you gentlemen know what you would like to order from our menu?"

I watch Lew stuff two tortilla chips in his mouth at once. "Do you have fresh tamales?"

She looks befuddled, like it's a novel word. "I don't think so. I can ask."

"That's okay. I'll have the burrito bowl. With chicken."

"Excellent choice. How about you, sir?"

"I'll have the steak fajitas," Lew says.

"That's our most popular. I'll be right back with your Corona and Wild Turkey. And your Budweiser."

"Miller," Lew says.

"I'm sorry, Miller."

She walks off. "I'm excellent, Lew. You're just popular. In a single stoplight town."

"Why did you ask if they have fresh tamales?"

"Because I like them."

"Nobody in the middle of Michigan makes tamales."

"You never know. It's a multicultural world. Stop pounding all the chips."

"What do you care, we can get more."

I look around the room. "I wonder how this town got so integrated."

Some fat white guy sitting at the bar turns around. "How'd this town get integrated?"

He smiles and elbows a fat black guy sitting next to him. "Hey Cal! This guy wants to know why we're integrated." He belches and they both laugh.

"You tell him," Cal says.

"Well, yo' people was my people's slaves!" They laugh their heads off.

Cal looks at me with a semi-drunk, seemingly sincere smile. "This town's been integrated forever. My people came here from Chicago, they were music performers. My grandpappy played the saxophone."

"Oh yeah?" I don't really give a shit.

"Yeah, man. They'd tour around the state and stop here for their August vacations. Go to the lake. Before they went back to the city. Some of them liked it so much, they retired in Gladkin, just up the road."

"I see." I'm having trouble taking in all this unsolicited info. Maybe they're messing with me. Grandpappy. Fortunately, they've returned their attention to the football game as Carrie drops off our drinks. Corona, it's like drinking frickin' water compared to a good Imperial stout like Samuel Smith's. But they wouldn't know that in Gladkin.

I quickly down the shot of Wild Turkey and take a slug of beer. "Hey, Lew, I bet Gladkin's not even the name of the town, even if there is one. And no stout. It's the middle of winter, and they don't have any fucking stout!"

"Be quiet."

"What were we talking about?"

"Fish guts."

"No, I mean before." Thoughts flicker like lightning bugs, and short-term memory's an issue.

"It probably wasn't that important," Lew says.

"We were talking about race. Although, to be honest, we have to qualify everything."

"Why's that?"

"Isn't it obvious? We can't possibly know what it's like to be black or brown."

"That doesn't mean we can't have an opinion."

"We can't have an opinion that's fully informed."

Lew's still eating chips non-stop, with big scoops of salsa. "That goes both ways, Dahd."

"Okay, but you don't have to turn it into an adversarial thing. The social situations are different. Whites have a more privileged status. In general."

Lew leans across the table. "That crap about so-called white privilege, it's loaded. It's code for, 'if you've got more than me, you're unfairly advantaged.' That's why you get such a reaction from the other side. They feel unfairly attacked."

"You can't deny that plenty of people have a lot of resources that others don't, and the vast majority of the 'haves' are white."

"News flash: most people who have a lot of money earned it. What's wrong about that?"

"Okay, Lew, but how'd they get there? How'd they get to go to a top business school, or law school, or medical school? They could afford it."

"That doesn't mean they're privileged. Their parents earned it, or their grandparents, or their great-grandparents."

"That's what makes them privileged."

"No, Rick, to label me as 'privileged' because I'm white and have money I earned, that's bull."

"It's not about you, Lew."

"It is, if somebody gets the job over me on that basis. This is a country built on the idea of individual self-determination, and there's nothing wrong with that."

"How can you eat that salsa? It looks like it came out of a big vat."

Lew takes another double-decker scoop of salsa. "I don't care."

"This country's also based on the idea of equality. There's a long history of the effects of discrimination on entire communities that don't have a way out of poverty."

"I'm talking about the here and now."

"Stop playing dumb, Lew. It's still happening in the here and now. But there's a way to make things better for everybody."

"Okay, Rick, so what's your big solution?"

"Make it easier for people to take care of themselves."

He pauses. "Sounds like socialism."

"Don't give me that shit. You say that words like privilege are loaded. So is the word socialism. Besides, I'm not talking about doing away with a free market economy."

"Then what are you talking about?"

"I'm talking about individuals. Everybody's stuck in their own body."

"Stuck in their own body? What does that have to do with anything?"

"I mean, the most practical way for people to live is to take care of themselves, right?"

"That's the way things already are."

"There's too much out of reach. The philosopher Jean-Jacques Rousseau said that in a state of nature, if somebody scares me away from one source of sustenance, like an apple tree, it's no big deal, I'll just go to the next one."

Lew finishes off the last chip. "We don't live in a state of nature."

"His point was modern society creates all kinds of unnecessary obstacles for people."

"Are we supposed to return to the wild?"

"I can't believe you just ate all the chips."

"Obstacles are the price everybody has to pay for living in a modern society."

"But if we truly believed in the importance of the individual person, we wouldn't tolerate all the unnecessary suffering."

"Anybody can take care of themselves," Lew says. "They just have to make the effort. And deal with some adversity."

"That doesn't work for millions of people. Is that their fault?"

"To a large degree, yes,"

"No, Lew! There's too much out of reach. Otherwise, you wouldn't have so many poor people. And I'm not talking only about poverty. I mean, we make it too hard for everybody. The stakes are constantly being raised. By nonstop increasing competition."

"How's that?"

"Let's say, somebody's fifty-five years old, has a job that pays a good salary, and loses their job because of competition in that industry. The only job they can get is for half that wage, and no benefits. They can't support their family and pay their mortgage on that. Fifty years ago, that wouldn't have happened."

"Then sell your house and go back to school. Get trained in a career that's actually in demand. Like web programming."

"That's not realistic for most fifty-five-year-olds who haven't been in school since they were young. Plus, it'd take years. Even if they could do that, who's going to hire them, over a twenty-one-year-old with the same degree?"

"Tough luck."

Carrie arrives with our food, a little too quickly. Suspiciously quick. "Here you are."

"Look at your steak fajita sizzle, Lew. Just like in Mexico."

"Let's just eat, I'm starving,"

"Would you like another Corona, or Wild Turkey?" Carrie asks.

Corona. Fake Mexican food on the outskirts of Gladkin or Gladbag or whatever. No Latinos. Makes no sense. America, the melting pot. Melted cheese all over my food.

"I didn't want all this cheese."

"I'm sorry, sir, it comes with it. Would you like me to take it back?"

"No, just bring me another shot of Wicked Turkey."

"Would you like another Corona?"

"Yeah. No, the last one tasted like piss. Give me the fish guts, even though it's from Canada instead of Ireland. And the Wicked Turkey."

"Excuse me?"

"I apologize for my friend," Lew interjects. "He means Guinness. And Wild Turkey."

"Would you like another Miller?"

"Um, sure."

Off she goes again.

"Why'd you say, 'apologize for my friend?'"

"Because you're being an asshole, Rick. And it's Wild Turkey."

"I know that."

"You said Wicked Turkey."

"No, I didn't."

"Yes, you did."

"She seemed to understand me. And even if I did, Wicked Turkey sounds a lot better than Wild. They should call it Wicked Turkey. Wicked. Wicked Wild."

"Just eat your frickin' burrito bowl."

"It's got cheese all over it."

"Stop making it so complicated. Just spoon it off."

"It's stuck to everything."

"Too bad. Just eat it."

"'Too Bad.' That's a good tune. Aerosmith."

Lickity-split, Carrie's back with the drinks. I promptly down the Wild Turkey and start on the Guinness.

"Are you deciding to get drunk?" Lew asks.

"It's been a long day. All the shit you've put me through."

"You mean all the shit you've put *me* through."

"Why couldn't you have just flown to Detroit Metro?"

"I didn't want to sit around in Toronto."

"What's wrong with Toronto?"

"Nothing. I took the earliest flight I could. What's the big deal?"

"The big deal is, Metro Airport is twenty minutes from my house, and Saginaw's like, three hours."

57

"That's because you drive too slow. Just like you walk. And eat. Eat your food."

Bar's gotten more crowded, the music louder. At least, that's how my sensory apparatus is working right now. Guess I am feeling a little tipsy. Not in shape for hard liquor. Big dude walks in wearing a shiny silver jacket with a logo that says, "The Bob Seger Silver Bullet Band 1998 World Tour" across the front. I watch him walk up to the bar near us. Big cowboy boots. On the back of his jacket there's a list of concert tour cities and dates. I could swear, he just ordered a Southern Comfort.

I hear my voice say, "Bob Seger sucks."

Lew glares at me. "Not so loud."

"I'm just saying, Bob Seger sucks."

The guy in the Seger jacket turns his head a little. Did he hear me? Hard to tell, not enough data.

"Keep it down, Dahd."

"Same with John Mellencamp, and Bruce Springsteen."

"Mellencamp, maybe," Lew says. "But Springsteen?"

"All that feigned, self-indulgent, running away from the man bullshit. Big rip-off."

"What's the rip-off?"

"Too contrived. Seems like a good guy, though."

"You're getting drunk. Mouthy drunk."

"I'm just exercising free speech."

"What you're calling free speech sounds angry drunk."

"I'm not angry drunk. Besides, even if I was, it's the Dead Boar's fault."

"Why's that?"

"Because if they had George Dickel, I'd be happy drunk."

"I think we should leave, Dahd."

"We need to finish our food and drinks."

The guy with the Seger jacket is standing near our table now, holding his drink, watching the stupid football game. Shit, he even looks like Bob

Seger, with a big beer gut and beard and long black greasy hair. Could be his kid, living off his dad's millions, in a cabin in the woods.

"Bob Seger sucks."

He turns his head and looks down at me. "Fuck you."

"Let's go, Rick."

"I have to piss first."

"I'll take care of the bill. Hurry up."

I stand up and put on my coat, feel for my catheter shit in the pockets. The Seger guy's in my way. Really does kinda look like him. Or Paul Bunyan. Or both. That's what Roger Daltrey sang, ain't it funny how we all seem to look the same. Even though the Brits got it from black America, at least they got it. As opposed to weak white American rock rot.

"Is-cues me. Bob."

Brush past Seger a little roughly, he turns around for a second, but I keep walking, stumbling through the crowd of bodies at the bar, toward the rest room in back. Didn't mean to brush against him like that, guess I don't have full control right now. A little unexpected trouble with balance, bump into a couple more people, didn't do that on purpose, sorry man, and it's darker back here, like in the Grosse Pointe South gym, at the prom. Guess I'm essentially intoxicated, in terms of being in full control of all bodily functions. Albeit by that definition, I'm drunk twenty-four seven, on account of everything that my body doesn't do or does too much of. Can't resolve that definitional issue right now, too many variables, brain cells scattered about, not enough usable info or reasoning capacity.

Alright, made it all the way to the back, there's the sign, GENTS, carved in the frickin' plywood door. A single toilet stall with no door, a communal urinal, and a sink. Fuck, why the communal urinal? Guess they didn't upgrade when they turned this place into a restaurant, too cheap. Gents. Musta been a barn once, the urinal a pig trough they just left there, added some plumbing. Imagine Calvin and his pal peeing in a pig trough. Hairy pigs. Wild boar, domesticated. While Bob Seger's taking a shit on the toilet. Grandpappy. Bunch of horseshit. Does the management expect me to leave the restroom door unlocked? I'm not into that Russian style restroom, ain't gonna happen, using a catheter's a private affair. In my world.

Dead-bolt the door and go to the urinal. Sigh, sick of doing this shit every time I frickin' gotta pee, just so my kidneys don't get damaged by air pressure. I'm usually pretty good at this but feelin' a bit unsteady at the moment from the beer and bourbon combo, and now the coudé tip's touched the wall. Fuck. Not gonna waste it. Don't feel like ripping another package open, fuck, I've had plenty of infections, don't need another right now, toss it and take another one out. Do the right thing. "Dream On," that was the theme of the prom. Aerosmith sucks, too, except their first few albums and I didn't stay at the prom very long. Caught my date making out with somebody behind a curtain. Let him take her home.

Okay, got things going here now as the urine falls. Think of a song to sing. Not Aerosmith. How about a pig song, since I'm at the trough. Like the George Harrison tune about the little piggies who like to crawl in dirt. Their life is getting worse. Burp, ahh needed that. Then there's other pigs, who wear starched shirts. Or something like that.

Somebody tries to open the door. Shit, I just got started. Tends to freak people out when they hear how long it takes me to piss. Sometimes they'll ask, are you okay? Forget the pigs, just count. One-apple two-apple three-apple four. Too loud out there, he can't hear the steady stream. Can't speed it up, only relinquish fluid as gravity allows. A steadily deteriorating plight, what my life has come down to, this shit. A knock. Turn my face toward the door. Whoever's there is turning the doorknob back and forth.

"Patience, please. It's a long one."

Said it loud enough. Loud enough for him to hear, without yelling like a maniac. Proper Grosse Pointe pronunciation, restrained. Explained the situation concisely. Decent. Objectively, even though there's no such thing. Shit, what apple was I on? How 'bout another pig song. Pink Floyd had one, about giant pigs flying around, over smokestacks. In an industrial zone. They're bored and in pain. Pretty grim. And somethin' about a dog and a bone. Another knock. Shit. Must expect me to be communal. Like a bunch of pigs bobbing for apples.

"I have a medical condition!"

A hundred apple. Whole numbers alone can easily take it to two or three hundred or so, depending. Hundred two, hundred three, hundred four, hundred forty. Another knock, louder. More like a pound, somebody's big fat fist. Getting pissed off, well same here, dude. What the fuck, go out back. What would Roger Waters advise in this situation? If there's a pig on the wing, that is. Lew would tell me to maintain. However, he's not here, so I have no such obligation. Two hundred thirty-two, thirty-three, thirty-four.

Two pounds on the door. All this pressure, on my bladder, on me.

"Alright, justa second!" Control your muscles, that's what the therapist said. Willpower. Thirty-three, thirty-two, thirty-one.

Three pounds, hostile. Okay, asshole.

Pee's still streaming as I turn around and open the deadbolt, can't waste the catheter. Whoever's on the other side of the door turns the knob and pulls it open. It's the big fucking Seger guy. From the look on his face, he ain't seen nothing remotely like this before.

"I just need a drummer."

He steps back, too late to avoid my piss on his boots.

"This must be the first time you've seen an alien. We're real."

"Hey Mike, this guy's pissing all over the place!"

In a flash, I yank the catheter out of my innards and extend it to him. Seger steps back as I step forward to my advantage, albeit my dick's hanging out. For a flash of a second, I think of one of those impressionist paintings, you know, in the Parisian salons, or whatever. By that little guy who looked like the Penguin, what's his name, with the hyphen. Backstage goings-on, at the Moulin Rouge. Don't ask me why.

61

Seger's pie hole's still open.

"See, nothing's coming out, I can't piss without it. Like I said, it's a medical condition. But you haven't seen a catheter before, have you? Watch. Nothing to be afraid of." I swing it over my head like a lasso. Some latent piss flies out across the dude's Bob Seger jacket. That's bad, that's a bad look, he might pop me. Fuckit.

Except he's still too stunned to do anything. Next thing I know, Lew's grabbed my arm and someone from behind the bar says, "You better put that away."

Clarify, man. My catheter, or my dick? Lew strong arms me through the bar crowd. He's grabbed my collar, he's in my face, I lose my balance as he drags me toward the door.

"Pull up your pants."

"Huh?"

"Pull up your fucking pants!"

"Oh."

Somebody says, "You'd better leave now."

"I have a medical condition."

"Ya asshole!" somebody else yells.

"Yeah! I just emerged, from *Plato's Cave*!"

"Shut up!" Lew says. Tersely. Almost to the door.

"The Oracle says you should all be listening to *Quadrophenia*!"

"Just shut up, Rick!"

"Instead of stupid Bob Seger! Lew, where's the wastebasket?"

Lew yanks on me again.

"For the catheter."

I swing it once more and let it go with a fling as Lew drags me out the door into the dark cold air. He loses his grip as I slip on a patch of ice and go down, face-first. Ouch. Huffing and puffing, Lew yanks me by the collar onto my feet. Bad dog.

"C'mon, Rick!" He leads me across the street as I wave back to the concrete bear. Shit, Lew's still strong as a tight end. Surprising, given his weight loss and generally emaciated appearance.

"I need to go back, Lew."

"No, you don't."

"I left my catheter."

"Never mind."

"It's recyclable."

Lew opens the door to our room, and I bumble into the bathroom.

"You just peed, didn't you?"

"I was rudely interrupted before I could complete the song-cycle."

This time, I don't bother closing the door. Pull out another catheter. Secret's out, all over town. Now Lew will hear my plight. I will be quiet and let him take in the full effect. Maybe he'll feel sorry for me, or awed.

"Playing in the dirt. Always in clean shirts." As I wait out the remaining dribble, I see Lew's pills on the edge of the sink. Feel my head clearing a bit.

A couple minutes later, done, finally.

"Jesus, it takes you forever." Lew is sprawled on the bed watching TV and smoking. I cross over to the sofa-bed, which he already opened for me, and even thrown a blanket and pillow on it. A true friend, still, after all these years. A rescuer. On the telly, white guy in a wheelchair, and a young black guy in a turtleneck.

"What's the deal with the catheters, Dahd?"

"*Streets of San Francisco*. That was a good show."

"It's *Ironside*."

"No, it's *Streets of San Francisco*. With Karl Malden."

"You're on drugs. Look, it's Raymond Burr in a wheelchair."

"Maybe they're both in it. Like when Batman met the Green Hornet."

Lew coughs. "Karl Malden was never on *Ironside*."

"He coulda been a special guest." I just wanted to say, Karl Malden. His real name was something like Ivan, or Igor. "Lew, do you remember, in college we used to do bong hits and watch those late-night *Ironside* reruns? Followed by *Marcus Welby, M.D.* With the other doctor on his motorcycle. Steven Kyling, or something like that. And their assistant, Consuelo. She didn't look Latina."

"She was a registered nurse. What's the deal with the catheters?"

"What's Ironside's assistant's name? That black guy there in the turtleneck, he was kinda slick. Mark, I think. Ironsides would bark out his name, Mark! Mark! I think he was in law school. He was my hero, kind-of. But not like Linc in the *Mod Squad*."

"What?"

"Mark, what's his last name?"

"Um, Mark Sanger."

"Yes! Good. Very good, Lew. I think he spelled it with a C, though."

"What? What C?"

"M-A-R-C."

Lew takes another drag on his cigarette. "How could you even know that?"

"I think at the beginning, you know, the actor's name so-and-so. 'As Marc Sanger.' Marc with a C. Same with Linc, on the *Mod Squad*. L-I-N-C."

"That's great spelling, Dahd, but what are the catheters all about?"

"I need them to pee."

"I get that. How come?"

"My bladder doesn't contract."

"Why's that?"

"Don't know. Could be drugs, or too much Diet Coke, or other filthy nasty habits."

"You mean like swinging a catheter over your head and your dick hanging out?

"That asshole kept banging on the door. And he was the one who opened it."

"Doesn't mean you had to pull that stunt."

"It wasn't a stunt. It was reality. I was fucking peeing. Like a reality show. I was trying to educate the dude. You didn't have to be so rough on me."

"Sorry, Dahd, but half the people there were probably packing heat."

"Heat?"

"Handguns."

"White light. White heat."

"Stop."

"It's gonna make me go blind. You know, Lew, you ruined my *Easy Rider* moment."

"What?"

"Like when Jack Nicholson goes ballistic at the diner."

"That was *Five Easy Pieces*."

"Did you really think somebody would pull out their piece and shoot me, just because I showed them how a catheter works?"

"No, but we coulda got our asses kicked."

"It was good Lew, what you did. Your quick reaction time. Like when you took a bullet for me."

"I didn't take a bullet for you."

"I told you about the catheters. Now you have to tell me something."

"About what?"

"About why, about the real reason you came back."

He sighs. "You already know that."

"Why now?"

"I'm just trying to help a friend. Make a difference for somebody, for once."

"But why now?"

"Because it's Cam."

"You haven't seen him in, forever."

Lew sighs. "Okay, it's not just about Cam. It is and isn't. But it's what got me out of what I was doing."

"What did you get out of?"

"The way I've been living."

"What do you mean?"

"I'm tired of bouncing around from one company to the next. I'm burned out. I quit."

"Why'd you bounce around?"

"Because my job was basically to break things down."

"Break what down?"

"Corporations. Fire people. After takeovers and mergers. Go in and straighten things out."

"I can't see you doing that."

"Well, I did. I've been doing it for twenty, twenty-five years."

"Why'd you move around?"

"Because the jobs were all over the place. Offices and factories in different countries. Europe. Africa. Asia."

"Who'd you work for?"

"Whoever hired me. European companies. I'd take over a division for a year or two. Cut payroll. Then move on."

"I still can't see you doing that. I can't see you going around and figuring out who loses their job."

"If I didn't do it, someone else would."

"Didn't it bother you?"

"That's how the world works. It makes companies more efficient. Which ultimately makes economies more efficient."

"Tell that to the people who lost their jobs."

"Get real, Rick. The world is flat now. It's an ultra-competitive world."

"It doesn't have to be."

"Yeah. Instead, we can make sure everybody's got a job. Then we'd all be poor."

"An ultra-competitive world, is that such a good thing? Has that resulted in a good society, a good world?"

"What's a good world got to do with it?"

"Foucault argued that freedom keeps people engaged. Not just the state, but big businesses, too. Like the companies you worked for."

"Yeah, well, guess what, Rick? The world's complicated. There's lots of people doing all kinds of shady shit. It's full of corruption. In fact, it's pretty much standard practice in most countries, you gotta pay somebody off to do business."

"What the fuck happened to you?"

"Maybe I wised up."

"If you're so wised up, what are you doing here, in the middle of fucking Michigan in the winter, with me?"

"Let's just go to bed, alright?" He turns off the TV.

"Just a minute." I reach down into my backpack.

"What the hell is that?"

"My BiPAP machine." I plug it in the wall. "See, watch. This is the mask. It turns on automatically as soon as I put it on and breathe. Cool technology. Great human innovation."

"I gotta listen to that all night?"

"It's soothing, it's a soothing sound."

"It sounds like a fucking jet engine!"

"Besides, Lew, you've got the bed. I gotta sleep on this thing I'm sinking into. I'll have a sore back in the morning."

Lew switches off the lamp light.

"Wait, turn it back on."

"Now what?"

"I forgot to take my meds."

"Hurry up."

I get the vials out of my backpack, unscrew the lids, and dump what I need into my palm.

"What is all that shit you're taking?"

"Various things." I step into the bathroom.

"What, are you a pill junkie now?"

"They're prescription." I tear the wrapping off a cup, fill it with water, toss all the pills in my mouth and drink all nine of them down. Back in bed, and Lew turns the light off again.

"They're probably not good for you in the long run, Dahd."

"I need them to maintain."

"What for?"

"Various maladies."

"Like what?"

"I'd rather not go over the whole list, it's boring. What about your pills?"

"Let's just go to sleep."

"Fine." I put on my mask and wait for blissful sleep. Thinking about this discussion and all of the adventures today. Maybe I overdid it in the Dead Boar. A little.

A couple minutes later, there's the sound of a vehicle and bright headlights shining through the curtain, then red, rotating, and a rap on the door.

"Who is it?" Lew asks.

"State Police."

"Fuck."

Lew goes to the door. I stay down, with my mask still on, and peer at the door through half-closed eyelids. Two young state cops in their royal blue unis, and behind them, a State Police muscle car flashing red and white lights across the open doorway. They look young enough to be my kids. One of the them's kinda skinny, with red hair and freckles, the other one's a black guy who kinda looks like Mister T. Without the tomahawk.

"We had a complaint about indecent exposure in the Dead Boar a little while ago," the redhead says. "The proprietor said someone came out of the restroom exposed, swinging a rubber hose and threatening customers."

"They said there were two Caucasians involved that no one in the bar recognized, and that they walked out and came over here," Mister T adds.

Lew looks a bit tense. "That's not exactly what happened, officer."

"I need to see some identification. You too, sir."

Shit, they noticed me. I pull off my mask and get my wallet out of my backpack. A tube of Surgi-Lube falls out. Lew hands the redhead his passport as I dig through my wallet for my license.

I hand them my license. "This is all a big misunderstanding, officers. I have a medical condition, and there was no hose. It was a catheter. Here's my doctor's business card. See, he's a urologist."

The cops look at me a little blankly.

"I'll show you." I pick up my coat and go into the pockets. Mister T puts his right hand on his holster.

I pull out a couple catheters. "See? I'll show you." I rip open a package. "You see, officers, my Johnson doesn't work right, so I have to shove one of these all the way into my bladder to get the urine out."

The redhead blushes. Or maybe his skin was already redneck red.

"And see, there's this lubricant I have to use, in this tube, it's called Surgi-Lube. What you do is, you put some of the Surgi-Lube up and down the catheter, these are the French tip model, which are easier to get in your dick than the American kind. I prefer the French style, more precisely, coudé tip. Americans can be crude. Coudé must be a French word. I'm not sure of the proper pronunciation. Coda? Cooda? Cood? Maybe just 'code.' But I can show you how it's intended to be used if you want. I've done it before; they made me do it in airport security once. In China."

"Sir, did you leave the restroom exposing yourself?" Mister T asks.

"Did you know that Rousseau used catheters?"

"There were families at the Dead Boar, sir."

"Not the artist. Jean-Jacques, you know, the philosopher? French Enlightenment? Actually, a little earlier. Did you know he had to use catheters to pee? Seriously, it's true. I wonder what they were made out of back then. I mean, we're talking eighteenth century. Although France was way more advanced than us. But what could they make then that you could get up your penis, not to mention a vagina. What materials could they fabricate? No coudé tip back then. Doubt it. I think, therefore I pee. Radical doubt."

"Sir, did you leave the restroom with exposure?"

"There could be an evil demon tricking me."

"Did you expose yourself, sir?"

"You mean, my privates? What happened was, this guy who looked like Bob Seger was pounding on the door of the Gents room, I figured he was in an emergency situation. Like maybe he had the runs or something. I tried to yell but the music was too loud, so in order to accommodate his concern, I thought I better play it safe and get out of there right quick. It was a normal human reaction to high-stress, a high-stress situation. Kinda like a battlefield reaction. You know, gut. Gut reaction. Normal. Plus, he was the one who actually opened the door."

"Did you throw the catheter, sir?"

"Negative. No, what happened, you see, it was slippery, I mean, I didn't have time to wash all the Surgi-Lube off my fingers, like in normal times. The priority in that situation was to get that other guy access in the john as soon as humanly possible. When I realized the catheter was still in me, much to my chagrin, I whipped it out to pull my pants back up. So as not to upset the other patrons. Unfortunately, it did slip from my grasp as we were leaving the Dead Boar. More of a fling, than a throw. Yeah, a fling. However, it was my left arm, and I'm right-handed. If it did hit somebody, which I'm not conceding, it was entirely unintentional, we were on our way out and I didn't want to add to any existing environmental risk."

"An eyewitness said someone was hit in the face with it."

"That's a design defect. You can't pin that on me, it's not supposed to do that. I went to law school. I know my rights."

Mister T looks at me with steely eyes. "Why are you here, sir?"

"You mean, like, in the Socratic sense?"

"Shut up, Rick," Lew says, giving me a stern look. "We're just passing through. We're on our way to Chicago."

"You'll be leaving in the morning, then."

"Yes, officer, first thing in the morning."

"Archie," I add. "Do you know Archie? The Archies? It was a band, sorry, I guess you're too young."

Mister T hands back our IDs. "We'll be here again in the morning. Since you're passing through, we expect you will be gone."

"Yes, officers," Lew says.

"Goon squad."

All three of them look at me.

"It's a song by Elvis Costello. There's another one, 'Oliver's Army,' that bears some relevance."

"Thank you, officers," Lew says.

"What is police?"

"Excuse me?" the redhead says.

"It's just a question Foucault asked."

"Good night, officers," Lew says. "We'll be gone in the morning."

I nod as they turn to leave. "Fare thee well."

Lew closes the door. "What the fuck was that?"

"It's from a Grateful Dead tune. 'Brokedown Palace.'"

"About Archie, and Rousseau!"

"That one cop, the ginger. Don't you think he looked just like Archie from the comics? You know, Archie and Jughead and Veronica. Et cetera."

"Yeah, I know, Rick. What the fuck! Goon squad?"

"That's a really good tune."

"Did you want to get us hauled in?"

"They were just kids. They weren't gonna do anything."

"How the fuck do you know? God, you're such an incredible asshole!"

"It was an educational opportunity for them."

"I didn't know you threw the catheter and hit somebody!"

"I just winged it. No, more of a fling."

"You know, this is just like what you did at the Ramones concert," Lew says.

"No, it's not."

"Yes, it is. And both times, we get in trouble because of you."

"That's not true."

"Rick, you hit somebody in the face with a used wet catheter!"

"First of all, like I said, that was a surprise, and second of all, you were forcing me out prematurely and I didn't see a wastebasket. And third, I didn't throw a catheter at Joey Ramone. I wasn't even using catheters back then. We were in our twenties and my bladder worked fine then; I think. Maybe not, and I just didn't know it."

"No, you threw a beer bottle and hit Joey Ramone in the crotch."

"I wasn't aiming for it."

"What were you aiming for, then?"

"I don't know, somewhere in his general direction."

"Yeah, that was another fucked up night thanks to you."

"Didn't we cover this already, like thirty or forty years ago? Everybody down on the dance floor was having a blast, bouncing off the walls, it was loud as fuck, we were up there on the balcony and there was no wall for me to bounce off of. I was just trying to participate. It was a historic event. Right after their debut album came out."

"You hit him in the crotch and we got kicked out, and missed the encore because of you. And we coulda got arrested."

"That was the encore."

"No, it wasn't."

"Yes, it was, Lew. He was singing, 'Hey Daddy-O.' It was a seminal punk rock moment in Ann Arbor.

"It wasn't 'Hey Daddy-O' they were playing," Lew says. "It was 'Beat on the Brat.'"

"Whatever. We were there, weren't we? I was the one who got the tickets. What does any of that have to do with now?"

"It's got everything to do with you pissing me off! It's got everything to do with, when you have a couple drinks, you're out of control. Here, here's a moment for you, now, this moment, right now, you're gonna shut up and we're gonna go to sleep. So just shut the fuck up." He turns out the light.

"Okay, Daddy-O."

"Shut up."

Darkness, stillness. "Lew."

"Now is the time for sleep."

"I need to ask you something."

Lew sighs. "What."

"What are your pills for?"

"Nothing."

"They must be for something, unless you're taking them to get stoned."

"I'm not taking prescription meds to get stoned."

"Then what are they for?"

"I want to go to sleep, Dahd. I've earned it. I'll tell you tomorrow."

"Alright." I put on my mask again and activate the BiPAP.

"Jesus!" Lew yells. "You're driving me insane!"

Well, we eventually got to sleep, Lew first, despite all his bitching. I could hear his snoring over the sound of the BiPAP. All I could do was lay there, staring into the dark above me, and think about the police, and Bob Seger, and the Dead Boar. And Joey Ramone, at the Second Chance Bar in Ann Arbor, so many years ago. Nineteen seventy-seven, I think. They kept breaking guitar strings. Even bass strings. How do you break a brand-new bass string? Hey Daddy-O. But thinking about the past got me time-tripping about other stuff in that direction, even further back in time.

Panic in Detroit

Grosse Pointe was surrounded. You had the blacks on one side, the south side of Alter Road, where the manicured green grass and pristine homes ended, and the Black Danger took over. That's all you could know about the other side of Alter Road. A black hole, don't go there, you'll never come back. To the west, on the other side of the Ford Freeway, and somewhere north of Eight Mile, lived those "Others," the working-class whites who fled Detroit for Macomb County. Known to some as the Union Hordes. To the east it's all water. Lake Saint Clair, known to Grosse Pointers as the Lake. Part of the Great Lakes waterway, it's never been particularly clean. You couldn't tell, though, at the surface, so it was clean enough to be the playground of Grosse Pointers on their sailboats and yachts, who never needed to look below the surface at anything. And on the far side of the Lake, way out on the horizon, was a vague gray indiscernible foreign land. Canada, populated by people you could comprehend only as facsimiles. They looked like us and spoke the same language but lived in a quiet, less affluent country with a limited army and badass hockey players. It was somehow fitting that you couldn't tell whether that grayish hue you saw was actually a distant land or just your imagination.

Within Grosse Pointe, there were, and still are, various class distinctions based largely on how close your house was to the Lake. The most visible sign of affluence is probably the two-mile span of mansions on Lakeshore Drive with commanding views of the Lake. Grosse Pointe Shores. On the lakeside, across the street from the mansions, there's a strip of lawn that descends gently down to a concrete break wall and the water. No sidewalk. No beach. Fishing and swimming are illegal because fishing poles and humans in swimsuits would be unsightly to the people living in the mansions. You'd end up with all kinds of people from outside—the union hordes and maybe even the blacks—piling on all over the place.

The unionists were bad enough as it was, cruising around wasted on their powerboats and tossing their beer cans in the water. When I was a kid, I used to bike down there with my trusty Zebco spincast rod despite the fishing ban. I'd lay my bike down at the edge of the break wall and crouch to avoid being seen by the Grosse Pointe police cruising up and down Lakeshore Drive. I still got busted multiple times. I guess they could see my fishing rod sticking up in the air. When the citations began to erode my meager savings account, I gave up a life of crime.

On one of my last few efforts, I had an encounter with a boatload of shop rats. Twentyish greaser guys with hairy chests and faces, and their women in bikinis with most of their sunburned tits showing. They decided it'd be fun to tear their boat about ten feet from the break wall and buzz me. The third time they came around I heaved a huge fucking rock their way, and although I missed their boat by a mile, it pissed them off enough that they turned around. I swear to God, a couple of those bastards actually got out and started after me while one of their women dutifully placed her hands over the boat's license plate. I fled across Lakeshore to the mansion side. They stopped in the middle of the road, glared, and swore at me, and retreated to their lives of general degradation. The looming mansions intimidated those dogs, as if they had come up against an invisible electric fence. Wealth, power, police.

If you lived in Grosse P and worked in downtown Detroit, you could take Lakeshore, which became Jefferson Avenue as you crossed into Detroit. Downtown was a straight shot through the collective devastation of the East Side to the Detroit business district. You did it with your doors locked and your windows up. Eyes straight ahead, though if you bothered to look, there were few signs of life. If you timed it right, during rush hour you could coast all the way through the traffic lights without having to stop even once.

The entire downtown business district consisted of a handful of high-rise office buildings, the City-County Building, the Renaissance Center, and the violent Detroit River, where blacks fished for food. Parking lots and garages, a small number of restaurants and cafeterias, a couple hotels, and some no frill bars. That was about it, unless you counted all the buildings that were vacant. Lots more of those. If you wore a suit, you were about ninety-nine-point-five percent likely to be a white male. During their lunch hour, none of the bankers and lawyers would venture on foot beyond the heavily policed business district for fear of getting mugged, or worse. All they could do was walk around the block.

So, there was this binary relation between downtown Detroit and Grosse Pointe. Two points, each end of a straight line. Whites were the ones, blacks the zeroes. That was reality, there were no other equations about here and now and the future for a kid in Grosse P. If you didn't become a doctor, or a banker, or a lawyer, or an auto exec, and your family didn't own a significant enterprise of some kind like an auto dealership or supplier, and you didn't want to sell shit like insurance or stocks and bonds, well, there was no place else to go. The crux of it for a kid in Grosse Pointe thinking about the future was that there were no other options. If you had question marks in your head, the lack of any information about how to live other than to conform was suffocating.

It was the downtown world of commerce in your business soldier's suit Monday through Friday, tennis and golf on Saturdays, and church on

Sunday mornings. Followed by tennis or golf afterward. The peaceful maintenance of homes, property, family, school, and God. On the weekends, you'd see whole families walking around in matching outfits, the Grosse Pointe leisure time uniform. A bright Lacoste shirt with the happy little alligator on the chest, khakis or shorts, Topsider boat shoes, and no socks. People looked like walking advertisements of what they were wearing. How could you walk around like that, knowing you were on the other side of apartheid?

In fact, most of the people in Grosse Pointe lived pretty modestly. They raised their kids to follow simple rules and do well in school, go to college and get into a well-paying career. Middle class, upper middle class, and yeah, some people had loads of old money. The Cadillacs and Mercedes you'd see up and down Lakeshore Drive were driven slow, below the speed limit, because they could. That's how the affluence was mainly expressed, by the cars, the stately homes, the pristine manicured lawns and shrubs, and the comfortable pace. No flash. Pastoral almost. Maybe like the pace of the antebellum, only with black laborers pushing power mowers instead of slaving away in the fields.

Once in a while, you'd see a little painted statue of a black servant in somebody's front yard. Facing forward, with one arm extended, waiting to welcome and serve guests. Or cheerfully reaching out to take the reins from the white master. Part of a continuous effort of physical and psychological resources directed toward maintaining the status quo. So controlled and deliberate, lawns never seemed to get high or turn brown, and houses never seemed to need paint. No change, except births and deaths. Slowness, and stillness.

Golf and tennis, tennis and golf. My dad, Sam, understood those weren't sports so much as social skills to learn. I hated wasting time on a golf course, and I wasn't very good at tennis. My personal exposure to the country club crowd was working as a harbor boy one summer at the Yacht Club. I got in trouble a couple times over the Commodore's flag.

"Commodore" was the title that designated the club president. Whenever the Commodore arrived, the old German guy who guarded the entrance would phone the harbor office. You had to run across the lawn and get that flag hoisted all the way up before the Commodore had finished parking his Caddie. I wasn't gonna bust my butt to the flagpole for anybody. I got canned by the harbormaster. Or maybe I quit before they could can me, I don't remember. Either way, I didn't give a shit. I was sick of hauling cases of booze to the beautiful people on their yachts in the harbor. Sick of staying awake most of the night to raise the bridge whenever a big boat returned from the Lake and blew its horn. Sick of having to help wasted yachtsmen guide their monstrosities to dock without crashing at three or four in the morning.

My dad's name wasn't really Sam. It was Saleem. He was eighteen years old when his family was forced out of their Palestinian village at gunpoint and fled to Beirut. They ended up in Ashrafiya, the Christian section of the city, where there was help from the local Maronite church. Beirut was beautiful, Sam said. Full of money and style. But not for a young Palestinian man with no money or connections, and he was ambitious. A little while later he went to Johannesburg to work for a Lebanese import-export business. He didn't like being barely above black on the social scale. A couple years after that, he came to the U.S. with a couple hundred dollars; to Dearborn, where there were a lot of people from the Middle East. He got a job at the Vernors Ginger Ale factory downtown on Woodward, learned English at night, became a citizen, then studied accounting at Wayne State and got promoted to the company bookkeeping office. He loved accounting.

"The greatest thing about accounting," he said, "is the balance sheet. There's always a solution. Keep things balanced."

After graduating from college, Sam was hired by the City of Detroit as an accountant, where he met my mother, Sarah. She was a secretary there, going to night school to be a teacher. Sarah was blonde, blue-eyed, the only child of a failed pig farmer from Tennessee who migrated north to work in a Ford factory. On their first date, they saw Casablanca at the United Artists Theater downtown. That's how I ended up with the name Rick. Never Richard, except on my birth certificate. After they got married, my parents moved to Grosse Pointe Woods. "I didn't come all the way to America to live mainly with people from the Middle East," my dad said to me once. "I wanted to be in the middle of things. In the center of the circle."

My dad fit Grosse Pointe perfectly—in a way. He spoke with measured statements and carried himself with the kind of formality that permeated the area, especially as you got closer to the Lake. Magnitude meant more than anything else. If you can't measure it, then it had little to no real value. The bigger the number, the better: house, car, land, bank account. After he got his CPA license and was on his way to becoming a partner at a Big Eight accounting firm, a ranch style house went up for sale in Grosse Pointe Farms, just a couple blocks from the Lake, and he jumped on it. Although a ranch, it was far too big for our family of three. Not big, so much as really long. So long that you couldn't find each other. But he had made it.

There was only one thing Dad didn't like about Grosse Pointe, and America in general. The standard bathroom didn't include a bidet. He didn't understand how everybody in the greatest country in history could walk around with dirty assholes. After we moved to the Farms, Dad had a bidet installed in each bathroom. That was the one thing we had over the neighbors. Our house might've been the smallest on the block, but we didn't walk around in brightly colored alligator shirts and Topsiders with stinky butts.

I was partly of Arab descent, even though I didn't really know it because Dad hardly ever referred to his background, and when he did, it was Palestine, which meant nothing to me. Never heard him say the word, "Arab." Ever. As far as I knew, that would be a guy in a desert astride a camel with a sword like in *Lawrence of Arabia*, or somebody from a place called Baghdad who rode a flying carpet or came out of a magic lantern.

That was what I knew until I went to college and took a Middle Eastern history class, taught by a Jewish professor, which was a momentary revelation without any lasting impact.

One evening, I sat with my dad watching the CBS Evening News, and there was a segment about the conditions of the Palestinian refugee camps in Lebanon. He put his hand to his forehead and rubbed it back and forth. "It's madness."

"What do you mean, Dad?"

"All the people in those camps, living like that. Hoping the Americans or the Soviets will do something for them, that they will be able to go home. It will never happen."

I never met my dad's parents because they never left Lebanon. I couldn't even talk with them on the phone because they didn't speak English. He would have to get on the other phone to translate. I learned from my mom that his parents told him he had married outside of the race. He went to Beirut a few times to see them, always by himself. I asked once if I could go with him but he said there was nothing there for me. After the Lebanese civil war started in the Seventies, he stopped going altogether. Sometimes during phone calls, he would have arguments with them. After one such call, I asked him why he was so angry.

"I plead with them to come here, and they refuse," he said. He wanted them to be safe, but they had already left their homeland once for fear of being killed. They weren't about to get on a plane and cross the ocean.

One afternoon, home from college during a semester break and sitting around the house bored, I flipped through an old photo album that had some pictures of my dad's family. There were just a few old brown and white pictures. Photos of his parents and extended family posed in a studio. My dad looked a few years younger than me, seventeen maybe. The complexion of that boy's face, it was different than he looked now. In the photo his pigment looked darker and smoother, his hair cropped close to the skin. He somehow looked familiar, like a kid I had seen recently. In Grosse Pointe? No. At college? Probably not.

A couple days later, I was watching the Evening News, alone. There was a brief piece on kids throwing rocks at Israeli soldiers. That's when it hit me. Right there. In that old photo, my dad looked indistinguishable from those Palestinian teens throwing rocks on TV. I understood then that where I saw my dad, some people in Grosse Pointe maybe saw somebody else. I also understood then why he preached golf and tennis, tennis and golf. He wanted me to stand on his shoulders and climb over the Wall. Be a member of The Club.

Since there seemed to be hardly any Arabs in Grosse Pointe, I imagine that if someone was asked where my dad came from, the answer would probably be Italy. If you had black hair and a complexion darker than a Swede, that's what you were. Or maybe Greek, there were a few Greeks in Grosse Pointe. Hell, there weren't even very many Italians. No Asians, no Latinos. An Indian doctor, here and there. No Jews, except for Lew's dad. Everybody else, white light.

Then there was the other side. Which was all one thing, too, as far as I knew.

"They don't show up for work," my dad would say of black clerical workers, when he was still working for the City of Detroit. "They take too many breaks and don't get the work done. They talk on the phone and eat potato chips at their desks."

Maybe they're hungry and bored, I thought. Or maybe that's what they can afford. Maybe they just like potato chips. So did my dad, on Saturday afternoons with his sandwich and pickle in front of a ballgame on TV. But what else could he think? That's all he ever saw of black people, everything else was the black hole on the other side of Alter Road, or hidden behind the empty storefronts on Jefferson Avenue. Black blight.

Potato chips. Where was anybody going to get any real understanding about the other side of Alter beyond the transient and superficial?

My mom didn't say much about the black and white or anything else controversial. Once, she announced that she was going to vote for McGovern for President. Dad admonished her, and that was it. She helped Mrs. Davis, the cleaning woman, clean our house, and she made her lunches that were better than I got. Not that Mom didn't have any opinions about the subject of Detroit. She taught in a Detroit elementary school just a few blocks past Alter Road. Most of the kids came to class well-dressed, better than the students in Grosse Pointe. A few times each day, one or another little girl in the class would spontaneously get up from her desk and walk up to my mom and give her a hug. The boys sometimes, too.

By December each year, over half of the class would be gone, replaced by new students. "Instability and poverty in the families," she said. The problem was that the parents hadn't grown up. Women too young to be mothers who had babies because they wanted to be loved. The missing fathers didn't have the discipline to hold down a job, or couldn't hack the responsibilities of being a husband and parent. "They need to stay put and sacrifice for the future of their children," she said. "Like everybody else. It's the easiest thing in the world to make a baby. Another thing to raise it."

One summer, a few years after Mrs. Davis retired, she called my mom and asked her to come to her home in Detroit. She had some clothes to give me that had been her son's, who was grown up and long gone in the Army. I was maybe twelve years old, and I didn't think I needed any clothes, especially second-hand ones. But Mom made me go with her to get them.

Mrs. Davis lived on the third floor of an ancient brownstone, dark and creaky inside. Hot as hell, and kinda dark because the blinds on the windows were down. She gave me a quick smile and a hug, then she got a serious look. She told my mom to return to the car, and I wondered if there was something to be worried about. It's not like the car's gonna get stolen, my mom never left her keys in it. Mrs. Davis handed me a neatly folded pile of clothes that looked like they were from the Fifties. Plaid collared shirts and dark pants.

"Now you get on down there, child, and give those to your mother. Then get back right quick."

When I got outside, there were a few people out watching. On the sidewalk, across the street, on the front step. Was Mrs. Davis afraid my mom and I were gonna get mugged for the clothes? When I got back, she was holding one side of a blind open a little and peering down, hunched over, tensed up, like she was on high alert. She quickly handed me another pile of clothes. It went on like that for four or five trips. Each time I went back outside, it seemed like there were one or two more people out, watching from the sidewalk or a stoop or a balcony.

On the way home, I said, "I don't understand why Mrs. Davis didn't just give the clothes to somebody in her neighborhood." I didn't want them, couldn't possibly wear them, they were ancient and way too big.

"We have to respect Mrs. Davis's wishes."

I wondered if her neighbors were gonna give her a hard time after we left.

All the serious crime, all the violence and murders in Detroit that you'd read about in the newspaper, it seemed like something terrible happened every day. Multiple murders, multiple articles. In bold black type, often front page. It was unsettling, hard to comprehend. The thing was, even with murders commonplace, it wasn't like everybody on the other side was dangerous. After all, there were well over a million people living there. But that's the impression you had from the local newspapers and TV news.

There was another thing about the TV news. It was the bare minimum, no commentary, no analysis, no context. It simply conveyed the fact of the murder and maybe a brief encounter with the survivors' grief. It was presented with a kind of sensitivity, but the compact approach and abrupt ending left one wondering where the humanity went. The tragedy was confined to the inside of the TV box. A video. The problem was—still is— there are lots of impactful facts. Where do you draw the line, what do you leave out? The news companies chose to provide the narrowest of accounts and call it reporting "just the facts." The only conclusion the white suburbanite could draw was, "black equals danger." Where else could you learn about blacks? The therapist, who was a kind of realist, said they couldn't be in my therapy group because the cultural differences were too great.

Once in a while, you'd see a feature article in the Detroit paper about somebody black who made it, gotten out of poverty, overcame major obstacles. The plight of the other hundreds of thousands is their own fault. They're free, it's entirely their fault if they can't rise above the poverty and crime and discrimination. See, this one person, he made it, so there's no excuse for the rest. We all have to do it. Doesn't matter that there's violence, doesn't matter that you're poor, doesn't matter if a better alternative wasn't a tangible, realistically reachable goal in your life. Doesn't matter that white people discount you because you look and talk different. Those are just obstacles. You're all to blame for your plight, each one of you, as an individual, and all of you, as a group. As a race.

Most of the kids on the black side of Alter Road wouldn't get through high school, but they didn't need a college degree, or even a high school diploma, to witness all the whites grabbing material gratification. It was right there on display, in the happy smiles on the giant billboard advertisements high above the Ford and Chrysler freeways. You didn't need a degree in economics or psychology or law or sociology to figure out that people are out for themselves, out to act on the world and take it. You don't even need to know how to read to figure that out. The images are all out there. Grab what you can for your own enjoyment.

If you rationalized all the media messages as "just advertising," or "just TV," then what about the businessmen who drove downtown on Jefferson every day in nice-looking cars? What about those big houses and green lawns and residents-only parks and private golf clubs? Freedom, and plenty. Besides, advertising is not just selling, it's advocacy. Here's the real way to live, here's how some people get to live. See how pleasurable it is. Look how valid the pleasure is. Feel its power. It's good, otherwise, it wouldn't be up there. Grab some, however you can, when you can, for yourself. Grab what's within reach, that's what those white people are doing. Rules? The game's practically impossible. You don't need a degree to know that either.

What was there in school except abstractions? What was the payoff for the boring brain work? What was there within reach, to persuade a kid that there was a tangible goal worth the immense effort to restrain desire, in favor of having the mind dulled by didactic lessons in math and reading and writing? How could any of those possibly give you a footing and a safe place through the invisible wall? On what planet could a broken-down school make apparent to an average impoverished black kid that it's practical to "delay gratification" for something years down the road if nobody who looked like you had it? Committing a crime isn't the right thing to do, but it can be explained. Within reach. It's only irrational according to the rulebook laid out and enforced by the people in the banks and the government and the suburbs. The one called The Protestant Ethic and the Spirit of Capitalism. Maybe the ignorant ones were the people making a big splash in finance or law or real estate or politics who expected everybody else to cooperate.

When I was a teen, my dad had pushed me into some of my summer jobs. Each one had a purpose. There were two general categories. One category included a mail room job at a big downtown bank, the harbor boy job at the Yacht Club, and selling suits at E.L. Dickey, a Men's Fine Clothing Store. Those jobs were about exposure to class and rank and status. Formality and proper communication. White-collar Anglo-Saxon culture. The other category consisted of dirty jobs: on a garbage truck, midnight security, cleaning public bathrooms at a park, and working on a road crew. "To learn how the other half lives," Dad would say. Thing was, I didn't really learn anything except how to tune out.

The road crew job was on the Detroit freeways for the Wayne County Road Commission. When I got that job I thought, cool, I'll get to do manly stuff like put up guard rails, repair roads, beat the shit out of something with a sledgehammer or a jackhammer. Get buff. Uh-uh. Most of the time I was poking paper and picking up litter with a dozen other young guys. Each morning at the Brush Street Yard, we crammed into an extended Econoline until we got dropped off to walk the freeways for miles and miles, to bag endless litter and junk that had been tossed from vehicles and made their way to the grass embankments on each side of the Detroit freeways or the concrete median. Every morning, they gave each of us a wooden pole with a big nail sticking out one end and a bunch of trash bags. And you better remember to bring your own work gloves, for all the metal and glass and plastic shit that you had to pick up by hand. You'd fill up a bag, tie it up and leave it on the shoulder of the highway, open up another bag, fill it up, et cetera. All day every day, for three-something an hour.

For the first few weeks that summer, I was the only white guy on the crew. It seemed that the only thing I had in common with the others was that we were teenage males. Almost all the other guys were tall and lean. They had impossibly long fingernails. I mean, long-long. An inch beyond their fingertips. Like the figures on the album cover of David Bowie's *Diamond Dogs* record. How could they do anything with nails like that? Didn't they get in the way, or break easily? How could that be a style? How could they touch or pick up things? Like catch a ball, or reach deep in their pockets for something? What sort of world did they live in, where nails like that on guys wasn't incredibly odd?

No way was I going to ask them about it. They didn't want to talk to me. They barely even looked at me. All I needed to do was to comply with the requirements of the job each day and otherwise pretend I wasn't there. I played white ghost in the back corner of the van. Hardly exchanged more than a word or two with most of them that whole summer. It was like we were inhabiting parallel universes. In fact, they didn't seem to have much

87

to say to each other, at least not loud enough for me to hear. Which really wasn't any different than a bunch of young white guys working really boring mindless manual labor in the hot sun. Even when a couple of them spoke loud enough to hear, I didn't know the language.

The driver was a Road Commission regular, maybe fifteen years older than us. Each day, he'd drive us around for a while, killing time. Then he'd stop on the shoulder of the Ford or Chrysler or Fisher or Lodge expressway. It always seemed random. We'd work for an hour or two, or several miles, until the next exit, or the one after that, whenever the driver showed up. He'd motion for us to get in the van, then he'd drive around awhile, park under an overpass, and everyone would nap. He hardly ever gave us any instructions, barely a word or two. There wasn't anything to learn. Sometimes he'd drop us off, drive down the road and wait for us to get there. Other times he'd just disappear for a while. Then he'd show up and we'd drive around and park and it was naptime again. Except for me because I couldn't nap. I'd just stare out the window at the traffic passing by and feel the sweat drip down my forehead and soak my clothes.

What I noticed that was interesting about the crew, looking over their slouched shoulders from the rear of the van, was what some of them did besides sleeping. They read the daily Detroit paper that the driver brought with him every morning. Not just the sports, like I did every night, or the cartoons. They read the fucking front section. Not just glance at it, or skim it like I did. They read it, intently. Maybe I wasn't supposed to be surprised, but I was.

There was one guy, the only guy who wasn't tall, who spoke up a lot in certain circumstances. Certain circumstances that happened frequently, like multiple times a day. It wasn't speech as much as a very loud deep bellow, and it was directed at any young female within sight.

"FREEEEK!"

Call of the Wild. It happened whenever we got off the freeway because invariably there would be a woman, or two or three, walking down the sidewalk or waiting for a bus. This guy would stick his head out of the window, yelling for her, just that one word. Freak. It was unreal how quickly he sprang into action. Sometimes two or three of the others would join him, desperately seeking a response. Usually, the women would try to ignore it. Sometimes they smiled. It didn't matter, he didn't stop. Even as we were driving away, he'd strain his neck and belt out the mating call. At least he didn't yell Freak if there was a child with her, or if the woman looked over forty. At least, not usually. He didn't do it with white women either, unless they were young and big. I thought he was insane.

If we were stopped, killing time, or even at a red light, the Freak would actually get out of the van and run up to the woman he had yelled at, sometimes followed by a couple of the others, and try to have what appeared to be a get-to-know-you conversation. The driver seemed to tolerate it, he never said anything. Maybe he was amused. I took it that he understood what they were all going through, he'd been there. Teenage hormone overdrive. He'd calmly call them back to the van when the light changed, or it was time to go.

At lunchtime, the driver would often take us to a little grocery in a neighborhood where the crew could get something to eat. The driver seemed to know where all of these little places in the city were, so no matter where we were working, he'd get us to one. The neighborhoods all looked the same to me. Ancient brownstones and clapboard houses that were falling apart, half of them with windows that were boarded up or blown out. Some that had been really nice, a few that still were. And always a little grocery store on a corner with barred windows and a cashier in a cage.

Other than liquor stores, those little groceries were the only places where you could get food because there were no fast-food chains, or supermarkets, or any other kind of visible commerce in the neighborhoods. More often than not, the liquor store *was* the grocery. Some of the crew would get a sandwich to go, while others would buy snack food. Going in those stores, it felt like going back in time. Kinda quaint, kinda cool, that somebody'd make you a sandwich to order.

Sometimes the driver would take us to a little park or broken-down ball field, where we could sit on a bench to eat for a little while. If there was a lot of trash in the park, the driver might tell us to clean it up a little. You'd see some shady-looking characters walking around in those neighborhoods, but I felt perfectly safe. Who was gonna fuck with a dozen young dudes, each standing six foot plus—the one short guy yelling "Freak" was clearly deranged—all of them holding long wooden poles with big nails on one end that were essentially spears?

After I'd been on the job a few weeks, a white guy joined the crew. He had hair as light as the sun, hazel green eyes, and a deep tan. Lean and ripped. He wasn't a big guy, but he was aggressive. It was like a hard-core punk surfer from Pismo Beach somehow landed in the middle of Detroit. What was this guy doing here? Apparently, he lived alone in a house somewhere in the city, which I couldn't imagine, but he was one tough bastard. Right off the bat, he didn't get along with any of the other guys. I didn't hear anything that might've started the animosity. It coulda just been his demeanor. He walked around with a big chip on his shoulder. He must've communicated a negative vibe they read as racial hostility. Probably was. After a few days, they started calling him Beach Boy. But he was a tough talking sonofabitch, and he and the Freak were adversaries from day one.

One day the Freak said, "I know where you live, Beach Boy. I gonna come by and torch your fuckin' house."

"Yeah, you do that," Beach Boy said. "Bring all your boys. Y'all come by, all you motherfuckers. See what I got for you."

Incredibly bold, considering Beach Boy was way outnumbered. He must've been a survivor of some kind. Like the bad boy Jules in the novel *Them,* by Joyce Carol Oates, about some marginalized whites in Detroit in the Sixties. Only that character ended up in California, not the other way around. Beach Boy was way more uncomfortable to be around than any of the black guys. He was like a ticking time bomb. I didn't talk to him, and he never acknowledged me. Shit, I don't think he ever even looked at me. Maybe once, and wrote me off. Which was fine with me. I didn't want to be associated with him just because he was white.

Why take sides with him? He was beyond asshole, walking around like he wanted to take on the whole world. I imagined that he had a bad family life, got kicked out by his parents, maybe. But what was he doing here, living by himself in Detroit, rather than king of the beach? No dad to drop him off on his way to the office and drive him home at the end of the day, like I had. What happened? I sure wasn't gonna ask him. All I could do was speculate about how this odd creature got to where he was in his life. He was an Other, maybe even more than the black guys. Guess he thought he had to be a hard ass to survive. Not that he seemed to be the kind of person who actually thought anything through.

One day, Beach Boy almost came to blows with the Freak. Hell, who knows what each of them coulda been carrying. We'd stopped at the curb by a little inner-city park to eat lunch and take a break. The driver was sleeping. There had been some mumbling and low volume back and forth between the two of them on and off all morning.

Suddenly Beach Boy got out of the van and said, "Come on, you motherfucker."

Freak got out, followed by some of the other guys. I wasn't gonna take sides when I didn't even know what the beef was about. Easier to play dead. All the other guys in the van started yelling and fortunately that woke the driver up. He leaned on the horn and started pulling out. That was the only thing that kept them from going at it. A couple days later, there was talk that some of the guys showed up at Beach Boy's house one night and both sides flashed guns.

A few times that summer, I got a break from picking up trash and all the tension that arose with the appearance of Beach Boy. On those days, I was assigned to work with the two guys known as the Dog Crew. They were a couple of Road Commission regulars, one white, the other black, who belonged to motorcycle clubs. You could tell from the lettering on their black leather jackets that their clubs were race-based. Each of these guys was hairy, with a Fu Manchu and long sideburns, and wore dark shades he never took off. They kinda looked like dogs, the white guy a hound, the black guy a bulldog. That's not why they were called the Dog Crew. Their daily job was to cruise around the freeways in a dump truck picking up dead animals, mainly dogs that had been dumped on the shoulder or had been hit by a car. Other than the few times I got to work on the Dog Crew, most of my summer at the Road Commission was spent in monotony with the paper poking crew and the daily tension between Beach Boy and the Freak.

Things got a lot better after another white guy joined us. He had a long last name, Italian or something. Zefferelli, maybe. The black guys called him Mister Z. Pale pudgy guy with a round face and a thick furry mustache and aviator glasses, Z had to be much older than the rest of us. Coulda been thirty. He didn't dress for the job in a t-shirt and jeans like we did. He wore a polyester Hawaiian pattern collared shirt and brown cords every day, even when it was high humidity and ninety-plus degrees, and a tan Fedora hat over his mostly bald head. He looked like he was on a budget group tour vacation cruising the Caribbean, strolling around the ship's deck with a constant smile. Or he coulda been a guest actor on *Hawaii Five-O*, playing a goofy shady bad guy. Or one of those round characters in a Curious George book. A zookeeper, or a baker.

What the fuck was he doing here? He hardly worked at all. But Mister Z quickly made friends with all the black guys for one reason. He had plenty of pot. They'd walk off somewhere with him and come back joyful. Whenever he appeared, the black guys would yell out, "Mister Z!" and follow him around excitedly, like happy little puppies in pursuit of a treat. Not Beach Boy. He just sulked and kept to himself. Didn't matter, Z and his perpetual pot seemed to cool everybody else out. Eliminated the racial tension, or turned it down at least. I could continue to be a ghost the rest of the summer.

The only other tension I experienced was riding the Woodward bus at the end of each day. I'd take it down to Dad's office building for a ride home with him. Getting on that bus, it would be hot and packed, barely room to stand, and I'd be the only white. Some people would glare at me, and I got spit on once, on the back of my neck. I turned around but couldn't tell who did it. Couldn't have done anything about it anyway, other than wipe it off with my hand.

Nothing I could've done the time Lew took a bullet for me either. It happened that summer, in the first week of August. It was Friday night, and Lew and I had gone to a ballgame at Tiger Stadium. The two of us would be starting college in Ann Arbor in a few weeks. Cam had already left for U. Chicago. The Tigers were getting creamed, so we left the game early, just as it was starting to get dark. I was driving cuz Lew had drank a few too many beers.

"Stop for a minute," Lew said.

"What for?"

"I need to hide the bong." His big purple bong was on the floor.

"Why do you have to do that now?"

"Because my mother's home and she needs the car in the morning."

"Why do we have to stop here?"

"So I can hide it in the trunk."

"On the freeway? Why can't we just wait 'til we get off?"

"Because I want to do it now. Just get on the fucking shoulder."

"Fine." I checked the rear-view mirror to make sure nobody was on our tail, then pulled over near the Connor exit, not far from where I had poked papers that day. We didn't have to stop there on the expressway, we could've stopped in Grosse Pointe on Mack Avenue before we got to his house. Hell, we could've stopped just down the block from his house. But

Lew, being Lew, doing things when they entered his brain, had to do it his way, right there on the shoulder of the Ford Freeway. Just to hide the stupid purple bong in the trunk.

There had been a lot of carjackings on the Detroit freeways that summer. It had been regular front page material and lead-in on the local TV news, everybody knew about it, talked about it. The more it happened, the more it got reported, which seemed to generate more incidents. I guess we weren't thinking about that when Lew told me to pull over for a minute. Well, I thought about it, but complied since it'd be just a minute and the ballgame traffic wasn't bad yet.

Since I was driving, I had the keys to the trunk. "Hand me the bong, Lew."

I expected Lew to be his usual bossy self and want to do it himself. I was a bit surprised when he handed the bong over without a word. I had the keys and the bong in my right hand, opened the driver side door with my left hand, and stepped out of the car. Right away, as I started to turn to walk to the trunk, a voice from nowhere yelled at me. A young voice.

"Gimme the keys!"

That was probably what he said, because the first time the words didn't register, I just saw this black teen standing on my side of the LeMans, at the rear. He was maybe a little younger and a little shorter than me, in a dark T shirt and jeans. And some kind of hat, an oversized blue jean cap like from a *Fat Albert* cartoon. He stood there at the back of the car, holding a little gun in his hand, aimed directly at me.

What ensued took just a few seconds, or more like forty-five seconds. What went on in my head while it transpired, I retrieved and thought about for weeks afterward, trying to figure out why things went the way they did instead of another way.

It started with a shot of nerves down my arms and legs, my eardrums went tight, throat dry and heart pounded. All of that in an instant. Thinking about it later, I saw that my mind was somewhere else. Something like, *This isn't real, can't be, there's something wrong with this picture. Something doesn't fit and therefore it's not actually happening. Black kid in dark t-shirt and jeans on the side of the freeway goes with daylight, poking paper in the daylight. Not a kid with a gun in the dark. How did he appear out of nowhere?*

When he yelled a second time, louder, that's when I actually took in the words.

"Give me the fucking keys!"

I remained scared stiff. Whatever he was aiming at me, he was now holding in both hands. How was I supposed to get the keys to him when he's got both hands on the gun? I wasn't gonna risk walking them to him. Did he want me to throw them to him? Had he fucking thought this through?

As if he read my mind, he stuck his left hand out toward me. Cooperative-like, but firm, it occurred to me later. Interesting, how people in conflict, potentially deadly conflict, can cooperate and work together, coordinate their speech and movement to see something through, safely.

Still, I had both the bong and the keys in my right hand, how was I supposed to get the keys to him? I can't throw the bong to him at the same time. He might think I was trying to hit him with it. If I manage to toss the keys, what if I miss? How would he find them since it's getting too dark to see anything on the ground? I wanted my heart to stop pounding, as if its movement was visible and could provoke him to put a hole in it. That little gun, I could barely see it in the dark, could it be a little squirt gun? Could it be nothing at all? No, there was a little bit of shine. More than anything, I wanted him to know that I was trying to act in good faith. I was trying. What other option was there? He took a step toward me. Okay, keep coming, I won't move, I'll just wait for you to come closer and hand the keys to you and get out of your way.

Never got that far. The intimate little bilateral relation that defined the entire world for me at that moment received an unexpected intrusion. I had forgotten all about Lew until I heard the sound of the passenger door opening, and there he was, standing on the other side of the car. Later, I thought, if only I could've forced my legs to walk toward the kid and given him the keys, Lew wouldn't have done what he did. On the other hand, maybe Lew would've got shot anyway because, well, Lew is Lew, and I'm a slow thinker.

One thing was certain. I wouldn't have said what Lew said to that kid. Lew was drunk and pissed, real pissed, scarlet scared pissed. Ready to go off. Lew was a new variable. It was gonna be taken out of my hands entirely, and we were going down a slippery slope river of no return. I thought, "Lew what are you doing, your dad just got killed last year on a deer hunt, is that why you're so red? What are you gonna do, Lew?" Just like that, I became a bystander, even though I still had the damn keys.

The kid pointed the gun at Lew.

"What are you doing!" Lew yelled.

He yelled at him. Lew actually yelled at the kid pointing the gun at him. You're not supposed to do that, it never happened like that on TV shows. The kid hesitated; he probably wasn't expecting Lew's aggression. His right arm with the gun might've shaken or trembled a little. Then he swung his arm back and aimed at me again. As if the kid didn't want to deal with the big angry drunk redneck, or didn't know how, so he went back to me.

"Gimme the keys!" he yelled again, now a hoarseness in his voice, like he was getting weary, or desperate.

"Fuck you," Lew said.

"Gimme the mother-fuckin' keys!"

I was just about to finally toss them to him, but I didn't get that chance.

"You don't even know how to drive, you little shit!" Lew yelled.

The kid swung the gun back at Lew. "What'd you say, motherfucker?"

"Fuck you, you little shit."

Then the gun went off.

Lew's body disappeared behind the car and the kid bolted. I got around to him; some previously unknown inner automata having taken me over. Lew lay there on the ground, looking up at me for once. He wasn't really looking at me, he was looking somewhere else, somewhere above my head. Like his mind had registered what had happened even though he couldn't see the blood coming out of his right shoulder, on the tie-dyed T-shirt his mom had wrecked by turning it pink in the washing machine. Bright red blood and run-on pink don't go together, the blood was spreading fast above the right side of his chest, coming out thick, blotting out the pink.

Do something! I pushed down to put pressure on it, I thought that was the thing you're supposed to do, but it seemed to only make it gush out faster, warm blood all over my hands and spreading all over him. What was I supposed to do?

I heard the sound of cars screeching, stopping, and quickly, there were people all over me. I fell forward while some people were yelling, others just looking down at Lew. A man who said he was a nurse inserted himself into the situation. I didn't know there were any male nurses. He was crewcut and square-jawed and hairy armed with tattoos and a lot of cheap cologne. Maybe former military. I couldn't see what he was doing. Sound of a siren and another, lights flashing, and the police and emergency personnel took over, worked on Lew.

There was room for me to move a little on the ground. I rolled onto my back and looked up from the ground at pure commotion above me. It registered in my brain then that it was now black out, because of all the lights. A couple people pointed at the service drive above us and some cops ran up there with flashlights. I looked at the freeway. Some cars were slowing to watch as they drove by, while others sped past them. In between people's legs I saw a stretcher on the ground, and the emergency people picking Lew up and putting him on it. As they carried him to the ambulance, a bottle of something held above him, I pushed myself up and tried to get a glimpse of his face, but others were in the way. Will I ever see him alive again? I asked a cop if I could go in the ambulance, but he refused and it was too late anyway, the doors were shut, and it was gone.

Another cop ordered me to sit in the back of a police car and tell him what happened. Why had we stopped? Where was the shooter standing, what did he look like? What did the gun look like, how many shots were fired, where did he come from, where did he go? Through the window of the police car, I saw lights flashing above, up on the service drive, everywhere. I told him everything, even about the bong, I didn't have any emotional resources left for a lie. The cop asked where Lew lived, which made no sense because he had Lew's wallet. Was he testing me for some reason? I asked about Lew's mom. They'd already contacted her. He abruptly got out of the squad car and told me to stay put. Gave me a towel to wipe up the blood even though I had already wiped my hands on my jeans and my shirt had red splotches of Lew all over.

I had to sit there and wonder about how all of this was going to get resolved, was Lew gonna die, and how would I know if he did? Road flares had been set up, and a Wayne County cop wearing a cowboy hat was directing highway traffic, keeping it moving. Lew couldn't die, we were supposed to go away to college in a few weeks, we were gonna be freshman dorm roommates. Getting shot on the side of a grungy Detroit freeway didn't square with going off to college. I got shaky, started sobbing, sitting there alone.

Eventually they had me get in a different police car for the ride home, and as I walked over to it, I saw that the bong had been smashed to tiny bits. Run over. The cop who drove me home said that Lew had been taken to Saint John's Hospital. I asked if Lew was gonna be okay, but he didn't know. Did they find the gun? First, he said no, then mumbled something about "single shot" and "Saturday Night Special." Maybe he meant the kid's gun could fire just one shot. Only one of us could get shot and Lew took the bullet.

Lew was lucky, he could've bled out, but I guess it was good that he got shot on a major expressway, where there was traffic and everything happened real quick, and pretty close to Saint John's on Seven Mile Road. There would be a permanent scar and he was drugged out for a few days. We joked about that, except when his mom was in the room. She was sick with worry and drove him nuts that whole week at Saint John's and after he went home. Actually, both his mom *and* sister drove him nuts the rest of August. He had to sneak to get out of the house.

I got to stay home for a couple days because my mom was scared about me going to work. I had to talk to the police a couple more times. Don't know if they ever caught the kid who did it. The first day back on the paper-poking crew, one of the guys in front of me was reading something in the *Detroit Free Press* about carjacking. He said something to his pal that I couldn't catch and they cackled. For a few moments I thought about telling them what happened but I didn't. What would be the point? How would they react? Probably just shrug. Surely, they had stories, too.

The funny thing was, after Lew got shot, it seemed easier to be around those guys. I even found myself interacting spontaneously with a few of them a little, goofing around. It didn't feel like I had to be such a ghost anymore. Maybe I could show myself a little. These guys, they're pretty innocuous, they came to work every day. They were just trying to cope with a shitty job in the hot sun, a job that maybe a family member or friend got them. Like me. Nothing to be afraid of.

There were a couple of other feelings I had on that first day back at work. Unexpected feelings. Actually, the other feelings came afterward. As I took the short walk on the service drive from the Brush Street Yard to the Woodward bus stop, it occurred to me that the neighborhood I walked by probably wasn't any different than the one the kid with the gun had come down from to the freeway. I suddenly felt exposed, visible, vulnerable, and walked faster than usual to Woodward. After I got on the bus and stood there, shoulder to shoulder in the heat and humidity and sweat, I felt something else. I thought, if anybody on this bus spits on me today, something bad's gonna happen. It wasn't just anger, it was stronger, like something had taken ahold of my brain. It was Beach Boy rage; *Come on, you motherfuckers. Come on.*

This is what happens with a racial divide. One summer, a few years later, after my first year of law school, I worked at a law firm downtown. For a little education, I signed up for a class on Saturdays at the Detroit Institute of Arts about the history of jazz and beat poetry, taught by a black guy named Kofi. After the first class, I introduced myself to him, and we shook hands the informal way that blacks did with each other. His eyes were alight and he grinned broadly.

About a week later, on my first day at the law firm, one of the partners showed me around, introducing me to each of the attorneys. They were all white except one young black guy in Jerri curls. He didn't look much older than me, must've been a recent law school graduate. As he rose from his desk to shake my hand, he looked nervous. Practically shaking. I figured, why wouldn't he be nervous, he's the only black, and it's a partner there in the doorway. When I walked into his office, I took his hand the same way I had with Kofi. He recoiled, as if I had buzzed him with one of those little gag shock toys. I don't think the partner noticed from where he was standing, but it didn't matter. I knew as soon as it happened that I had done something terribly wrong.

I saw the young lawyer the next day sitting outside the office, eating lunch, and he glared at me. I wanted to say I was sorry, but I was too afraid. I was scared of making it worse. Scared of crossing the line. Scared of bringing something out into the open that I didn't get. Scared of embarrassing myself and offending him more because I would fuck up again, say something wrong, not know the right words in the right order. I did what everybody else on the Grosse Pointe side did. Easier to go back to the white side, that's what I could do at the end of each day. Where what I had done had no meaning, no impact, like it hadn't even happened. Even

100

though I thought about it every day I stepped into the law office that summer.

At the end of my last day of work, I went to each attorney's office to do the "thank you and goodbye" ritual. When I got to the young attorney's office, I made sure to shake his hand the same way I did everybody else. I could tell by the way he extended his right hand, and the resolute look in his eyes when they met mine, that he wanted to make sure I got it. I had to leave it at that, let him resolve it instead of me. That was probably the best possible outcome.

I wanted him to know that what happened was out of my own weakness, my own insecurity, that I wanted to be liked, that Kofi had shaken my hand differently on Saturday at the Art Institute. That I knew better. But I didn't know better, otherwise it wouldn't have happened. Was I culpable, for not knowing better, for not knowing at all? Okay. Was the binary relation culpable, for me not knowing? I think so. My sincerity, my ignorance, my naiveté, my wanting him to know that I was a decent person who didn't accept the falsehoods of Alter Road; it didn't matter. Nor did it matter that a complete explanation went beyond black and white. What difference would that make? It happened, and the fact that I didn't know better, if nothing else, reflected the reality of the divide.

Rick and Lew get back on the road

In the morning, I wake up to the sound of the shower. Bathroom door opens. There's Lew, all six foot four inches of him. Butt naked.

"Get up, Dahd."

Though pale and underweight, he still has the barrel chest and shoulders of a swimmer. That scar below his right shoulder from when he took a bullet for me.

"What time is it?"

"Almost eleven. C'mon, the car's fixed, let's get the hell out of here while we can."

"I need to take a shower first."

"No, you don't. We need to go."

I earned that last night. "Alright. But I want to get pancakes somewhere."

Lew coughs. The heavy smoker's morning hack kind of cough. "We gotta get out of here."

Twenty minutes later, we're on the road again. Still gray out, and cold as always, but we're mobile. Lew with his frickin' Diet Pepsi, cigarettes, and two packages of Twinkies. Me with my morning forty-ounce Diet Coke, another one on ice, and a couple chocolate granola bars.

"You know, Lew, that thing with the State Police, it's just like what Foucault was talking about."

"I'd like to be done with police. In all of its manifestations."

"There was no need for the Dead Boar to call the police. Just because nobody there had seen a catheter before."

"Maybe nobody had seen one hanging from somebody's dick in public before."

"I was doing my thing privately until Bob Seger started pounding on the door."

"Look, Rick, you were lucky you didn't get arrested for indecent exposure and assault."

"You're not a lawyer so don't act like one. If anyone could've gotten arrested for assault, it was Seger."

Lew lights a cigarette. "He was on the other side of a locked door. You said so yourself."

"I had reasonable fear he was gonna break it down and assault me."

"Well, he didn't."

"Doesn't matter, Lew. Reasonable man standard. Reasonable fear. Of a guy with no taste in music."

"Just consider yourself fortunate we don't live in a police state. They listened to your explanation, however bizarre, and didn't do anything when you started to mess with them."

"That's right. They minded their elders. It was the right thing to do."

"No, Rick. You were messing with them, they knew it, and unlike you, they acted with restraint."

"I was managing them. Like Foucault said, in a liberal democracy, freedom is managed."

"We have more freedom than we've ever had."

"That's the neoliberal in you talking."

"I'm not a liberal. I'm more of a moderate."

"Neoliberal doesn't mean political liberal. Neoliberal refers to hard core advocates of unlimited free market. Foucault called it American anarcho-capitalism."

"Hold on for a minute," Lew says.

"What?"

"Open one of those Twinkies for me."

"You want me to open your Twinkies?"

"I can't open the Twinkies and smoke and drive at the same time."

"Jesus." I reach down into the bag between us, take out a package.

"What are you doing?"

"I'm looking for a seam to tear it open."

"Just pull it apart, Dahd."

"I can't. The plastic's too thick."

"Don't put it in your mouth!"

"I'm just trying to rip it open with my teeth."

"What are you, twelve years old?"

"I wish."

"Do I have to stop the fucking car and do it myself?"

I finally manage to tear it the package open. "Here, enjoy your stupid Twinkie."

Lew takes a big bite. "You were talking about American anarcho-capitalism."

"The free market is a model throughout society. Everything is interpreted in economic terms. Even the individual human being is viewed as a piece of capital."

"That's just an academic theory."

"It's been the ideology of the far-right wing of the Republican Party across our lifetimes. Now it's their center."

"Are you trying to say that's all people do, compete with each other? There are all kinds of activities people do that aren't about competition. Like doing stuff in their community, donating to causes."

"Yeah, on a voluntary basis. Kinder, gentler. In other words, I will decide what you get, instead of you taxing me. If you aren't competing like you should, there must be something wrong with you. So, you only get my charity."

"Wealth is created, Dahd. Economies have to be run. By competition."

"The economy is not just the economy."

"What are you talking about?"

"It's about managing an ostensibly free population to maximize its production while keeping enough people happy to minimize social disruptions."

Lew lights up another Marlboro. "Are you saying it's all about the government?"

"It's not all about 'the government.' It's about governing. Am I gonna have to smell your smoke nonstop for this whole trip?"

"I've got the window open."

"Barely. That's what you've always done, Lew, it's always pissed me off." I wait in vain for him to lower the window some more. Asshole. "All kinds of organizations are involved in managing people, including big business, not just government."

"Now you're saying there's one big conspiracy. Military-industrial complex."

"No, it's not all coordinated from some central power. It's localized."

Lew wolfs down the rest of his Twinkie. "That sounds really vacuous. Maybe all you're describing is simply the way modern societies function."

"Just because it's not one big grand conspiracy doesn't make it benign."

"Then what's the big issue?"

"Expecting too much out of the individual. There's this basic clash between the demands of our everyday lives and our predisposition to do what's convenient and pleasing."

"Like what?"

"Like, grab a big sub or a burger, both of which everyone knows have tons of calories that are bad for you and eventually result in serious illness. Then we blame that person for their health problems and the costs to keep them alive."

"Give me the other Twinkie, Dahd."

"You just had one."

"And now I need the other one."

"You don't need another one right now. You just want it."

"Give me my Twinkie!"

"Fine." I take the other Twinkie out of the package, hand it over, and watch him take a big bite. "You eat like a feral pig."

"Nobody's making you buy a burger."

"Burger King puts their restaurants where a lot of people work and travel. Totally rational from the context of Burger King. Then we blame the individual for ending up obese. Like it really was their free choice to buy a Whopper."

"Well, it is. Not everybody pounds Whoppers."

"You're working hard all morning, doing tasks requiring concentration and patience, dealing with pressures, repressing desire to do something pleasing. You've got a half-hour for lunch, what are most people gonna do? Satisfy desire."

"It's still a choice."

"But see, your whole line of thinking is flawed, Lew. You're assuming it's entirely on the individual to manage their desires. Even Burger King's gonna blame the individual."

"Why are you picking on Burger King?"

"Burger King's just a placeholder. You could pick any fast-food place. Although I'm not sure what's in those things that McDonald's sells."

"What about Wendy's?"

"I don't care for the little Wendy girl and her dad shit. Burger King will say, 'Well, we're not telling people to have a Whopper every day.' But they want to sell as many as they can."

"Of course they do, Dahd. It's a business."

"They don't say, "Gee, Mister Rosenberg, you just bought a Whopper yesterday, you can't buy another one 'til next week.'"

"I wouldn't want them to."

"And we justify it all on the basis of individual freedom. Same with bars having happy hours so you buy multiple drinks, then telling people, don't drink and drive."

"Would you rather have the bar say nothing?"

"Then people end up with chronic illnesses, and a shitty health plan."

Lew finishes off the Twinkie. "That's why you have to maximize competition. Not government health care."

"Here's what you get with maximum competition, Lew. The hospitals and doctors and medical equipment companies and Big Pharma all want a lot more for their services and products than is necessary for a reasonable profit, and it all ends up getting imposed on the individual."

"Even if that's all true, Dahd, people still have to take care of themselves."

"It's putting all this pressure on the individual person, pushing it down to the individual brain, the individual body, the individual's personal resources."

"Everybody has to deal with a little adversity from time to time."

"It's about the terms of our adversity. Unnecessary things happen all the time that are adverse to the individual."

"You think Burger King's just out to cause adversity?"

"I'm not saying that CEOs make decisions to intentionally hurt people. But since the sole context for their decisions is the company's bottom line, there's no reason for them to care about unintended effects. They might as well be throwing a bomb in a crowd."

"But Dahd, almost by definition, business is all about taking calculated risks. They have to compete. Otherwise, we wouldn't have tasty golden Twinkies. With cream in the middle."

"We don't have to take it so literally. We don't have to emphasize that one aspect of human psyche or behavior over all others. It's about the drive to 'succeed.'"

"Somebody has to be the motor."

"Most people aren't wired that way, Lew."

"There's a slow lane for them. Give me another Twinkie."

"You just had two."

"Open the other package."

"No."

"Then give it to me."

"You don't need to smoke and drive and open a package of Twinkies at the same time."

"You gonna have a law that says I can't do that? I can choose what I want, when I want, as long as I'm not hurting anybody else."

"What about my safety, Lew?"

"Tough shit. It's called liberty. Life, liberty, and the pursuit of happiness."

"That's Locke."

"What's that?"

"Not what, who. John Locke. He was an English philosopher. Life, liberty, and the pursuit of property. Those were his words, not Thomas Jefferson's. In the Declaration of Independence, Jefferson changed pursuit of property to pursuit of happiness, as a universal right."

"Happiness instead of property," Lew says. "That seems like a good move. You don't necessarily have to own a lot of property to be happy."

"At the time of the American Revolution, it was thought that the essence of individual happiness is to have control over things. Dominium. Locke said what drives the pursuit of happiness is the desire for things you want. He called it, 'uneasiness.'"

"Are you gonna open the other Twinkies for me, or not?"

"In fact, he believed people experience a more or less continuous stream of uneasiness."

"That's bull. Everybody's not frantically running around trying to satisfy themselves. Open the Twinkies."

"You don't need to inhale any more Twinkies."

"Was he saying it's good to have uneasiness, or not?"

"It's good if you can manage it. He was into the whole Protestant thing. You know, God created earth for people to develop. Like strip malls and Toll Brothers subdivisions and all the shit you can buy on the Internet."

Lew sighs. "What's any of this got to do with life and liberty?"

"Locke said you're free to the extent you can make rational choices."

"That's exactly what we have in this country."

"People are confronted with too much outside their control."

"Shit. Now what!"

The LeMans is shaking again. No, more like heaving and bouncing, hard. Feels like maybe the left tire's gone flat. Lew holds onto the wheel tightly as we veer onto the dirt median for about thirty yards before coming to a stop.

"Shit," he says. "Must be a flat."

Lew gets out and looks down at the front left wheel well. His jaw drops. "Where's the fucking wheel?"

Screech from the other side of the highway. A red Subaru completes a nice fishtail, narrowly avoiding our entire tire and wheel, which rolls up the opposite embankment. Now it's rolling back down, picking up speed, and flying back across the road. Heading straight for us.

"Look out, Lew!"

He does a kind of backward spring to the ground as it slams into the quarter panel with a sound like an explosion, just missing him, and ricochets, finally coming to rest a few feet from his sprawled body.

I walk around the front of the car to see for myself. The left end of the axle is partially ground into the frozen earth. Big dent in the quarter panel. The spent tire and wheel loom motionless nearby, as if possessed by some kind of demonic supernatural entity, waiting to pounce and do more harm. Like something from a Ray Bradbury novel. Alive and dangerous in its stillness.

"Are you okay?"

"I'm fine." He grabs the edge of the car and pulls himself up.

"How could the entire wheel come off?"

"All the lug nuts must've sheared."

"What're lug nuts?"

"You don't know what lug nuts are?"

"I missed Auto Mechanics in high school, Lew."

"They're what holds the wheels to the car."

"Oh, those nuts."

"This is crazy. I thought you got a tune-up."

"I did."

"They put new tires on the car, why the fuck didn't they put new lug nuts on? They should've replaced lug nuts on all the wheels. Didn't you tell them to put new lug nuts on?"

"How could I tell them to replace something I didn't know existed?"

"What do you think holds the wheels to the car?"

"Um, lug nuts?"

"Those idiots!" Lew exclaims. "The nuts must've been totally rusted. We've probably been losing them, one by one, and we didn't know it until now, when the last one came off."

"How're we gonna get the axle out of the ground?"

"Axle hub. We're not. Fuck this car. We need one that works." He slams the driver side door and starts to cross the highway.

"Where are you going?"

"Where do you think? To get another car."

"How are we gonna do that?"

"How do you think, Rick? We'll have to hitchhike a ride to the next town."

I watch Lew finish crossing to the shoulder. The back of his trench coat's got dirt and wet on it from the dive he took a minute ago.

"You forgot your shit, Lew!"

"Get it for me."

Why the fuck doesn't he come back and get his shit himself? Now I gotta yell to him across the fucking road. "Where are the keys?"

"What do you need them for!" he yells back.

"To get in the trunk!"

"My bag's in the back seat!"

"I know that! Where are the keys?"

"They're probably still in the ignition! And don't forget my Twinkies!"

Jesus Christ. I get his suitcase from the back seat and set it down on its rollers next to my backpack. Grab the other fricking package of Twinkies from the front seat. Walk around back and open the trunk.

"What do you need from the trunk!" he yells again.

I'm done yelling to him. I take out the two fly rods and slam the trunk, only it won't close. Fuckit. Sling my backpack over my shoulder and cross the road, dragging Lew's luggage, fly rods in my other hand.

Lew's lit a cigarette. "What do we need those for?"

"I like them."

111

"They're warped."

"I don't care, Lew. I just want them."

"That makes no sense."

"Yeah, well, none of this does."

"Do you have the Twinkies?"

"Yes, I have your fucking Twinkies."

Lew starts walking down the road, fast. As a car approaches, he turns around and sticks his thumb out. Looks like an idiot, dragging his wheeled luggage along like he's at an airport. A big pale dude in a dirty trench-coat. Bald head in the cold and cigarette between his thin lips. Compelling cinematic image, kind of. And me, carrying a couple old bamboo fly rods.

A white Range Rover blows by us. "Hey, Lew. What was that film we saw a long time ago with Gene Hackman and Al Pacino, about the two down-and-out guys who hitchhike across the country?"

"*Scarecrow.*"

They end up in Detroit. Standing in the big fountain on Belle Isle, Pacino has some kind of mental break and ends up in a psychiatric ward. Pretty grim. Lew and I were the only people in the theater. Which one of us will break first? My legs have that pain again, and Lew's not even that far ahead yet.

A few minutes later, a dark blue Lexus blows by.

"We're just going in circles, Lew."

"No, it isn't, we're going in a straight line. Due west."

Due west. More like *True West*. Fuck. Down the road in the freezing cold. Bones and joints are feeling kinda creaky. Wish I had some Advil. At least this time, I've got my wool gloves, and the fly rods. "Shit."

"What's wrong now?" Lew asks.

"I forgot the tapes."

"What tapes?"

"The 8-tracks. They're still in the back of the car."

"What the fuck would we do with those?"

"We could get a used 8-track player at a second-hand store if we make it to Chicago."

"You're on drugs, Dahd."

"Or at least keep a couple. As mementos."

"There's nothing memorable about any of this. We just gotta push through."

Over the next three-quarters of an hour or so, Lew valiantly raised his thumb whenever a vehicle approached, to no avail. While I thought that I couldn't go much longer in these flatlands with all this cold emptiness. Nothing memorable about this journey, and we're too old for it, at least I am, with all my maladies and misgivings. All the uneasiness.

"There's something else that Jefferson took out of the final Declaration, which was there in his original draft."

"Will you stop with all that shit?"

"You're being unpatriotic."

"You're being a pain in my ass."

"Jefferson's original draft said, 'preservation of life, liberty, and the pursuit of happiness.' Not just, 'life, liberty, and the pursuit of happiness.'"

"What's the fucking difference?"

"He took out 'preservation.'"

"Seems like it wasn't needed."

"Preservation shows up a lot in early political philosophy. It's not real explicit, but it meant more than mere survival. I think it meant access to all things needed to maintain your life in reasonable comfort."

"You're just giving your own spin on things."

"Actually, Locke said to have true happiness, you need to be able to care for yourself."

"That doesn't mean other people should do it for you."

"I didn't say that, Lew."

"That's what you're implying."

"It's access to all necessary things. It doesn't mean you don't have to work. Just don't make it harder than it needs to be for people to take care of themselves."

"But that's the deal, Dahd. A person has to be realistic about what they can and can't do."

"How are people supposed to take care of themselves, if the constant message is, you're cared about as a source of revenue? Otherwise, we'll pay attention only if your frustration manifests itself in an abnormal behavior that poses an imminent danger to others."

There's another car approaching, going maybe ninety. The wrong way. An old lady, I think, her head barely above the dashboard, blows by us, alone, in a rusted black Dodge of some kind. Dragging the exhaust pipe, sparks flying. She was staring straight ahead, clutching the wheel. Scared shitless, possessed by an evil demon, or both.

"Shit, Lew, she's gonna kill somebody."

"It's still daylight, maybe somebody with a cell will call the police."

Here comes another one, going the right way. It's an old Econoline with plenty of room. Purple, for god's sake. Goes right by us. Wonder if he almost crashed head-on with that old she-devil driving the Dodge.

"This blows, Lew. Hey, check out that billboard."

Up ahead, a billboard proclaims, "Spend some time doing time. Visit the Michigan Prison Museum."

"Wow, Michigan's got a prison museum," Lew says. "Bizarre."

"Figures, they've got so many people locked up, why not make the experience entertaining for all? I wonder if it's like a haunted house, with fake prison guards and shit. Foucault woulda had a field day with that."

"Put your thumb up, Dahd. We need to get a fucking ride."

"We don't need to both do it. I don't have a spare hand anyway."

"If you put your backpack on both shoulders, or just dump the fly rods, you'll have a free hand."

"Why are we doing this?"

"Because you didn't get the lug-nuts replaced."

"I mean, this whole thing."

"Find Cam."

"Chicago's huge."

"I'm aware of that. I told you, I have an address."

"If he really wanted to see us, he would've called you. Not just a text."

"People don't talk on the phone anymore. Except you."

"He might not want us to find him, did you ever think of that?"

"Don't be such a downer, Dahd."

"I'm being realistic."

"Since when have you been realistic about anything, with all your talk about righting wrongs with handouts?"

"Historical wrongs. Not handouts."

"Yes, there are historical wrongs. But there's a lot about American history that's not evil. There's a lot of good about the quest for individual freedom, and not having government tell you what to do."

"You mean like conquering the land, killing Native Americans, and developing a robust agriculture on the backs of people who were kidnapped and forced to work as slaves?"

Lew stops and lights a cigarette. "That's all really bad shit. But don't pretend native tribes were all peaceful with each other and rolled out the red carpet for the Europeans. You can't throw out the baby with the bathwater."

"I don't think marauding invaders can be analogized to innocent little babies."

"Take critical race studies. Bunch of radical professors getting off on saying the center of American history is slavery and discrimination. So, they can feel important and get published."

"That's not exactly what it's about."

He resumes to walk briskly. "They want to rewrite American history. To replace the current system so they're in charge."

"Where on earth do you get that? Have you been reading white supremacist websites?"

"No, but see, that's the problem, Dahd. All that white supremacist shit, they're a bunch of losers and dumb shits. But it's a reaction to a reaction. You've got people on the far left rejecting everything white, and then you get overreactions from whites who are too far right. People just spouting off, instead of having an open and honest conversation."

"I don't think militias are capable of having an open and honest conversation."

"You mean guys who go around playing soldiers in the woods on the weekend? Bunch of morons. They're harmless."

"That's not true. Look what happened at the U.S. Capitol."

Lew sighs. "That was sick, okay? People died and the whole thing shouldn't have happened. But half of those nitwits walked around like they were sight-seeing."

"What about the other half?"

"Look, I'd like to see the FBI bust all those neanderthal hate groups. But there's an honest and open discussion that needs to be had by ordinary people on a national level about what individuals are responsible for and what government's responsible for. Involving all races and political persuasions. Look at all the social programs."

"What about them?"

"I bet if someone did a truly rigorous study, the vast majority are a waste of taxpayer money."

"You don't know what you're talking about, Lew. You have to apply for money to do social programs, it's a competitive process and the ones that get accepted get evaluated."

"I say there's way too much waste and political graft."

"You gotta expect there's gonna be some unsuccessful programs when you're trying new ways to help people get on their feet."

116

"I don't have a problem paying taxes for effective programs, Dahd. But how many of them rehash stuff that was already tried and failed years ago?"

"Maybe some of them."

"Same thing with the billions of taxpayer money that goes toward university research."

"Is that really what you want, Lew, to defund universities, and have a shitty education system? Where do you think that would put the U.S.? The right-wing says they want a stronger America. You can't have that without public investment. It's for the common good."

"Common good? That's like when politicians say they want to make America better for 'all Americans.'"

"What's wrong with that?"

"The 'all' part. It's a lie."

"How's that?"

"It sounds nice, good for all," Lew says. "But it's always put out there by social groups who've got a point of view they want to become dominant. Single issue groups. Me and people like me."

"Maybe there are some people who think like that. But just because a group is advocating for itself to be treated equally, doesn't mean they think other groups should lose out."

"Dahd, my basic point is that there should be an honest national conversation about individual responsibility instead of all the code words."

"I wouldn't have a problem with that. But the invocation of 'individual responsibility' by conservatives is a code word."

"For what?"

"It implies that it's entirely up to each person to take care of themselves regardless of their station in life."

"That's what works. That's how you have a better economy. And the better the economy, the less need for government. Better for everybody."

"But Lew, the historical truth is that the less government, the greater the inequality. That's what the rural and working class don't get. They're totally mistaken about what's in their economic interest. It's not capitalism. It's not getting rid of unions. Government is not their enemy. They've been brainwashed by Republicans for fifty years. They spend all their time waving flags cuz it makes them imagine they're powerful, and send their kids off to wars that get them killed. In the name of nationalism and God and apple pie and shit jobs."

Lew tosses his cigarette butt. "Are you done with the speech? Give me a Twinkie."

"My hands are full."

"Then dump the warped fly rods."

"I'm not opening your fucking Twinkies for you." I stop, put both fly rods in my left hand, and reach in my coat pocket. "Here, do it yourself. Take them."

Instead of taking the package, Lew continues walking. Fucking asshole. I heave the package of Twinkies over his head.

He turns around. "What'd you do that for!"

"Sorry, I missed. I was aiming for your head."

"Dickhead." He walks briskly to the package, scoops it up from the ground, and slowing his pace momentarily, rips it open with his teeth. Then he squeezes a Twinkie halfway out of the package and starts to devour it. "There's a very good reason why people think the U.S. should be more nationalist."

"What's that?"

"It's a country, Rick! And people live in it! Of course, Americans should be prioritized, instead of wasting money on other countries!"

"It's actually a puny percentage of federal spending."

"It's billions and billions of dollars a year!"

"You can't just pretend the rest of the world doesn't exist."

"I agree the U.S. should be involved internationally, for its own sake. But what about the people in this country? Why focus so much on immigration when so many people in this country, of all races, have needs? People who are citizens, paying taxes. What about them?"

"Nobody's excluding them, Lew. Immigration's always been a part of this country's values."

"Legal immigration."

"If we let more people in legally, they won't have to enter illegally. They're coming from poor, oppressed, dangerous places."

"That's not our problem."

"Really? Latin America has a history of American corporations making deals with corrupt governments to extract their resources while tolerating dictators. You know that."

"What I know is that those countries are thoroughly corrupt democracies," Lew says. "Military dictatorships are a viable option for them. Besides, America can't control what goes on in other countries."

"What do you think international policy is largely about? Creating a red carpet for American corporations to make a lot of money."

"That benefits everybody, Dahd. Would you rather have China do it?"

"We can do better, for the people in those countries, than we do."

"They get jobs. Better than in their own companies. Trust me, I've seen it. In Africa. In southeast Asia. In lots of countries."

"But what happens to the culture? American corporations are there for one reason only. To make a killing."

"Wake up, Dahd. There are all sorts of companies from lots of different countries that make and sell products outside their national borders. It's not just the U.S. and Western Europe and China and Japan. The world is flat now. It's much better to compete through capitalism rather than to wage war."

"You can't pretend that capitalism doesn't diminish the indigenous culture."

"What you don't get is that most of the locals *want* McDonald's burgers. They *want* Nike Air Jordans. They *want* Apple iPads. Isn't that far better than countries invading each other with armies?"

"But Lew, when you push products, you're pushing on other people's ways of life. It creates resentment and conflict and sometimes violent reactions."

"I see it very differently. If you want a better world, then the goal is to break cultures down."

Ollie Biteman and Queenie Bitch

A couple years after my family moved to the impossibly long ranch house in Grosse Pointe Farms, I transferred to Grosse Pointe South for high school. A few days after school started, I recognized Lew in a crowded hallway between classes. He was going one way, I was going the other, and our eyes met for a second. There was a mutual acknowledgement and the briefest of a verbal exchange, just a hey, before the sea of students carried us past each other. We hadn't seen each other since he left Tuna Tech in fifth grade. Now he was a big dude, and not at all chubby. Looked like a jock, except for the long straight brown hair below his shoulders. The following weekend, I saw him at the Harmony House record store on Mack Avenue. He was holding *Sally Can't Dance*.

"Who's that?"

"Lou Reed."

Like I should have known. He invited me over for a listen. As soon as we got outside, he lit a Marlboro.

"Want one?"

"No thanks."

We walked around the corner and down a block to his house. Lew's street was neat and leafy, and the houses were close enough to each other that you could hear neighbors yell at their kids. Sturdy brick two-story with a garage out back. The kind of house I had lived in before Dad got his promotion and we moved near the Lake. Being with Lew felt promising, like I was returning to a familiar, less formal environment. Or maybe it was just being around him that felt promising, an old friend from childhood, and we could've been any place where you didn't have to give a shit about where you lived and how you were gonna measure up.

I followed him up the stairs to his room. It was pretty small, barely room for two people to stand, on account of all his electronics. He had a Technics turntable atop a Sony receiver and a monster pair of five-foot Pioneer speakers. Brown shag carpet with a few cigarette burns. Next to the dresser, there was a stack of four wooden fruit crates full of records, and on the two walls adjoining the bed, big posters of David Bowie as Ziggy Stardust and another glam rocker I later learned was Marc Bolan of T. Rex. And in the corner, an electric guitar on a stand. Burnt orange.

"You play guitar."

"Yeah."

"So do I."

"That's cool."

I walked over to it. "Nice Telecaster."

"What do you play?"

"I've got a Strat."

"Cool."

I had no posters, no smoke, no shag, and all I owned in terms of hi-fi at the time was a portable Panasonic cassette player with a radio. Didn't have nearly the number of records Lew did. Some of them I had bought only because the album covers looked cool. I played them on my dad's four-foot-long Fisher cabinet stereo in the living room, the kind that looked like fine furniture, on four legs with built-in speakers, AM/FM, and the turntable hidden inside. On which he played Andy Williams records and Neil Diamond's *Hot August Night*, which, compared to Andy Williams, rocked.

While I started looking at his records, Lew closed the door, tore the plastic wrap off *Sally Can't Dance*, and laid the vinyl on the turntable. Then he lit another cigarette and sat on the bed.

"Check this out."

I hadn't noticed Lew turn up the volume on his receiver all the way to ten, so when the sound of guitars and drums hit, I nearly shit my pants. Then a low foreboding vocal kicked in, if you want to call it a vocal, it was more like somebody reciting a script. Something about a son who gets electric shock by doctors and then runs away from home.

Lew lit a different kind of cigarette, the kind with a twist at each end instead of a filter and tobacco. A joint. And I had my first toke.

That was my first intimate moment with Lou Reed. "Kill Your Sons." The righteous down south in white capes and hoods burned this kind of stuff in solemn offering to the gods. I was worried about my ears. Lew said something I couldn't make out; it was too fucking loud.

"WHAT?"

He took another toke, put his head down on the bed, closed his eyes and nodded to the music. I started to feel dizzy and nauseous from the combination of pot and cigarette smoke and extreme volume and hard hitting vocal and guitar. Kinda like when I passed out in seventh grade science during a movie about African people with elephantiasis. I remembered seeing a bathroom in the hallway, so I went out and closed the door behind me.

On my way to the can, there was another doorway open, and the sound of bubbles and a TV. A fish tank? I didn't look to find out, just went straight to the toilet. Sat there for a minute and tried to collect myself. Just fifteen minutes ago, it was leafy trees and sunshine and chirping birds. On the way back to Lew's room, I paused and looked in the room I had passed.

123

In the near corner, a small unshaven man sat in his underwear, holding a cigar and a can of beer. There were a couple tubes attached below his nose that went down to a machine on the floor between his hairy legs. His feet were missing. He nodded and smiled. I mumbled hi and made it back to Lew's room. He was still lying on the bed.

"That's my uncle," he said without looking up. "He's dying of diabetes and a few other things."

I examined some more of Lew's records. There was one album cover that stood out. It was a double album, with a cover comprised of little black and white photos that looked like they were taken in the deep South. Old New Orleans, or Memphis, I imagined.

"What's this?"

"It's the Stones. *Exile on Main Street*. It's a great album. You should listen to it. You can borrow it if you want."

So, I did. The first time I gave that record a listen, it sounded like incoherent mush, so I put it away. But that album cover, with those archetypal Fifties photos of funeral processions and freak show acts, interspersed with street shots of the Stones, kept me interested. Keith Richards holding a bottle of Old Granddad while singing into a mike, I wanted to do that. Who was that one guy in just a couple photos, with the long fair hair?

A week or two later, I gave the record another try. This time it sounded different. What had been mush now blew me away. Horns, multiple guitar tracks, piano, organ, and rhythm section. And a little gospel choir. I eventually figured out who the guy with the long fair hair was. Mick Taylor. Exceptional guitarist. Jesus, he ripped it, though you gotta listen close to hear him. Every tune was a jumble of sounds, as if the musicians were competing for primacy. The total effect was so raw, it sounded like it was recorded in somebody's sweaty hot basement.

And it was. Most of *Exile* was recorded in the basement of a nineteenth century mansion on the French Riviera. Villa Nellcôte. It had an unseemly past in that it had allegedly served as the local Gestapo headquarters during the Occupation. Years later, Jagger thought the record was overrated, and Richards disparaged it in an interview once as drug music. The band didn't have a very good time, dealing with people coming and going and trying to get a piece of them, never feeling straight, no separation between work and play. But on that record, they created a place, a culture, not entirely their own, not exactly real, but it was an immersion. A rough-and-tumble English immersion in bluesy black South, there on the fucking Mediterranean. A couple albums later, Taylor got bored and quit, and like other bands of their era, the Stones realized they could make a shitload of money if they just settled down and made clear-headed music.

When we were in high school and college, we had our own Villa Nellcôte. Villa Biedermann. It was our friend Ollie Biedermann's big house in Grosse Pointe Shores, right on the Lake. On Ford's Cove, just a little way past the Yacht Club. A three-story mansion built before the Civil War, painted white inside and out, with matching white carpet throughout, two winding staircases, a screen porch two stories high, and balconies that faced a big backyard and the Lake. At Villa Biedermann, we could pretty much do whatever we wanted. Which meant play music and party a lot.

Ollie's name wasn't really Ollie, it was Ottokar. Everybody except his parents called him Ollie. Unless when we wanted to give him a hard time, we called him Biterman. That got reduced to Biteman. Like hey, Biteman, bite me. Ollie's main claim to fame, though, was that he was one of the biggest pot dealers in Grosse P.

Ollie's father, Odolph, was a coroner. The Chief Wayne County Coroner. Odolph had been a kid in Berlin during the Second World War when the Allies bombed the shit out of it. Odolph's own father was a foot soldier who died of malnutrition in a British prison camp. After the war, Odolph had to scrounge for scraps of food to keep his mother and himself alive. It was hard to understand what he was saying most of the time, which could be attributed partly to his broken English and partly because he drank a lot. It seemed like he didn't think in English, just German. Hard to tell if it was the booze or the language. Probably both.

The Biedermanns' mansion was our Villa Nellcôte, though we usually called it Club Maya, on account of Ollie's mother, Esperanza. She was the daughter of a Mayan Mexican and a German Marxist filmmaker who had fled Berlin in the Thirties for a little artists' colony near Guadalajara called Ajijic. Esperanza was round with a weathered complexion and dried out jet black hair that had the stiffness of straw. Like Odolph, she was a heavy drinker. She liked to wear big white Mexican dresses with colorful stitching year-round. She'd do these spins, dancing to Bunny Wailer and Jimmy Cliff, and her big colorful Mexican dresses would rise and fall. We called her "Parachute Woman." A Stones' song. Well, maybe not to her face, although she probably wouldn't have minded much.

Ollie's two sisters were twins. Marta and Ursula. They were a few years younger than Ollie. Like Ollie, they had light blonde hair and features, which made no sense because Esperanza had black hair and Odolph didn't have any. Sometimes in the summer after a party, in the wee hours of the morning, Marta and Ursula and a bunch of us would sit on the big porch, in the legless wicker chairs from Mexico that hung from the high ceiling. Odolph, if he hadn't crashed yet, would bring out the good Russian vodka he kept hidden in a freezer, spiced with rosemary or mint or some other herb from his garden. Lew and I might take out our acoustic guitars and play mellow singalong tunes, like "Willin'" and "Coming Down Again." We'd try to stay awake and wait for the sun to rise over us and light the Lake.

Club Maya was our nonstop party escape, our only escape, from all the Grosse P uniformity. Odolph and Esperanza were way too whacked for the Grosse Pointe prim and proper. They were Others with a boldface O. Their only friends, besides a few artsy fellow expats they knew from the Detroit Institute of Arts, were their kids' friends.

It was in Ollie's back yard, before we headed off to college for the first time, that Cam made a kind of prediction about my future, as we laid on towels in our Speedos, bodies slathered in Hawaiian Tropic, sharing a spliff of marijuana in the sun.

"Hey, Ace, you wanna know something?" He rolled over and looked in my eyes with a kind-of intimate smile. "I think you're gonna be an artist. An intellectual."

The way he spoke, it wasn't clear whether it was a compliment, or something else. Like a warning, maybe. Artist and intellectual? Were they the same thing? Where did that come from, anyway? Why would he say it with such assurance, like he was divulging a secret? It didn't feel very sincere. I couldn't draw, and I didn't have the patience to paint. And intellectual, what's that? I didn't say anything, I didn't want to risk giving him the opportunity to act all-knowing and superior, like he was prone to do. Besides, how would he know what an artist or an intellectual looked like if he had never been out of Grosse P? How would he know any more than me about anything, much less about myself? Just because he scored near perfect on the SAT and was about to head off to Chicago on a full ride? Fuck you, Cowboy.

Sharing a spliff on the lawn. At Club Maya, we must've always smelled like pot, but Esperanza never said anything, and Odolph, shit, he took some tokes with us more than a couple times. Maybe they even knew their son was a pot dealer. There were other drugs available, too. Somebody discovered that Esperanza liked pills. Darvocet, codeine, and a few others. The Club had six bathrooms and the medicine cabinets were practically full of them. Mother's little helpers, prescribed by Odolph. We figured, well, one or two or three here and there wouldn't be missed. After a few weeks of nabbing a few pills like that, somebody got bolder and thought, a bottle or two wouldn't be missed. Or another. And another. And another after that. Coulda been Cam who started it, wouldn't have surprised me. He could be shady.

After a while it seemed like everybody who hung out at Club Maya had them. Then one Saturday afternoon, Esperanza had a fit. Somebody must've swiped the last bottle in the house. She stormed all over the place, swearing and hollering, demanding her pills. Probably going through withdrawal. We took off in the LeMans in a hurry, including Ollie. That's when Parachute Woman became officially known as full-bore Queenie Bitch, the Fucking Witch.

We stayed away for a week or two. When we returned, the medicine cabinets had been replenished. After that we went back to taking just a couple pills at a time, although Cam was always pushing it, taking more than I thought he should have, the asshole. I didn't want to face anymore wrath from Queenie Bitch.

An unusual feature of the house was that the garage was in the basement. The cement driveway descended from Lakeshore Drive and curved right under the house. There had actually been a boat well down there, and an underground canal that ran under the back yard to the Lake. The story was that the house had been used to ferry blacks who escaped slavery to Canada, then later, during Prohibition, it was used to sneak alcohol the other way, from Canada to Detroit. A vehicle would back down into the basement and unload its human cargo or load up on booze, out of sight. The underground canal was long gone, but there were two big doors on the floor that swung open. Must have been a boat berth. It was a perfect place to store all our instruments and electronics because it never got too humid or too dry. The basement was also a great place to practice because we could play as loud as we wanted, and the neighbors couldn't hear it.

On the weekends in the summer, if it was nice outside, we might wheel all our sound equipment up the driveway on dollies and set it up in the big back yard, right by the break-wall at the edge of the water. We had to run long strings of power cords all the way across the lawn and through the porch into power outlets in the house. Sometimes Lew's girlfriend Anna, who we called Anesthesia, would sing background vocals. Lots of boats with young people would anchor in Ford's Cove to party, so we had a captive audience. It was an unusual mix on the water, blueblood Grosse Pointers and Macomb County mongrels. It didn't matter, we played to the masses. There'd often be young women sunning on the boat decks who might cheer, or yell, "Hey, you guys suck!" In the latter case, Ollie, manning the soundboard, would instruct, with a kind of deep flat Lou Reed intonation, "Show us your tits." Invariably, they'd yell back, "Fuck you, assholes!"

At some point, a friend asked us to play at his house party and we hadn't thought about an official name for the band. We had been tossing around some names for a while, but never agreed on anything. I don't remember how we came up with it, but we eventually settled on Schlachthof Fünf, which is the German title of the book, *Slaughterhouse-Five*, by Kurt Vonnegut. Ollie was our manager, sort of, because he had business experience dealing pot and couldn't play any instrument, except this huge Mayan drum the rest of us tolerated at the summer lawn gigs.

We played at a bunch of house parties our senior year of high school. It seemed like every weekend, there was a big party at somebody's house whose parents were out of town. Amazing how kids got away with that. When we played at those parties, which wasn't often, we didn't get paid much. Basically, all that happened was Ollie would pass the hat, this stupid sombrero he used to wear because he thought it made him look like a hard-core drug dealer. Passing the sombrero never amounted to much cash. It seemed that people would take money out of it almost as much as they put money in it.

At one of the last parties we played, in the winter at some chick's big house in the Farms who none of us even knew, things got ugly when her parents arrived home unexpectedly. Her dad, red skin livid, came down into the packed basement where we were playing and stormed across the room, creating a path in our direction by physically grabbing kids and shoving them out of the way. I didn't even notice the guy on account of it being so crowded and noisy until people started backing away from him, like the sea was parting. He wasn't a big guy or anything, but he was real ticked off, an enraged elder, it was his house, and the whole basement smelled like pot and spilled beer and sweat and cigarettes. He might as well have been Thor. Making his way toward us. Straight toward me.

Something flashed in my brain, he wasn't gonna grab me, my guitar's in the way. Right? If I just kept playing, that would make it awkward for him. As he got closer, however, it didn't seem like he'd be deterred by any of that, so at the last second, something else popped in my head. Do what the pros did in the old days, if someone rushed the stage, before they had all that security. They'd turn around and go into a self-protective crouch position, cradling their guitars. That's what I did, at the last second, I turned my back on him. He couldn't do anything then, could he? It worked for the Stones and the Beatles, and he wasn't a big guy. All he could do would be to give me a shove, or at worst, maybe punch me in the back.

Or kick me in the ass. He kicked me in the ass so hard, I went down, hard. Headfirst, practically jaw first, on hard black basement, my full weight on the guitar, and there's a loud buzz coming out of the guitar amp. He wasn't done. The lunatic grabbed my guitar cord and ripped it out from under my arm, right out of my guitar. Then he reached down and actually grabbed the neck, trying to yank it out from under me. I rolled off of it, because I was afraid if I didn't, he'd break my beloved Strat in half. Looking up at him, I could taste blood coming out of my mouth. The room had gone totally quiet, everyone anticipating a climax of some kind.

"Take your shit and get the fuck out of my house! Now!"

"Okay." I wiped the back of my hand across my mouth and looked at the blood. Felt a loose tooth with my tongue. My whole jaw felt like it had been hit with a sledgehammer. And the guy was holding my guitar by the neck with both hands, like he's gonna swing it at somebody.

"Take it easy," Lew said.

He looked up at Lew. "Don't you tell me to take it easy, you punk! Get your goddamn asses out of my house, now!"

"Okay man, we're going," Lew replied.

"Don't 'man' me!"

The guy just leered up at Lew, and Lew turned red. Everybody in the room stood there silently, waiting for what would happen next. I thought, "is he gonna swing it at Lew, please don't swing my guitar at Lew. You'll break it."

"Mark."

It was his wife, presumably, standing halfway down the stairs. Mark? I thought, that's not a dad name, that's a kid's name. Or a teenager's. Who the fuck lives here? Oh yeah, some chick. The dad turned around and they looked at each other silently while everybody watched, like it's a TV drama. All you could hear was the dad fuming through his nostrils, which sounded kinda gross, and I thought, this dynamic doesn't seem to be an entirely new narrative for them. Where the fuck is the daughter, why isn't she down here protecting us, saying Daddy, don't, please don't, Daddy?

Finally, the dad walked across the basement toward the mom and followed her up the stairs. Kinda like he was in a trance. Dragging my guitar! What the fuck! He's dragging it up the stairs! He's scratching it, where the fuck's he going with my guitar! What's he gonna do to it? I imagined him in the driveway, swinging it over his head and chucking it into the icy street to be run over. Somebody said, fuck, man, party's over, bummer. We packed up, and all I could think about was my Strat. Which I eventually found outside, leaning against the side of the house. Asshole. The tooth came out the next morning. My butt was sore for a week.

We had one real gig at a concert venue where we actually got paid. There was this kind of groupie named Vicki, a thirtyish woman who tended bar at the Purple Pickle, and graciously taught us a few things in the parking lot behind it. We called her Vanilla on account of how white her skin was on the other side of her dark tan lines. Give me more Vanilla, we'd say. French Vanilla. Anyway, she knew the manager of Harpo's, a cavernous dance bar in what had been the old Harper movie theater on the other side of the Ford Freeway, in mongrel territory. Harpo's needed a one-night warmup band for somebody named Eddie Money. This was before he had any hits. We didn't know or care who the fuck Eddie Money was. The main thing was the opportunity to be on a real stage in front of real paying customers. The manager said we could play just five songs, but we'd get paid something depending on the gate.

After the sound check, Lew and Cam and I went backstage to chill and use the bathroom, and we found a kind of lounge area. Nothing fancy, looked more like a little outdated kitchen in a mobile home. On a counter, there was a stack of Little Caesars Pizza boxes, the lid of the one on top open. Cans of Miller High Life on ice, and some sorry-looking hors d'oeuvres. Three guys sat at a table playing cards and smoking, tough-looking bearded longhairs in black leather and jeans and boots. They didn't look like musicians. Big beefy guys, older than us. I thought, maybe that's what roadies look like, in the flesh. Wow, this must be the big-time.

Cam walked past them and nonchalantly picked up a slice of pepperoni pizza.

"That's Eddie Money's pizza," one of them growled.

I thought, "Who the fuck's Eddie Money? If all he qualifies for as headliner is Little Caesars Pizza, who are these dudes to tell us we can't have some? What's Cam supposed to do with it, put it back?"

"Put it back," another roadie bellowed.

"What the fuck," Cam said. He was wearing his stupid Harvey Wallbanger t-shirt. "Can I take a bite first?"

"Put it back, now, or I'll kick your ass!"

I thought, "Cam you asshole, now you got them all pissed, just put the pizza down. Let's not get fired before we even get on stage and our chance at fame. Plus, we could get our asses kicked. Just put the pizza down, Cam, it's not that big a deal." But Cam decided to tease these guys. He held the pizza up in the air, opened his mouth, and got ready to take a bite. It was a freeze frame moment of silent anticipation, like, what's Cam gonna do? Then he took a big bite and dropped the rest on the floor. The three of us tore out of there, down a hallway into the bathroom, slammed the door shut, and locked it. They swore and said they were gonna beat the shit out of us.

"Man, we're gonna kick your ass!"

Lew yells back, "Don't 'man' me!"

Then we yelled it out together, "Don't man me, don't man me!" over and over, which really pissed them off. They pounded the door so hard; I thought their fists would come right through. After a few minutes they went away, but our new circumstance created the question of how we would know when it would be safe to exit. We opted to go conservative and stay put for a while. Finally, somebody else came and knocked and said that if we wanted to perform, it was time to go onstage.

It's one thing to fuck with people backstage. It's another to actually get up onstage, where fucking up isn't funny at all. There's no magic elixir. You actually have to have your shit together and perform. It's not like playing at a party full of friends, when nobody really gives a shit if you fuck up, and most aren't even listening. Being on a stage, up high where everybody could see you, in front of maybe a hundred and fifty people, even in that dump, an old movie theater with all the seats torn out, I didn't realize how exposed I was gonna feel. The whole crowd standing, looking up at us. And stage lights. I wanted to hide. In fact, I got so nervous as we were being introduced, I went behind Cam's drums and barfed. Even though we were all jittery, we actually got through the first three songs and played okay. And the crowd bought into it, like we were legit. Until we got to the fourth one.

We'd been breaking in a new lead guitarist, some guy we met named Nick Longnecker. Who we called Dick Limp-pecker. He was tall, thin and goony with oversized, teardrop shaped, gold rimmed glasses. Looked kinda like a young Jorma Kaukonen from Jefferson Airplane before he could shave. Limp-pecker tended to sweat real easy; he'd get big stains around his armpits on his print polyester. His glasses were always slipping down his long nose, and he'd be pushing them up all the time, even during songs. He was a pretty good guitarist, better than me for sure. But neither of us knew "LA Woman" before we first practiced it a couple days earlier. In the safety of Ollie's basement, it seemed okay. We shortened and simplified it some, although Limp-pecker and I didn't practice the mojo rising part much. I told myself it wouldn't be a big deal; I knew the lyrics and chords and Limp-pecker said he'd work on the lead guitar part.

There were premonitions that something was going to go badly. Plenty of kids from our high school were there, but most of the other kids in the crowd looked pretty rough around the edges, and out for entertainment by blood. Even though they clapped, and a few people even whooped after the first three songs, they didn't look like they came to hear us. Back then, the legal drinking age was just eighteen, and you could get a fake driver's license pretty easily. We found out afterward from Ollie that while we were still locked in the bathroom, there had been heavy drinking and a fight between a couple of our friends and some of the union horde, and they got thrown out. And Vanilla, who said she'd be there "for moral support," got in trouble as soon as she arrived. I didn't see it happen, but Ollie did. Actually, "arrive" isn't exactly the right word. More like, erupted.

Apparently, Vanilla showed up in a white limo she must've rented for the occasion, wearing something risqué. She was so wasted that she fell out of the limo, tore her dress and broke one of her heels, then she stumbled right into the glass door of the theater and went down. When they wouldn't let her in, she kept banging on the door with her broken heel and screaming, so they called the cops. She spent the night drying out behind bars. So much for Vanilla's coming out party.

You know that saying, about biting off more than you can chew? This was one of those moments. "LA Woman" started out alright, but Limp-

134

pecker and I totally fucked up the mojo rising part. Either my mojo was rising too fast, or Limp-pecker's guitar was running ahead of mine, and we were both trying to fix things instinctively, but we hadn't played with each other enough to pull it off. The whole thing kinda blew up. We had to cut the song early and a lot of mongrels booed loudly. A few of them threw plastic cups of beer at us so we left the stage. It was embarrassing. Didn't stay to listen to Eddie Money or eat more of his pizza.

That show was the beginning of the end for Schlachthof Fünf.

Even though Odolph never looked very healthy, no one was prepared when he died, the summer before our junior year of college. He had a massive heart attack in the back yard. Esperanza found him lying there in the grass near the break wall. A good man. The Biedermanns were godless so there was no question of a formal religious funeral. We had a kind of made-up ceremony in the yard, lots of kids came, all the girls cried. Including Parachute Woman, as she released Odolph's ashes in the Lake.

Esperanza had to sell Villa Biedermann. Turned out they'd been living paycheck to paycheck on account of their lifestyle. Odolph hadn't kept up his life insurance, and there was only a small pension and a little savings. She couldn't continue to make the mortgage payments, and besides, the old place was falling apart and there wasn't money to fix it. A young couple from out East bought it, did a tear-down, and built a monstrosity with a mock lighthouse on top. The remaining Biedermanns moved to a modest look-alike colonial in Grosse Pointe Woods, far from the Lake. When Villa Biedermann came crashing down, it felt like a second death. Like an era had ended and nobody had prepared for it. We had been too busy living in the moment.

Lew and Cam and I, we had nothing to fall back on after that. All the freedom and fantasy, like a never-ending costume ball, was over without warning. We'd lost the only place in Grosse P where we get away from the overdetermination of our surroundings. Esperanza and Ollie and the twins didn't seem the same after that, they were swallowed up by the conformity.

She got a job at the Grosse Pointe Public Library and we lost track of the family after Ollie transferred to Cal Poly in San Luis Obispo. There was no sense going back to Grosse Pointe in the summers anymore. Lew and I stayed in Ann Arbor. Cam decided to go to school year-round so he could graduate from U. Chicago early, since he already had a job offer.

Kid stuff. How, then, to explain why Cam mattered, in a way that does justice to why he mattered? Since anything that really matters, I mean really matters, is grounded on doing justice by or for someone. Not so much justice to Cam, who could be an asshole. Justice to the idea of Cam, the idea I had of him. It's not simply about trying to relive a fond, even an imaginary fond, memory of youth. For the most part, I don't have good memories of high school, or of my early years in general.

Why do I care about seeing Cam now, after several decades have gone by? A guy I always had mixed feelings about? I'm not sure. Maybe on a superficial level, I want to see how he turned out. Had he made a ton of money in the commodities market, as some had said? Did he sell out? Or get in some kind of trouble? Was he married, or divorced, or neither? Maybe he was normalized, living in one of those upper middle-class suburbs north of Chicago. I couldn't find anything about him online. There were some guys named Cameron Miles, but they weren't him, most weren't even American. If he was, or had been, a high roller, you'd think he'd be on the Internet, but he might've made it big well before that, then flamed out, or checked out. Or died. The text he sent Lew coulda just been somebody's random hoax.

Those are superficial reasons to find Cam. Lew and I had spent so much time together, we instinctively knew what to expect from each other, even now, after all these years apart. Whereas Cam was a kind of wild card for some reason I couldn't put my finger on. Those two used to disappear on me sometimes. Cam's somebody in the middle, between Lew and I in some way. Not on a linear scale, more off-center. Uneven. Maybe that's what I'm hoping for, a jolt, like that first time in Lew's room. Kill your sons.

If we find him, with all the time that's passed, I'll be able to see through what had been opaque. I'll see the culmination of a life, the truth about him would be revealed, in some kind of change. Whether he wanted me to know or not, I'll be able to tell; I'll know what became of him. Regardless, I'm sure I'll learn something significant about myself, in some sense unknown to me right now. Something in the relationship. Maybe something about myself that I couldn't find in isolation, something that could only come to consciousness in an encounter involving the three of us. A three-headed dynamic with time that hadn't been resolved, couldn't be resolved, due to our dispersion. Before we could really know each other, except as kids, when we thought the world was open to us.

A bad move at the Welcome Center

We'd been walking along in silence, mostly. Due west, toward Chicago and the question called Cam. Just a few cars had driven by, and nobody wants to pick us up. We must look dangerous. Maybe it's the fly rods. Not to mention a big bald dude in a trench coat dragging travel luggage along the freakin' highway in the middle of winter. Ruminating on that, and what Foucault might've had to say about our plight, my sensory apparatus doesn't register the pickup truck that slows as it passes, pulls over on the shoulder in front of us, and stops.

"C'mon, Dahd."

It's a big red F-150, jacked up, running boards and a German Shepherd standing in the back, wagging its tail as we approach. Dark blue tarp in the back, too. Something big under it. No place for us to sit in the cab, there's two guys in there and a lot of junk in the back seat. The guy on the passenger side opens the window.

"What're you guys doin' out here?"

He looks vaguely familiar. Shit, is it . . . it is! It's the fucking hunters from yesterday, sans orange outerwear. Now they've got army green jackets on, and caps with those furry ear covers turned up, like the guy wore in *Hogan's Heroes*. The heat's blowing high, nice and toasty warm in there. The bigger guy's at the wheel, his gut pressed up against it. Other guy's staring at the fly rods in my hand. On his jacket, over the right chest, an oval patch says, "Jerry."

"You goin' ice fishin'?"

"Our car broke down," Lew says.

"Was that it, back there?" the driver asks. "The one in the median, with the wheel missing?"

"Yeah."

"You left the trunk open."

"We know that."

"You really shouldn't be out here," Jerry adds. "It's too cold."

"We need to get another car. Can you take us somewhere we can rent one?"

"We could take you to Kalamazoo, you could get a car there. You'll have to sit out back. Don't mind Missy."

"Thanks, man. C'mon Dahd."

"Just knock on the rear window when you're all settled in."

I follow Lew to the back of the truck.

"We're gonna freeze out here, Lew."

"It'll be fine."

"Fuck. With a dog?"

Missy wags its tail.

"Look it's friendly. Hi, Missy."

"C'mon." Lew steps on the rear running board and pulls himself up into the truck bed. I follow, struggling a bit with the fly rods in one hand, while Missy watches, still wagging its tail. There's just enough room for us to fit on either side of the tarp with our backs against the cab. Missy sits down by Lew.

Lew raps on the rear window and we're off, picking up speed on the shoulder, and then enter the highway with a big bump. There's a red emergency light on top of the cab, inactivated. Looks like the revolving flasher you'd see on an EMS truck or a police car, except smaller and ancient-looking.

"Lew, why do you think that light's on the roof?"

"Maybe he bought the truck at a police surplus auction or something."

"Police don't drive pickup trucks."

The tarp starts flapping against the bed, making loud snapping sounds. We bounce as the truck goes over a pothole. Missy bounces and stands up.

"Hey, Lew, that dog's got a dick."

"Yeah, so what?"

"Maybe we didn't get the name right."

"Maybe it's Misty."

"That still sounds like a female name. Like in *Play Misty for Me*."

Lew pets him. "Maybe it's gender fluid."

"Why can't they keep it in the cab?"

"Maybe he likes it out here."

"What is this junk?

"What junk?"

"Whatever's under the tarp."

"What do you think, Dahd? It's a deer carcass."

I lift the edge and take a peek. Shit, he's right. Frozen stiff, legs bound, glassy eyeballs staring at the sky. Disemboweled. One, two, three … six points. "Could this be the same deer?"

"Probably."

"Shit, Lew. Is this what our voyage has come to?"

"Just be glad we got a ride at all."

I look back at the road we've left behind. The LeMans is back there somewhere, grounded for good. I can imagine scavenger types descending upon it right now, breaking it apart with giant wrenches and hammers. Like vultures ripping flesh off rancid carrion.

140

"What about the LeMans?"

"Fuckit," Lew says.

"It's in my name. The State Police'll track me down. That Archie dude, and his sidekick. Mister T."

"It doesn't matter, we'll be out of the state by then."

"That's just great, Lew. On the run, have to leave the state."

"Don't worry about it."

"They'll hassle Ginny, and she'll get all worried. And pissed off."

"Tip her off. Maybe she can hide."

"That's not helpful."

"Then quit bitching."

"I'm freezing."

"Look at it as a challenge," Lew says. "Tough it out. Everybody has to be challenged."

"Challenge. What a bunch of bullshit. You're an American hard-core even though you've been gone for thirty years. Did you notice what the sign in front of that school said?"

"What school?" Lew asks.

"Before we got on the highway, we passed a school."

"What about it?"

"It had one of those school announcement message signs out front. It said, 'Be Focused.'"

"Be focused?"

"Or maybe it was 'Stay Focused.'"

"Stay focused," Lew says.

"We passed it twice. Probably one on each side. Be Focused, Stay Focused. It's perfect."

"What's so perfect?"

"It epitomizes what schools are all about, to prepare kids to compete for vocational slots. You can't waver, or digress, or you don't have a slot. So, get focused, and stay that way."

Lew tries to light a cigarette. "What's wrong with that? It doesn't mean you have to be focused."

"Yeah, then you're just an anonymous consumer of what's produced by people who fill in the higher slots."

"How would you have it otherwise, Dahd?"

"If I was running for political office, I'd say we need to lower educational standards."

"You want to lower the quality of education? That's insane. Fuck, I can't get a flame out here."

"I didn't say lower quality. Make it easier for kids to learn what they really need to know to take care of themselves."

He gives up trying to light his cigarette. "What, so we should stop at two plus two equals four?"

"I didn't say end school after kindergarten."

"You'd never get elected, Dahd. People would say you're anti-American."

"You see, that's a problem. Education's all wrapped up in national competitiveness, in a race for global domination against with the Chinese. This ethos, this achievement ethos, is fucking destructive for everybody. For the learner, for the society, for the globe."

"You gotta provide a competitive education to give every individual an opportunity to be successful."

"Okay, Lew, let me ask you about what you just said. You said, 'opportunity to be successful.' What exactly does that mean?"

"Opportunity to take advantage, to make your life better."

"Why should anyone have to take advantage of anything, to make their life better?"

"Nobody has to."

"What happens if you don't?"

"Nothing. Isn't that what it's all about, equal opportunity?"

"That's my point, Lew. It's interesting that we equate fairness with the idea of giving people an opportunity."

"What else is there?"

"I question the basic idea that a person should have to take advantage of opportunities in order to have a reasonably comfortable and secure life."

"Dahd, here's something very simple you don't seem to get. Everybody's out for themselves. Even the basket weaver squatting at the side of the road in Malaysia or the Ivory Coast."

"That's not a very nuanced way of describing somebody trying to make enough money to eat."

"Even if what you're talking about was feasible, of everybody having access to reasonable things needed or whatever, you can't get around global competition. What if other countries don't treat their people the same and then outcompete us?"

"Who's to say that we couldn't have a society where everyone is assured that they will always have what they need to care for themselves, even with global competition?"

"Good luck with that, Dahd."

"My point is, why doesn't this question even get raised?"

"Because it's completely ridiculous."

"Is it? Well, so is sitting in the back of a pickup truck with a deer carcass and a dog with a penis named Missy. Freezing our asses off."

"Just be quiet for a while."

"Fine." Cold whips my face, like sharp little needles, over and over. My extremities are near frozen. I feel like a bag of guts, slowly freezing to death, to meet and greet this deer who's already reached the safe zone, where no hunting is allowed.

"Hey, Lew, why are we slowing down?" We've been on the back of the truck for what seems like an hour, though it's been less than that.

"Looks like he's turning into a rest stop."

143

"Shit, I thought he was taking us straight to Kalamazoo."

"Nobody goes straight to Kalamazoo."

A big sign says, PURE MICHIGAN WELCOME CENTER. We pass the rest stop building and enter the parking lot. It's mostly empty, just a couple cars. We pull into a spot near a gap in a split rail fence. Behind the fence there's a big open grassy area, frozen over, with patches of snow. A sign says, DOG PARK. PLEASE PICK UP YOUR POOP. STATE OF MICHIGAN DEPARTMENT OF TRANSPORTATION. The dog park's maybe forty yards deep, and beyond it, dense woods. Missy stands up as our two buddies get out of the truck. Jerry heads for the Welcome Center and the other guy, the driver, walks around back.

"Come on, Missy!"

Missy jumps off the truck and bounces toward him. The patch on this guy's jacket says "Larry." Great. It's Jerry and Larry.

"How come your dog's named Missy?" I ask.

"Oh, well, the story goes that when he was a puppy, the people who owned him had a little kid who called him Mommy, so they taught the kid to call it Missy. To avoid confusion. The name just stuck. How you fellas holding up back here?"

"Alright," Lew says. "How much further to Kalamazoo?"

"Not far. Come on Missy. C'mon boy."

Larry jogs off into the dog park with Missy. He's got a bit of a limp in his jog. Maybe he's got a fake hip like me.

Lew lights a cigarette. "Well, there's your answer on why it's Missy."

"Wonder how confused the kid's self-concept is turning out."

We watch Missy and Larry run around, they're way out there now, at the far end of the dog run, near the edge of the woods. Missy takes a shit, and Larry takes a poop bag out. Good job, Larry. He starts walking back toward us, but Missy isn't following him. She, or he, rather, has turned toward the woods. There's a couple young deer in a little clearing, probably looking for a handout. Missy takes off in their direction.

144

I sigh. "Oh-oh."

The deer bolt into the woods, and Missy leaps over the far fence after them.

Lew yells, "He went into the woods!"

Larry stops, looks at us, confused.

"In the woods!" Lew points. "He's in the woods!"

Larry turns around, sees Missy's gone. He limps toward the woods.

"This blows, Lew. Why didn't he have him on a leash?"

"Shit."

"We're never gonna get out of here."

Larry struggles to make it over the fence, then loses his grip and falls to the ground on the other side.

"Yeah, could be a while," Lew says.

"I'm gonna take a piss." I head for the Welcome Center with my backpack. Inside the lobby, there's an enormous map of Michigan behind glass. Must be about five by eight feet. It's got a red arrow that says, 'You Are Here,' and above the map in big letters, PURE MICHIGAN. Pure Michigan what? There's a bunch of vending machines down the hall, maybe they've got Pure Diet Coke.

In the restroom, five stalls. Somebody's in one of them, farting and grunting. Probably Jerry. I go down to the one on the other end for the disabled. Figure I qualify and it's easier cuz there's usually a hook to hang my backpack and get my catheter shit out. If it is Jerry in the other stall, he's gonna get to hear all my alien sounds, above his farts and grunts and plops.

I'm well over a hundred seconds of dribble before I hear him flush. Peering through the gap in the stall, I watch him go to the sinks. Yep, it's Jerry. He activates the towel dispenser, rips off the paper, and dries his hands slowly, looking my way. Looks a little uncertain.

"Are you okay?" he asks.

No, man, I'm Nosferatu, come for your soul. That Klaus Kinski version, from the Werner Herzog film; yellow-eyed, otherworldly. Let Jerry wonder about something different for the first time in his life. Finally, he leaves the room.

I reach a count of two hundred and twenty, finally finish up, and get out of there. Lew's standing in front of the vending machines. Jerry's at the last machine, looking his options over.

"Is Larry back yet?"

"No."

"What are you buying?"

"Diet Pepsi."

I look at the list of soda options. "Fuck, no Diet Coke?"

"Must not be pure enough."

I follow Lew back outside. Fucking cold, I put my gloves back on. Not that they help much. An army green Jeep that wasn't here when we arrived is parked a few spaces from Larry's truck. No Larry or Missy in sight. There's another guy with a dog in the park, in a big blue parka and a fur-lined hood, just a short distance from us. He holds a leash on a big dog that looks like a pit bull mix, black and white.

"There they are," Lew says as he lights another cigarette. Larry and Missy have just emerged from the woods. He's got a little extra oomph in his limp, like he's accomplished something super.

"Thank God."

Suddenly Missy takes off full bore again, only this time, he's coming in our direction. Straight for the pit bull. Larry slips and falls behind Missy as the pit strains on its leash, preparing for war.

"Oh, shit!" Lew exclaims.

Jaws open, Missy crashes into the pit, both dogs go flying, and the guy in the parka falls down as he loses hold of the leash. The dogs fight for position, each of them trying to come down with its jaws on top of the other's neck. Larry's still getting up from the ground. I find my legs moving through the opening in the fence toward the fray.

"Rick!"

I launch my body onto Missy, trying to grab ahold of his collar with my arms. Only I more or less roll off of him and hit the ground as the pit bull chomps down on my right hand, right through the glove.

"Aaaah!"

A couple seconds later, somebody's fist comes down hard on the pit's head, once, twice, three times. Lew's fist. The pit finally releases my hand and runs off, whining to its master, while blood gushes out of the holes in my glove left by its teeth. Lew pulls me up from the ground by the armpits.

"Missy!" Larry yells as he reaches us, limping hard. He gets on top of Missy while the other guy's holding his pit.

"What the hell are you doing out here with that beast unleashed, you mother fucker!" he yells at Larry.

"Missy's a good dog!" Larry yells back.

My glove's getting soaked red. "I think I'm gonna puke."

"Jerry!" Lew yells. "He's bleeding pretty bad; do you have first aid?"

"That's Larry, not Jerry."

"It's in the truck!" Larry yells back.

"Get it! Take your glove off," Lew orders. My whole right hand's red blood.

"C'mon, hurry up with the first aid!"

Larry fumbles around in the cab and returns with the first aid box. Lew opens it, takes out a bottle of alcohol, and dumps it on my wound. Searing pain hits me, like I got bit again.

"Aaaah! Fuck, Lew! You didn't need to do that!"

"Shut up." Lew takes out a roll of gauze and wraps it around my hand, over and over, until the blood's not showing through.

"I'll tape it, no problem," Larry says. "No problem, no problem."

"No, I'll do it!" Lew commands as he grabs the white adhesive tape from him. He wraps the tape around the gauze a couple times.

Jerry's back from the Welcome Center. "What the hell happened?"

"Dog bite," Larry says.

147

"Dahd, we need to get you to urgent care."

"No, Lew."

"You gotta get assessed, you might need stitches."

"I don't wanna go to the fucking ER, it'll take forever."

"Just shut up for once."

"Jerry, I need you to get out back with Missy," Larry says.

Larry gets behind the wheel and starts the engine as Lew pushes me in the passenger side and climbs in behind me. Shit, I'm squished between these two big guys.

"Where's the closest urgent care?" Lew asks.

"Kalamazoo. Hang on." Larry backs out with a jerk, hits the brake, then goes down hard on the accelerator and we're off. As we exit the parking lot, he flips a couple switches on the dashboard. A siren goes off and beams of red light revolve in front of us from the light on top of the cab. A couple more seconds and we're back on the highway.

The revolving red's making me more nauseous. Siren's loud as hell. "Why do you have a siren and emergency light?" I ask.

"Tipton volunteer."

"Huh?"

"Volunteer fire department. Town of Tipton." The speedometer passes eighty, eight-five, hits ninety.

"It's just a dog bite. No need to break any land speed records."

"Don't worry, we'll be there in no time. This truck's seen plenty of fires."

"Let's not start one."

Lew looks at me. "How are you doing?"

"Just peachy. My hand's killing me and you wrapped it up so fucking tight I feel like you cut off all circulation."

"You'll be fine, Dahd."

"They're probably gonna have to amputate."

"Raise your arm above your head."

"Why would I do that? I'd just be taking more blood from my hand."

"Just do it!"

"Alright, cool out. Jesus." I raise my right arm, but I have to keep my elbow bent on account of the tight quarters.

"What were you thinking?" Lew asks.

"About what?"

"Back there. Why'd you get in a dog fight?"

"It was a gut reaction. My body just took over. Freaky. Instinctual."

"I didn't think you could ever do anything like that."

"Iggy Pop used to do it all the time. Stage dive."

"You're not Iggy Pop."

"Thanks for getting that fucking pit to let go of me, Lew."

"I'm real sorry that happened," Larry says. "Missy's never done anything like that before. I couldn't keep up after chasing him in the woods. I don't know what got into him."

Yeah, right. "It's not your fault," I reply. I wanna say, *Larry you fucking asshole, why didn't you have him on a leash?*

"Why didn't you have him on a leash?" Lew asks.

"Never had to in a dog park before. Don't know why he went after the deer, to be honest. He sees deer all the time. Same with other dogs. Don't know what got into him."

I close my eyes and try to leave this reality. "Maybe we've entered *The Twilight Zone.*"

"Huh?" Larry asks.

"Never mind." It'd be nice if he thanked me just once for quite possibly saving Missy's life at risk of mine. Maybe he's programmed to think everything's in the hands of God. I drop my chin to my chest and keep my eyes closed. Pretend I'm back in my little guitar room in Ann Arbor, with a bottle of stout, room temperature.

Before long, I feel the truck slowing down a little. Open my eyes, there's a sign that says, "Kalamazoo, ¼ Mile," and we're getting off the highway. A few minutes later, we pull up to a decent-sized hospital, at the emergency entrance. Thank God, it's not some itty-bitty mom and pop place.

"Here we go," Larry says.

A young guy in a uniform with a buzz cut approaches as Lew opens the door.

"C'mon Dahd."

"Do you need a wheelchair?" the young man asks. He's looking at my hand, wrapped up like a club.

"No." This must be the path of decrepit old men. Should I walk gingerly? Sure, why not.

"I'll get our bags," Lew says. Jerry hands them down from the back of the truck, climbs off the truck with Missy, and walks up to me. The truck's flashing light is revolving red on us.

"How're you doing?" he asks.

"I'll be fine." God I wanna be done with these dudes. I look down at Missy and our eyes meet. Screw you, Missy. I might've saved your life, and you'll never know.

"Good luck." Jerry and Missy get in the truck with Larry, and they pull away, light flashing, siren wailing again. Weirdos.

Just inside, there's a couple young women at a reception desk. "Hello," one says. "What happened?"

I notice that the waiting area is nearly empty. "Got bit by a dog."

"Oh, I'm sorry. Do you have medical insurance?"

"Yeah. Lew, my wallet's in my left pocket."

He rifles through my wallet. "Dahd, you've got too much shit in here." A couple cards fall out, and the old picture of Cam and Lew.

"It's the blue and white card. That's it on the floor."

"Great," the receptionist says as Lew hands it to her. Would they have sent us someplace else if I didn't have insurance? Then we'd be fucked since we have no vehicle. We'd have to hoof it again or take an ambulance.

Maybe all the way back to Ann Arbor. Guess I'd be liable for all the costs cuz it'd be all my fault, for saving a dog's life. At least we're free, and American.

A little while later, I'm sitting in a bed in a room, and a nurse is preparing to put me on an IV. She's got dark brown hair and a little tattoo just below her right ear. Not sure what it is, a little red something. Not a heart. She's thirty, maybe thirty-three. No wedding ring, although a bunch of other ones. Costume jewelry. Don't get that term. Doesn't make a lot of sense unless you're in costume. A nurse costume. Badge says, "Rachel Grosinki, RN." Sort of attractive in a semi-biker chick kinda way, a little rough around the edges.

Lew sits in the corner. My wallet is on his lap. He's looking at the old photo of Cam and himself.

"Remember that, Lew?"

"Yeah."

He looks at it a few moments longer, then puts it back in my wallet.

"A little poke," the nurse says, and sticks in the IV needle.

"Ouch."

More like a jab. She makes a tight smile. Or grimace. A smile-grimace. Looks like she can't wait to get the fuck out of here, maybe it's late in her shift. Probably goes straight to the bar after work. Plays darts and drinks a lot. Lives an Other life of some kind. Maybe at a co-op pot farm.

Beep. "Ninety-seven point six," she says.

She sits down in front of a computer and types.

"You were bit by a dog?"

"Yes." She's gotta know that already, the receptionist punched that in, you'd think. Is she testing my short-term memory?

"Did you know the dog?"

"What?"

"Were you familiar with the dog?"

"No. We just met."

Not even a corner of a smile, she gives me nothing, just keeps typing. Nurse Rachel. Nurse Wretched.

"Have you had a rabies shot in the last seven years?"

Jesus Christ, how the hell should I know. "I don't know. I don't know if I've ever had a rabies shot."

"Then you'll need to get one." Touché. She stands up.

"The doctor will be in here shortly."

And she's gone. Off to the dart bar.

"This sucks."

"Don't start bitching," Lew says.

"I can't believe I got bit by a dog."

"I can't believe you tried to break up a fight between a screwy German Shepherd and a deranged pit bull."

"We could be here for hours."

"Yeah, I know. You're lucky you didn't get your hand ripped off."

"Do you see the TV remote?"

"It's under your right arm."

"I wish I could get this coat off."

"Then take it off."

"I can't get my hand through the sleeve, the way you wrapped it up so much."

"You can at least get the other sleeve off."

"Then get up and help me, asshole."

I pick up the remote with my left hand and turn the TV on, flip through the channels. *CSI*, exercise equipment commercial, fantasy heroes, junk news, junk news, antique guns for sale, and Apple commercial. *Law & Order* rerun, living off the land somewhere, and high stakes cooking show. Desperate people competing on an obstacle course, jewelry for sale, and *Ninety Day Fiancé*. Fast-food commercial. Sprint commercial. MSNBC. I hit the mute button.

"You know, Lew, you'd think when we went from three to hundreds of channels that somebody would cover topics in real depth. Instead of these hosts play acting to the viewers and panels of talking head publicity hounds with their intense expressions, like they're gonna wet their pants if they don't get to talk next. People talk about fake news. It's staged drama."

"If they went any deeper not very many people would watch."

"Okay, so we'll just give people images and minimal real analysis. Leave it to the individual viewer to concoct the story based on what they already believe."

"The media is supposed to be about reporting. Not education."

"There's education going on all the time. Miseducation."

"Like I said before, there's no straight news reporting," Lew says. "But you can't just have an official truth clearinghouse."

"What's most important is that nobody talks about what isn't said."

"You mean the implicit message."

"No, Lew, I mean, what is it the speaker wants to persuade you about that isn't spoken?"

"What isn't spoken? What isn't spoken is nothing."

"We have the right to free speech, but we don't have the right to know what's behind what is spoken. What is said, and how it's said, derives much of its meaning from what's behind the speaker's goal. Which is often hidden."

"That's why we need to have a national conversation among ordinary people."

A woman enters the room and quickly walks up to me, followed by Nurse Wretched. "I'm Doctor Stone. Mister Had-dad?"

"It's Huh-dahd."

"Excuse me?"

"Nothing."

She's kinda tall, a little taller than me, maybe five eleven. Thick black hair and a few freckles. Maybe forty. Her employee badge says, "Tricia

Stone, M.D." Sounds like a stage name. Could be Irish. Who else could have that combination, of black hair and freckles, and the name Stone? She's got a wedding band. Maybe her husband's a doctor, too, or a broker. Or a mover and shaker, in Kalamazoo.

"You've been bitten by a dog," she says, as she puts a pair of surgical gloves on. "Let's take a look." She sits down on a stool and turns to Wretched. "Give me one of those trays and a large cotton bandage."

"What size?"

"Four by six, six by eight. Doesn't matter. And saline."

Wretched hands Stone the bandage and positions a little plastic tub under my hand. Stone begins to slowly unwrap the bandage from my club arm. Wretched stands next to her, holding a clear plastic bottle with a nozzle on one end.

Bad memory flash of me naked, quartered, and splayed on the parallel bars. Four women in black leather and whips, four cats hiding their privates, my bladder filled 'til it explodes.

"I understand it was a stranger dog," Stone says.

"Pardon me?"

"A dog you didn't know."

"Yeah, it was strange. I was traumatized."

"You were wearing gloves."

"The women, there were four of them, in black leather. Photos of four cats."

"I don't understand. What women with cats?"

"Never mind."

"This is quite a wrap job."

I nod toward Lew. "He did it."

"You must be a guardian angel." She's definitely Irish.

Lew chuckles a little, a chuckle with an edge. "It was bleeding pretty bad." He's got that look, that dying for a cigarette look.

As she unwraps the gauze, more blood is exposed with each turn, and her eyes hone in. With the last couple turns, the blood's flowing, but not like before. She takes ahold of my hand firmly but gently with both of hers, as Wretched squirts warm saline over it. There goes my blood, into the tub. I'm being diluted.

"One, two, three, four, five, six puncture wounds on this side," Stone says and turns my hand over. "One, two, three, four on this side. Goodness."

Goodness. The blood comes out faster with my palm down. Saline feels good, though, everything's fine. Doctor Stone's warm hands, bloody water dripping, life slowly slipping away, but these women don't know what that's like yet, they're too young. They're doing what they've been trained to do, which is to carry out technical procedures. Focused on the here and now only, on getting done what needs to get done. That's alright. I can die here; I've faced worse in a clinic. Women and cats in bondage.

Stone turns my hand back to its original position, palm up. "Most of these are not deep, that's good. Good thing you had gloves on and that it didn't cut through any tendon. Or your fingers."

"It's not bleeding like before."

"Your friend did a good job."

Good job, Lew. If I could just sit here and close my eyes and listen to her talk some more, and she could hold my hand and tell me about the poetry of the Irish hills, life would be good for a little while longer. I might even pee in my pants without the aid of a catheter. Cured by a woman after being abused by the Evil Four.

She peers more closely at my palm and touches a couple of the wounds. "I don't like these two, they're from the upper fourth premolar. It was starting to grind there."

"Grind?"

155

"It's good you got the dog to let go pretty quickly. You see, with their location, you're going to be aggravating these two every time you move your thumb and fingers. They'll need to be stitched."

Shit. Stitches. I wanna get the fuck out of here.

She turns to Wretched. "Get Doctor Reuss." Wretched leaves and Stone looks at me again.

"And you know you're going to need a rabies shot."

"I heard."

"We're a teaching hospital for Western Michigan University."

Why is she telling me that, is it a warning of some kind? Is she bragging, or is it just something she had to say? Maybe it's required by the corporate sponsors. What's Western doing with a medical school anyway? When I graduated from high school, Western was the college where all the stoners went who couldn't get in anywhere else and wanted to keep partying hard at the next level. Did she go there? Does she party hard? Delirium, I'm feeling it, and they haven't even offered anything for the pain.

"Can I get something for the pain?" She'll probably say no, but as an old friend advised once, if you don't ask, you don't get.

"Sure. We'll write you a prescription for Tylenol with codeine."

Cool. That was easy. "Can I get those tape stitches?"

"No. They'd come off too easily."

Fuck. Can't you say, sorry? At least I'll get the pain med. Wretched reappears accompanied by a young guy, maybe all of twenty-six years old. Another young person with black hair. He looks a little pale, too. What is this place, everybody's got black hair, except Wretched and hers is dark brown. Is it some kind of Goth hospital, in the middle of southern Michigan? Or the home of the freaking Munsters? Or *The Rocky Horror Picture Show*? Maybe they'll all suddenly rip off their outerwear and do a macabre, promiscuous dance. That would be okay.

"This is Doctor Reuss," Stone says.

Did she say, ruse? No, I see from his badge, it's spelled, Reuss. She said the E and the U like the French. "Rooze." Maybe it's properly pronounced "Ruse," as in, this is a big ruse. He looks a little soft and unsure of himself. Pretty straight. Jogs every morning, doesn't eat a lot, plays by the rules. He's probably from someplace like Miami or Philly, or Long Island, and this was the only residency he could get, in the flatlands of godforsaken Pure Michigan. At the edge of a town called Kalamazoo, where it's below freezing, and right off the Interstate.

He puts out his hand, as if we're meeting in drastically different circumstances. Like he's working at Bank of America in midtown Manhattan and I've come in for a business loan. Then he realizes I can't shake his hand, yeah, my hand's the issue, you dumbfuck. Stone's still holding it anyway, please don't let go.

"See this?" Stone instructs Ruse, pointing at the two deeper wounds. "Canine. They'll need stitches. Let's put some triple antibiotic on the wounds. And give him some samples to use later."

Still holding my hand, she looks in my eyes. "The biggest issue for you is going to be avoiding an infection. You're going to need to keep it very clean. Try to keep it from getting wet. We'll give you everything that you'll need. Do you live in the area?"

"No. We're on our way to Chicago."

"Tonight?"

"Well, no, we don't have a car right now."

A momentary look of incomprehension passes. She's probably thinking, I'm not even gonna try to understand what these two are doing on a trip to Chicago, without a vehicle, in the middle of the winter, one of them with a dog bite, from a stranger dog encountered at a Welcome Center. "You should make an appointment to see your primary care doctor to check on the wound in a few days."

"Alright."

"If you get a fever, or redness, or swelling, or worsening pain, or a persistent headache, go to the nearest ER immediately."

Now she's thinking, not sure how the fuck you'd be able to do that, since apparently you're walking your way to Chicago. Doesn't matter, none of what she said registered. Maybe Lew was listening.

She stands up and says something technical sounding to Ruse that I can't hear. Maybe it was, don't fuck up like you did last time. Then she looks at Lew. "Make sure he keeps it clean."

Why'd she do that, doesn't she think I can take care of myself? Keep it clean. Wounds, or my life in general?

"I will," Lew says. Another chuckle with an edge. He's climbing the walls for that cigarette.

"Good luck, Mister Had-hat," Stone says, and she's gone, just like that, forever. And so, our brief relationship abruptly ends.

Ruse and Wretched. She could be Missus Munster and he could be little Eddie. Lew, he'd be Uncle Fester, or something like that. No, that's not *The Munsters*, that's *The Addams Family*, I think. Same thing. Ruse glances around like he doesn't know how to get to Point A, while Wretched watches him, like she knows he doesn't know what to do and doesn't wanna help him. Just wants to watch him fry, since he's gonna be a doctor and make a lot of money someday, while she throws darts and harvests pot.

"Excuse me a moment," he says, and splits.

Where the fuck is he going? Wretched looks at me, as if we now have a legit relationship, above board.

"How are you doing?" she asks.

"Fine. Can I get a cup of water?"

"Sure. I'll be right back."

"I'm gonna go have a smoke," Lew says.

"Alright."

"And I'm gonna see about renting a car and getting a phone."

"Don't leave me in this place."

"Relax. It's not useful for me to just sit here. You're gonna be here for a while, and we need a reliable vehicle."

"It's not gonna be that much longer."

"By the time they're done, and you go through all the checkout shit, it'll probably be another hour, at least."

"Fine, go. But bring me some food."

"What do you want?"

"I don't care, just not something from a vending machine. Get me a couple of fishwiches from McDonald's."

"What's a fishwich?"

"You know, a piece of fish in a bun. A steamed bun."

"You mean the Filet-O-Fish."

"Whatever, Lew. Without cheese. Light on the tartar sauce. And a large Diet Coke. Light ice."

"Any other special requests?"

"Yeah. Don't take too long. And a chocolate sundae."

Just like that, he's gone. Now it's just me, defenseless against the medical Munster people. I turn the sound back on the telly, flip around the channels, it's still all shit. Poker competition between a bunch of lowlifes. Jesus Christ. I look at the tub under my hand with the blood and saline, a warm stream no more.

A few minutes later, Ruse reappears. With a syringe.

"What's that for? Is that my rabies shot?"

"No. I need to numb your hand before I can do the stitches."

Great. He sits down on the stool so that he's facing, away from me, and takes my right hand. I can't see what he's doing now because his back and left shoulder are in the way. Must be his way of dealing with the pressure. Don't let the patient watch him fuck up. Where's Wretched with my water?

"This might sting a little."

"Ow!"

"Sorry."

Why did he just give me a shot on the back of my hand if the wounds he's gonna stitch are on the palm? I feel him turn my hand over, so I squeeze the metal arm of the bed with my left hand, bracing for the needle's next impact.

"Ow."

"Sorry." Ruse stands up. "Let's give it a few minutes for the numbing agent. I'll be right back."

That's weak, taking off again. Real weak. Fucking little shit. I look at my hand, wanna be comfortably numb now. Fucking pit bull. Fucking Missy, fucking Larry. Fucking Jerry, although he did do the noble thing and sat in the back of the truck so we could sit in the cab. And Lew, you asshole, you're probably gone two hours minimum. I'm gonna need to pee pretty soon, how am I gonna use a catheter with my right hand like this? Maybe Wretched can help me, that could be interesting. Why the fuck do they put poker on the sports channel?

A few minutes later Ruse returns. With another syringe.

"How's the numbing?"

He taps around my hand. "Can you feel that?"

"A little. What's that for?"

"This is the rabies vaccine." He walks around to my left arm and rolls up my sleeve.

"This one won't be too bad."

"Ouch!" Little liar.

Wretched walks in with a tray that's got pieces of light blue plastic thread and a bunch of needles. The stitches. And my water.

Ruse walks around to my right side and sits back down like before as Wretched stands there with the tray. "Okay," he says, and exhales.

He said that like he's trying to talk himself into being confident. Like the second-string QB who hasn't played all season, suddenly called into the huddle. No, third-string.

"Am I getting all those stitches? For a couple puncture wounds?"

"I don't know yet."

Maybe he means, it depends on whether he does it right or screws it up a couple times. He takes my hand and taps it again with his forefinger.

"Numb?"

"Pretty much."

"Can you remove the basin for me?" he asks Wretched.

Basin, that must be what they call plastic tubs where he's from. Remove the basin. Wretched frowns, like, I've got my hands full already, do it yourself, little prince.

"Okay," he says again, and hesitates.

C'mon, dude. Call the play.

Ruse picks up one of the stitches and attaches it to a needle. I can't see his hands, but I imagine they're shaking a little.

"Ow!"

"Okay?"

"Yeah." Not enough numbing, you little shit. I feel him stick me two, three, four more times.

"There we go."

Feel him tying the stitches, like a little kid tying his shoes. Wretched frowns again. Not a good sign. Finally, he gets up and I can examine his handiwork.

Looks like one of the stitches isn't tied tight. "That one there, isn't the skin supposed to be closed tight like the others, so it heals and doesn't bleed?"

Ruse looks at it for a moment. "It has to have room to breathe."

Room to breathe. That's bull. "Doesn't it need a third stitch? You did three for the other one."

"It should be alright."

Now I know for sure. These people are total hacks.

"We're going to give you some bandages in case there's more bleeding and an antibiotic application to put on your wounds every day, to avoid infection. It's important to keep it clean."

"Doctor Stone said I could get a script for Tylenol with codeine."

"Right."

Ruse and Wretched split, and I'm alone again. On the TV, the poker match must be over. Now they're showing a fucking video game competition.

Bad karma

Some years back, I went to a kind of interdisciplinary disease doctor. I asked him to look at all my medical records to see if there was some underlying explanation for my maladies. He couldn't find anything. In other words, my problems are piecemeal.

There's one malady of mine that I never had checked out. A chronic one. It's the extreme difficulty I have whenever I've tried to do anything that requires the placement of words in an order that conforms to a prevailing discourse. Like law school.

At the elite law school that I attended, you had to really screw up to get a grade below a C. They figured it would look bad if they accepted only those with the highest LSAT scores and GPAs and then failed them. I managed to get a grade below C once. A D-plus in Legal Ethics and Professional Responsibility. Which is kinda funny, or ironic, at least, since I couldn't keep from questioning the whole ethical basis of the American legal system.

Here's something even more amusing. There were these two guys in my Legal Ethics class who were straight arrow buddies. The class was taking the final exam, which determined your entire grade in the course.

About an hour or so into it, one of the pair left the room for about ten minutes. After he returned, his buddy did the same thing. Then after he got back, the first one left again. Because it wouldn't have been ethical if the second guy got the benefit of the first guy's answers, and the first guy didn't get the benefit of the second guy's answers.

Ethics. I imagine both of those guys got A's in that class, and lots of A's in the other classes they took together, like Property, Tax, and Contracts, and that they're now sitting in large corner offices with nice views of the Golden Gate Bridge or the Statue of Liberty. And both of them feel perfectly valid because their profession rewards aggressive personalities who can find clever ways to win and do what it takes to generate big revenues. Men of good fortune.

They earned their stripes the American way, bucking the system, managing the odds. Devising strategies and tactics to find ways to push the edge or make it fuzzy. Grab assets. None of the other hundred-odd students taking the exam left the room, so you could easily say those two guys were exceptions. But Foucault said it's not just a matter of law or rules, it's about what people do outside the law. Which is really what the goals of business and law are about, aren't they? Getting there first to control the language and the context. Tell a good story, not just any good story, but one that establishes what can be believed as true, in order to win and collect your reward before somebody else changes the language game on you.

In the interest of full disclosure, I probably made Legal Ethics a lot harder than it needed to be. You see, it was taught by a federal judge on Fall Saturday football mornings, and at that time, I was usually parked on the front porch of my old fraternity house, right across the street from the Law Quad. Drinking beer with the other bros around the house keg. Honestly, that D-plus might've been charitable. What the fuck, Legal Ethics on Saturday mornings with some old judge? Football Saturday mornings? Are you on drugs?

"That D-plus in Ethics was your own fault," my conformist conscience tells me.

"It wasn't really Ethics. It was Legal Ethics," my alternative conscience protests.

"What's the difference?"

"Legal Ethics is about being fully committed to your client's interests. What I'm talking about is the ethics of law. Training in law ought to include analysis of law at a fundamental level, from the standpoint of social justice, broadly construed."

"That's not why people go to law school. They go to law school to be lawyers."

"I know that. But when it comes down to it, many judicial decisions are pretty darn arbitrary. Decisions are often based on personal values. Which remain hidden."

"It's based on precedent and argument. Applying law to the facts."

"There's often more than one plausible interpretation of the evidence and the law. In those instances, a judge's personal sense of right and wrong can factor into the result. Consciously or subconsciously."

"Isn't that pretty obvious and well understood? That judges have different views about right and wrong, different views about society and so on, that they bring to their work?"

"It's glossed over. But when you talk about right and wrong, you're talking about what is just. You see it all the time in split appeals court decisions all the way up to the Supreme Court. Why not bring right and wrong out in the open and debate it?"

"But that's not how the game works."

"That's the problem."

What happens when you've got no place in law school to seriously address these kinds of questions? Inner conflict, bound to spill into interpersonal conflict. Like Aristotle said, nature abhors a vacuum. Nature manifested itself one day in an exchange with my professor in Contract

Law. It was an afternoon after a night I may have slept on a pea, or something like that. It wasn't my plan to have an existential debate with Professor Smith when I fell out of bed that morning.

"Mister . . . Had-dad, is it?" he asked.

"It's huh-dahd."

"Alright, Mister Had-hat, what about the contract in this case? The plaintiff says, 'I relied on the man's word. I committed four hundred dollars with the reliance that we had a deal. If this contract is not enforced, that's unjust.'"

"Professor Smith, if we're gonna talk about justice in the context of contract, then I think we need to consider John Rawls's work on social contract."

"That's not what we do here. The method we use to analyze cases is the Socratic method."

"Professor, Socrates engaged in rational dialogue to think through the nature of being and reality and justice. What we do here is basically jousting between adversaries with technical lingo. We're just going in circles."

Silence. So, I added, "We're only sitting here because the rhetoricians won out over the philosophers a long time ago."

"It's called the law, young man."

"As opposed to justice. Because if it was about justice, we wouldn't be spending all of our time stuck in the reasoning of court opinions."

"Do you want to be a lawyer, young man?"

"Actually, probably not."

"Then I don't know what you're doing here."

It got real quiet then. So, I thought I might as well fill up the space. To keep from losing my lifeline and floating off in the galaxy, like Major Tom. Actually, I wasn't really thinking, I just kept going. Like every good lawyer, I didn't want to lose, even if I knew I couldn't win. I said something like this.

"That's a reasonable point, Professor. I guess I'm naive. I should've understood that this is a vocational school. Like for beauticians, or embalmers. Only the trade we learn here is how to be manipulate words to win the language game. The only class in the entire curriculum dealing with anything other than money is maybe the First Amendment. And the guy who teaches that is a dandy."

Oops. I was referring to the dean of the law school. I bumped into him once, years later. Literally. I was doing my usual thing, reading philosophy while on a walk. On the right side of the sidewalk, following standard American custom. He was jogging when we nearly collided. He said, "What are you doing." Not like a question, not like, how's it going? What are you doing. Like an accusation. Hm. What am I doing. As a citizen? As a commoner? As a tool? Maybe he meant, what am I doing at the moment. I'm doing the Philosopher's Walk, what the fuck are you doing, hotshot?

I saw Professor Smith once, too. On a fine fall day. He was sitting on the edge of the big fountain in front of the Women's League, eating his lunch. As I walked by, I cheerily exclaimed, "Hello, Professor Smith!" He looked up and dropped his sandwich. It fell apart in a pile of leaves, looking impoverished. One piece of salami and a piece of lettuce. Too much mayo.

I had no one, no place, to take my concern in law school. What can you do in this kind of conundrum? You seek a comrade for relief and amusement. At least, that's what I did. I found somebody on my wavelength. Or rather, he found me, at a Friday afternoon cocktail party in the Law Club. It was just a day after my exchange with Professor Smith. I was in a room full of people talking about nothing but law school, while gargoyles carved into the walls leered down at us from above, angry they were immobilized and couldn't pounce upon all the blasphemy. As I scanned the room for some kind of relief, something caught my eye, something out of place. Something wrong with this picture, something that didn't fit.

I did another scan and saw what stood out. A guy sat cross-legged in a chair with a shit-eating grin. In a blue blazer and a pink Oxford and khakis and Earth Shoes. Something around his neck—what's it called? —an ascot, a fucking turquoise ascot. A cigarette in one hand, a cocktail in the other. And he's grinning right at me. I thought, what the fuck, who invited Hunter S. Thompson Junior? Why's he staring at me with that shithead, what-me-worry look? What's his deal?

His name was Paul John Wall. To his friends, he was known as P.J. or Wally. His friends, I learned soon enough, were a bunch of townies who worked in late-night restaurants, bars, and the local U-Haul in Ypsilanti. A couple of them worked at the Howard Johnson's Motor Inn out on Carpenter Road, a stone's throw from the mobile home park where Iggy Pop grew up. P.J. never sat well with me, too predictable a nickname, too lowbrow given his idiosyncratic mode of living. His omnipresent navy blazer and handkerchiefs with initials, the button-down Oxfords, his bolo ties, and the old emerald-green Eldorado he drove. And his cats, Alexandra and Cleopatra. When either of them acted out, he'd put it in the freezer to chill for a little while. He deserved a name that was more formal or sophisticated, but still kinda pop culture. So, I called him Jonathan Paul. Or, like what the law professors called him. Mister Wall. Or sometimes, for a casual alternative, since Johnny Rotten and the Sex Pistols were the latest thing, I'd call him Johnnie Wall.

At that party, I didn't know any of this yet. All I could think of that moment was, what is wrong with that dude? Why is he fixated on me? Is he staring at me like that because I look funny? Did I walk in with a big splotch of bird shit on my shoulder or something? So, I looked away and wandered through the party for a little while, seeking in vain to find a conversation with someone who would talk about something, anything, other than law school.

A bit later, I turned around and he was standing right there with the shit-eating grin. Skinny little guy, with a cigarette and a cocktail. Dirty blonde hair short and a bit spiky. Heavy whiff of cheap cologne, that Clubman aftershave shit. Probably hasn't showered in a while. Is that a hint of green eye shadow? Overall effect is twenty-year-old David Bowie if he'd been raised somewhere in the Midwest instead of working-class London.

"I liked what you said in Smith's class yesterday."

It took me a few seconds to recognize what he was talking about. Didn't even know he was in my Contracts class since there were a hundred students in it.

"Oh yeah, thanks."

He offered his hand. It was wet and limp like a fish, so I wiped my hand against my hip.

"I'm Paul. Wanna get high?"

I hesitated, not sure what this guy was all about. "Yeah, alright." Figured he wanted to go outside to share a joint somewhere. Instead, he pulled out this little metal thing and offered me a toke.

"It's smokeless. And odorless."

I took a hit and coughed. Whoa, strong shit. The only people who get pot with this potency are tight with a well-placed dealer.

That was my introduction to Johnnie Wall. You know how rebellious teens, and overaged ones, tend to find each other. That shit-eating grin. Johnnie even wore that look in class. He always sat in the back row. I figured he was going to class stoned. That was until I started sitting with him. I realized then why he had that little tool. Wall wasn't just going to class stoned. He was actually getting stoned in class. Which was impressive. Pretty ballsy. I mean, this isn't high school, it's the third ranked law school in the country. Alright, yeah, like you, I'm goin' through a teenage rebellion again, but do you really want to risk getting suspended or kicked out of Michigan Law just to get high in Contracts or Criminal Procedure? I did it a couple times with him, but it made me so paranoid that I'd burst out laughing at the pseudo-holy sanctimony of it all.

169

Johnnie and I soon became bestest law school buddies. Studied together, sort of, partied together, frequently, often both at once, and generally tried to cope with law school together. One of the ways we did that, besides getting high, was to express ourselves creatively, and make a little money off of our affiliation with U-M Law. Johnnie Wall discovered that there was a dormant student film society called Gargoyle Films. There were a couple of sixteen-millimeter projectors that more or less worked, and a little annual budget funded by Student Activities. Like an aspiring lawyer, he analyzed the rules and concluded that there was no reason we couldn't make money showing films. He proposed that we get it going again. Which we did, hooking up with a distribution company, selecting films and printing up a schedule and flyers and so on.

Nobody affiliated with the law school was around the Law Quad on Saturday nights when we showed our films in Room 100. After we collected the dollar admission and started the first reel, one of us would hike down to the Blue Front for a six-pack, then to the back door of Dominick's to buy a couple plates of bun bo xao and some Thai stick from the Vietnamese woman who worked in the kitchen. We'd sit in the back of Room 100 and drink beer and get high and eat the bun bo xao while preparing to switch to the second reel. Nobody in the audience ever seemed to mind.

Dear Johnnie Wall. May the gods rest his soul. He actually finished law school and managed to somehow get a good job with a firm in L.A. I heard he did well out there for a few years before he got stoned one time too many and fell off a cliff while hiking in Bryce Canyon. That's one story, at least. Another one is that that he'd been farming pot on a big piece of land somewhere in central California and managed to get thrown from a tractor. Broke his neck amid the devil weed. Maybe he died twice. I don't want to believe that Wall's bit the dust. I'd like to think he's just gone off radar.

Johnnie's undergrad degree was psychology, whereas mine was philosophy, which had ruined me for U-M Law. Unlike Johnnie, I quit and went back to philosophy, this time, the Ph.D. program, just down the road

170

from the law school. I thought I'd finally found my home. Turned out that wasn't exactly the case. The stuff I wanted to study, political critique of social institutions, starting with higher education itself, was not sufficiently academic. As the British department chair said in the Queen's English, "Faculty are generally very conservative when it comes to their work. They don't like the idea of critiquing the ivory tower."

As a result, I wrote papers that had no home. Actually, I did get published in obscure journals. Journals that were not recognized in Anglo-American philosophy. One was out of South Africa, I think. Another was based in some university in Scandinavia whose name I couldn't pronounce. Petit journals. The kind that only maybe twenty people in the world read, and half of them only did so because they were on the editorial board and got free issues.

That was not the proper method to go about getting published. The proper method was to do it the other way around. You're supposed to pick a couple journals that are well established, read some back issues to figure out what they accepted, and then write specifically for them. That way you could concentrate on doing what you really needed to do to get a tenure track job and eventually tenure. Which is to churn out papers that are largely variations on one topic with different little twists and push your ideas at conferences. You could be efficient. Hence strategic. Cunning, even. Made perfect sense, from a practical standpoint. Practical for both the functioning of the individual and the institution. But it seemed wrong, counter to what learning and thinking and teaching were supposed to be about. Especially in philosophy. Turns out, philosophy professors pursuing advancement were just as means-ends as lawyers. Marketing yourself, marketing philosophy, to philosophers. In a word, it seemed kinda perverted.

When I complained to the chair about this state of affairs, he replied, "This is a profession, the scholarly profession."

Profession? What's the worth of a so-called advancement in knowledge if it has nothing to do with making the world better for everybody? And that word, scholarly, made me cringe. Sounded wimpy. If you put it all together, you get professional wimp.

The chair said, "If you wanted to critique social institutions, why didn't you pursue a doctorate in sociology?"

"All they do is conduct repetitive statistical studies about social inequalities based on demographic groups."

"Aren't those important topics?"

"Yeah, but they don't do any real thinking over there. They seem to presume they've got it all figured out, and it's simply a matter of grabbing big grants and getting their hands on new datasets to crunch numbers."

"Well, everybody has to pay their dues until they get tenure, then you can pursue whatever you want. You must first make an academic contribution."

Hm. Why should somebody have to pursue clever slants on redundant topics in order to qualify to pursue significant ones? Is that what intellect is for?

It didn't help matters that by the time I made it to dissertation stage, half of my committee had retired, and the other half had died of old age. Eventually, when the department chair and I agreed that we'd had enough of each other, they gave me a master's degree as a sort of consolation prize, and I said, goodbye, Mister Chips. Ever since then, I've eked out a living of sorts, doing a variety of things that eventually led to a series of part-time teaching gigs at community colleges, while helping to raise a couple kids. And reading lots of thoughtful philosophers with illuminating ideas about where we are in the West that you weren't allowed to study in American philosophy departments, because they were too thoughtful. Such as Michel Foucault.

I encountered Foucault for the first time by accident, one weekend at Borders. In fact, I might never have read Foucault if not for my little toddler

Timmy. It happened in the real Borders Bookstore, back when there was only one, the original store in Ann Arbor. Borders consisted of two floors that were deep and not very wide. Nothing at all like the megastores that came later, with aisles wide enough to drive a tractor through and more empty space than books. In the original store, books and bodies were crammed in everywhere, which gave it a little charm. It was also a great place for kids, not only because it had a large Children's Books section, but also because there were lots of narrow aisles they could explore and stacks of books they could knock down and climb over. Kinda like an indoor playground for bookish tots.

On that particular day, little Timmy toddled out of the Children's section with a copy of *Thomas the Tank Engine*. I figured he'd made his choice and we headed toward the cashier. On the way, however, Timmy took a sudden forty-five degree turn down an aisle, and wouldn't you know it, we ended up in the Cultural Studies section. On display atop one of the shelves, a single book in large black letters against a white background shouted, *Power/Knowledge, Selected Interviews*. I'd heard of Foucault and knew he was associated with "power" in trendy lightweight literary criticism circles. Which meant he wasn't taken seriously in philosophy departments west of France. I was still a doctoral student at the time, albeit proceeding well along an irreversible downward path toward all but dissertation. Given these circumstances, I was beginning to dedicate mindful activity to reading and thinking about whatever I wanted to read and think about.

I don't typically latch onto anything with large letters. Anything that pushes itself like that usually repulses me. In this instance, the association of power and knowledge grabbed me. Power, because, like most grad students, I had none, and knowledge, because if I had managed to find a niche in Anglo-American philosophy, it would've been in some kind of intersection between epistemology and political philosophy. Which didn't exist. I felt like there was something terribly wrong with how theories about knowledge and justice were treated separately.

Those block letters that grabbed me shouted that there was somewhere to go with the relationship between knowledge and power, and not just theoretically. I put cute little Timmy back in the stroller with *Thomas the Tank Engine* and spent a few minutes examining the more substantive books by Foucault. I bought a bunch and spent the next six months trying to figure out what he was trying to say. That critical event, of Timmy and Thomas and Michel, is long gone.

Gone too are the days when Lew and I went to war with nature, fly fishing in upstate Michigan for trout and salmon. If the weather was right, and even when it wasn't, we'd often skip Friday afternoon high school and drive four or five hours up north, directly to a river, and fish into late Friday night, to cover any tardy bug hatches that would draw the big fish to the surface of the water for their bedtime snack. Then we'd get up from our tent before dawn Saturday morning, fish all day into night, and do it all over on Sunday, before finally driving home, and arriving in the wee hours of the morning. After we got to college, we'd go up whenever we felt like it.

The topography of the northern Michigan trout streams stoked us. Winding through dense woods in constant twists and turns, the course of the rivers meant that we often couldn't see downstream more than twenty yards, or even less. There were sudden changes in width and depth and current, endless jumbles of rocks and branches and logs, and massive trees that had uprooted and crashed across the river. If you went off the beaten track and fished for ten or fifteen hours in a single stretch like we did, it was less about matching your flies to fogs of bugs and more about fishing to habitat. We couldn't cast much because the rivers were frequently narrow and the elm and maple tree branches covered the air overhead. More often than not, we had to lightly fling the fly and use the tip of the rod to get it close to the nooks and crannies where the fish might be, for a few precious seconds at a time. A fling, I became pretty good at.

To tell the truth, those stream conditions mean that fly fishing in northern Michigan is frequently a bitch. One exception is the Au Sable River, the most well-known and overrated of all Michigan trout streams. From our young and cocky point of view, the Au Sable was reserved for old men who would stand and cast from one or two places for a couple hours before retreating to their well-appointed living quarters. They looked like they just walked out of an LL Bean catalog, smoking a pipe. There was a name we had for the Au Sable. Old Man's River. We stayed away from there.

Catching fish was our telos, I mean, why else go through all the hassle? But there was a lot more going on that made it infinitely more meaningful. The Kennebec or Yellowstone, these rivers are not, but for us, there were all kinds of possibilities in the rugged complex intoxication of it all. Although whenever I waxed poetic about fly fishing to Ginny, she'd frown.

"It's not like hunting," I'd say. "We always release the fish back in the water."

"How would you like to be hooked through the lip and dragged around the water against your will?" she'd retort. Which is interesting.

As much as Lew and I were on the same page about rivers, at some point we started to grow apart. He'd disappear downstream for the ever-elusive big one while I tried to stay immersed and connected to the particular moment and place. After Cam joined us, things changed some more. Instead of Lew disappearing down the river, it was Lew and Cam who disappeared. That was okay, I'd tell myself. Eventually they'd have to wait for me to catch up or come back for me. They'd often boast about the fish they caught. I only believed half of it. I didn't make shit up, well, maybe I did a little. Everybody bullshits to some degree, the way they market themselves, their public persona. Which is one of the ways we delude ourselves.

Cam was a pretty good guy, he really was, most of the time. But I didn't like how he acted as if he knew what he was doing with a fly rod when he was still new at it. Didn't like how he'd say, "Hey Ace, how'd you do?" when I caught up with them. A few times, I'd wake up in the tent in the middle of the night and they'd be gone. Fishing for the monster browns and rainbows, they'd say in the morning. I guess I resented how Cam waltzed into this thing that Lew and I had. It didn't exactly coincide with a change in vibe between us, but it might've indirectly hastened it, because it changed what we did. And how we did it.

After Cam joined us, we started partying more, fishing less. Fishing high. That posed a new challenge. Try to keep yourself together, try not to fall in, try not to be blown off your feet. Then we needed something else. Cam wanted to strip. We started to wade in just our vests and boots. Shades and a cap for the sun. But no waders or anything else.

The second time we did it, a Michigan Department of Natural Resources officer busted us for indecent exposure. Unbeknownst to us, some asshole property owner had seen us walking back to the LeMans for our lunches and complained to the local office. The officer appeared out of nowhere. By then, we were back in the water well above our waists. He ordered us to step out of the river. We thought he was just gonna ask to see our fishing licenses. Lew asked the officer if we could just show them to him from the water, but he told us we had to get out. Pretty embarrassing. Had to walk all the way to the LeMans and get dressed in front of him. He wrote up big tickets and told us to go home and never come back.

Then one weekend we really took fly fishing too far. It was our last trip together before we went back to college for our senior year. We decided to do a kind of challenge. We'd camp like always, except we wouldn't bring any food. Instead, we would live off what we caught and boil our water from the river. We went way up to an obscure river in a remote area of the Upper Peninsula somebody told us about. Someplace way off the grid. Supposedly the water had great habitat, and was accessible and wadable.

And it was located in a pure virgin birch forest. This somebody claimed he'd caught lots of big browns and rainbows there, even monster brook trout. We'd heard rumors about monster brooks in the U.P. but we'd never seen them on our previous trips.

The river turned out to be a major bitch. It was ice cold alright, and good habitat. Fast, deep, really rocky. We caught just two twelve-inch browns and a few small brookies on the first day, not enough for even one person to get by food-wise. Cam fell in the water, and we had to quit fishing to build a fire for him to warm up and dry out his waders. Lew tripped in the woods looking for kindling and hit his head on a downed tree, got a little woozy. Big bruise on his forehead. We got the fire started, dried Cam, and grilled the fish. He had some backup clothes, but he couldn't fish for a while. Lew and I got back in the river, fished downstream 'til dark, hooked but lost fish, and came back to camp with several more modest ones. We went to sleep that night pretty hungry. I wanted to quit but Lew and Cam said we'd made an agreement and had to gut it out.

The next day was bad. It got real hot and humid, there were enormous swarms of horse flies that seemed to defy DEET, and it poured rain in the afternoon. Like a fucking monsoon. I had one of those cheap single use ponchos that ripped so I got soaked, though that wasn't too bad. We caught just a few more modest browns and rainbows the whole day.

That night, we were so hungry, we decided to eat the psychedelic mushrooms that Lew had brought. Along with passing around the fifth of Cam's Wild Turkey. Bad move. I got up to pee and became disoriented in the woods. The birch seemed to be swaying all around, so I got down on all fours and started crawling in the muddy wet ground, trying to find my way back to camp. That didn't help much cuz the tree roots were slithering like snakes in my hands, and there was buzzing around my head, like bees or little faerie voices. I rolled onto my back, put my hands over my ears, and closed my eyes. Opened them just in time to see an oversized black bear hovering over me on its hind legs. It was about to come down on me and I thought I was a goner, when a light shined in my face and the bear spoke.

"Dahd, get up. I can't find Cam. Come on."

I got up and followed Lew closely, grasping the back of his t-shirt, getting mud on his back. This time, he actually walked slow. He must've been seeing things too and trying to keep his head.

"Lew. Where's Cowboy, where's Cowboy?"

"I don't know." He spoke calmly but I was paranoid something was going to fall out of the trees and kill us.

"Creatures up there, look. Big ones, mushrooms and creatures. They're gonna fall and squish us."

"Maintain, Dahd."

"Monkeys. Yooper monkeys, Lew."

"You gotta maintain, man."

"Cowboy, oh Cowboy, where are you?" I called out.

We found Cam lying in a little freezing cold feeder creek. Lew almost stepped on him. He was spread eagled on his back, his face barely above the surface of the water, quivering in the cold flowing over him, next to the half-empty fifth of Wild Turkey. When we stood him up, he shivered uncontrollably. Lew shined the light in his face. Cam's eyelids were drooping, lips blue. Saliva and mud and blood and soaking wet in his stupid Harvey Wallbanger t-shirt. We got him back to the tent and rolled him up in a blanket, but it didn't seem to help much. He just kept shivering and shaking. Lew said we had to get him to the car and turn on the heat. Since Cam couldn't walk or stand by himself, we had to get on either side of him and hold his arms over our shoulders.

It was tough going three-wide on a narrow deer path through the woods, stumbling on surface roots, scratched by buckthorn and wild raspberry. Cam was dead weight, and everything was moving. I had trouble keeping my side of him upright. At one point we were half-carrying, half-dragging him, but we made it to the LeMans. Unfortunately, it was locked. Lew didn't have the keys, so he went back to the tent to look for them. I hoped they weren't hanging from the ignition. Couldn't tell in the dark. Lew never locked the LeMans. Why here and now?

Waiting for Lew, I attempted to keep Cam upright against the car but lost leverage. I tried to gently ease him down to the ground. Unfortunately, I couldn't hold him and had to kinda drop him the last foot or so. What was taking Lew so fucking long! Cam's eyes were fully closed now, and he wasn't mumbling or saying anything. I talked to him, as if it could bring him out of his stupor. Slapped him hard a couple times, felt his neck, and yelled for Lew. How would he find the keys? They were probably in the river, and we were all gonna die of exposure.

Lew finally made it back with the keys. He insisted it had only been a few minutes. We laid Cam on the back seat, which wasn't easy since the LeMans was a two-door. Lew decided it wasn't gonna be enough to turn on the heat in the car, we needed to get Cam somewhere, someplace indoors, warm, maybe even a hospital. He got behind the wheel and drove through the narrow curvy two-track, bouncing off rocks, turning the wheel back and forth as if we were being chased, punching the brake before stands of birch that seemed to suddenly appear in the headlights and lurch at us. Cam's body rolled back and forth on the back seat, building momentum until he finally fell to the floor.

"Is he breathing?" Lew asked.

I looked back at Cam on the floor. How was I supposed to tell? I couldn't exactly check his pulse with the way we were bouncing along, jerking back and forth, amid my paranoia.

"I think so."

Somehow, Lew got us out of there and onto the smooth state road.

"See if he's breathing!" he said again, sounding scared.

I leaned down to Cam's face. "Turn the light on, Lew. I can't hear anything."

"He's not breathing?"

179

"Just a minute!" I put the index and middle finger of my right hand near Cam's nostrils.

"Is he?"

"Yeah."

I sat back. In the sky, stars flew about randomly, collided, and exploded. The northern lights in psychedelia. How could I know he was breathing for sure or if I was just imagining it? Lew hit the accelerator again, he was all over the median. On his forehead, the blue bruise from the night before had gone purple, grown bulbous, and pulsated in and out. What about Lew, shit, what was he seeing from behind the wheel? Good thing it was one in the morning, or whatever, and there wasn't another car on the road. Why would there be, I thought. We're in the middle of fucking nowhere in some kind of horror film.

Eventually we came upon a little town with an Econolodge. We got Cam out of the car, he was a little coherent in that he was mumbling again, his eyelids fluttering. He shuffled his feet a little as we carried him inside. Got his clothes off and sat him in the bathtub under a hot shower and harsh bright light. The sound of the water hitting him was incredibly loud. Felt antiseptic, like we were preparing him to be embalmed. We dried him off and put him in bed under a couple blankets.

The room was spinning a bit but not as bad as the stars had, maybe I was coming down. Started to go outside to shake my head and puke but Lew made me stay.

"You'll get lost again. I can't go looking for you, we gotta keep an eye on Cam."

I sat on a chair and looked out the window at the starry night for what seemed like hours, waiting for the hallucinations to subside while the two of them slept.

In the morning, I woke up on the floor in my boxers, still kinda wet from the river. Birds chirped, sunlight. I heard Cam laugh a couple times and sat up.

"Hey, Ace."

I looked around, nothing was moving except for Cam crossing the room, fully clothed. Lew stood outside the open door having a smoke.

"How'd you get your clothes dry?" I asked Cam.

"They have a laundry room. Wanna go fishing?"

"Fuck you, Cam."

"Here, Dahd." He tossed me a two-pack of Hostess Chocolate Cupcakes.

"You put us through a lot of shit last night."

"Sorry, Ace." He laughed.

That pissed me off. After last night, he fucking laughed. I sat up and devoured a little of my aggression by eating the cupcakes with lust.

"You alright, Dahd?"

"Yeah. Are you?"

"I'm good. Good karma."

I was about to say, "No Cam, actually, you're really bad karma." And maybe take a swing at him. Lew stepped back in and interrupted.

"Let's go get our shit before somebody takes it," he said.

Forgot we'd left our stuff at the river. Everything was still there, though wet. We packed it all up and drove straight home. On the way, Cam got high and joked about the night before. I kept telling him to shut the fuck up, but he didn't, which pissed me off more. Lew hardly said anything at all, probably because he was the one who had brought the mushrooms.

That was the last time the three of us fished together. I fished with Lew a few more times that autumn. After that it was over. Lew moved out east to begin his MBA at MIT, I stayed in Ann Arbor for law school, and Cam graduated from U. Chicago, got a job with some bigshot consulting firm, and worked like a dog on the road all the time.

I stopped fishing altogether. Years later, I would occasionally get motivated to go up to a river for the beauty and challenge, but I found myself impatient with the effort it took to fish and wade where we had fought mighty wars. The water seemed faster, deeper, colder. Handling a fly rod in tight quarters became pure aggravation. Fewer fish. Some of the old paths seemed to have disappeared and I found myself fighting my way through dense woods and brush.

One morning a few years ago, having not picked up a fly rod for I don't know how long, I headed north to hit one of our old haunts. Three hours in, I was about to pass the exit for M-72 and the Au Sable. On impulse, I got off the highway, parked at the first access site, put on my waders, assembled my 5-weight rod, and stepped into Old Man's River. Old-timers were there in their clean, neatly pressed LL Bean vests, casting to the same spots, barely moving. Now I'm one of them, I thought, and took my place. But I couldn't cast like they could. I'd spent my youth taking on rivers with an edge, putting a fly in difficult spots. I'd been so busy defying nature that the mind-body connection necessary for casting a fly the ordinary way had been severed. I could relearn. But with friends gone, why relearn how to do something without them?

Rick and Lew get prepared

I had to wait what seemed like hours for Lew. Wretched eventually made me go to the waiting area to make room for the late-night emergency crush. Just when I was feeling settled and part of a crew. Felt like getting kicked out of a band. Lew finally returned with a rental vehicle. A real car, a new model Camry. With GPS and heated seats. And all other kinds of high-tech shit that I sure as hell don't know how to use. Lew, on the other hand, is the kind of guy who never admits he doesn't know how to do something. Now, he's fucking around, pushing buttons, clicking on screens, acting like he's getting to know the car. While he's driving. Lew also managed to get himself a smart phone. He got my Filet-O-Fish, only he forgot to tell them to leave the cheese off and go light on the tartar sauce. I had to use a bunch of napkins to wipe off the tartar sauce and the edges of the cardboard to scrape off as much of the cheese as I could. Some of the tartar sauce got on the car, which pissed Lew off, but what's the big deal, it's a rental. The Diet Coke tastes like it's from a bad batch. Sickly sweet. Plus, no chocolate sundae. He claimed he didn't hear me ask for it. Asshole.

"Lew, let's just stay here tonight. Find a motel and leave for Chicago in the morning."

"I've already made reservations at the Days Inn."

"Oh, okay, good. Wait a minute, where are you going? Kalamazoo's on the other side of the highway."

He lights a cigarette. "Where do you think? I'm getting back on the highway."

"Why are you doing that?"

"Because we're going to Chicago."

"You just said you made reservations at Day's Inn."

"I did. In Chicago."

"In Chicago? It's like three in the morning."

"If we leave now, we'll be in Chicago before dawn."

"What are you talking about, before dawn? We're not trying to sneak up on somebody. I wanna stay here tonight and sleep."

"Too late, Dahd. I've already made nonrefundable reservations. See how disadvantaged you are now that I have a smart phone and you don't?"

"I'm not disadvantaged. You're just an asshole."

"Yeah, well, I'm an asshole with a smart phone. You're an asshole without one."

"I didn't realize we were competing for advantage."

"It's technology, Dahd. Get with it."

"But I'm really tired."

"You said you slept in the waiting room."

"Not really. It was packed with overly wasted college kids. No room for me to lay down with my BiPAP."

"Then sleep now, it's quiet and we've got a ways to go."

"I can't sleep in cars. And there's no place for me to plug in my BiPAP."

"Good. I need you to take my Diet Pepsi."

"Why?"

"Because it's too big for the cupholder and it's getting the seat wet between my legs."

"So what."

"It's getting my pants wet," Lew says. "And I need a free hand to eat my Chicken Nuggets." He extends his Diet Pepsi to me. "Here, take it."

"What am I supposed to do with my drink?"

"Put it in the cupholder."

"Fine." I put my Diet Coke in the cupholder and take his stupid Diet Pepsi. I can barely hold it in one hand. I notice the cup says 'Big Gulp.' "Since when does McDonald's sell Big Gulp?"

"I got it from Speedway. Their cups are bigger."

"What if I don't want to hold it all the way to frickin' Chicago?"

"Then put it between your legs."

"What if I don't want to get *my* pants wet?"

"I can't help you with that. I'm driving."

"You know what, Lew? You're beyond asshole. You're a royal asshole."

"We can sleep once we get to Chicago. This way we miss rush hour."

"We could stay here and miss rush hour and sleep."

"But this way, we'll have a full day to look for Cam. Plus, I want to get there in time for the free breakfast."

"What free breakfast?"

"At the Lincoln Park Days Inn."

"You mean, make your own waffle?"

"The website says they have a variety of stuff."

"Like every Days Inn in the world, Lew. Including the one in Kalamazoo."

"Look, you're the one who slowed us down with your pseudo-heroic act back at the Welcome Center."

"I didn't choose to get bit by a pit bull. The whole thing was the result of those two douchebags Jerry and Larry. Aw, shit."

"What now?"

"I left the fly rods in the back of Larry's truck."

"Big deal."

"We need them."

"We're not going fly fishing in December in the Chicago River."

"But now they're gone forever."

"They were warped."

"Maybe they could be repaired."

"You can't repair warped bamboo that's been sitting in a car trunk for decades."

"They mean something, Lew."

"They're history."

"Our history."

"That's nice, but history's just history."

"The past impacts the present."

"Well, that's obvious."

"No, I mean, change the past to change the present."

"What are you talking about? You can't go back in time."

"You can do what Foucault did. Start with something in the present that you think isn't right. Some practice, some social situation you think is brutal, that people blindly accept without questioning it."

"So, he just made things up. Like fake news."

"He didn't claim his accounts of the past were the only right ones. There are multiple histories, they're all narratives that leave things out. Like the photo of you and Cam."

"What about it?"

"Somebody who didn't know you guys and looked at the photo would think, here's two guys smiling, two buddies with their fly rods and fishing vests. What a nice picture. Can't tell you weren't wearing anything below your waists."

Lew takes a final drag of his cigarette. "We were warped. Warped kids, doing stupid shit."

"We need to prepare for Cam."

"Prepare?"

186

"We need to talk about what we might find."

"We have no idea what to expect."

"That's all the more reason why we need to prepare, Lew."

"I need a sip of my soda."

I sigh and extend the giant cup to him. "Here."

"I can't hold it while I'm driving. I need you to hold it so I can drink out of the straw."

"You're kidding me, right?"

"It's the least you can do, if I have to tolerate all your philosophical indulgence."

"Fine." I lean over and point the straw toward him while he takes a long slurp. "What about those texts Cam sent you? Let me see them."

"They're in the cloud."

"What cloud?"

"Never mind."

"I want to see them, Lew."

"It's just gibberish."

"We came all the way here because of gibberish? Give me your fucking phone."

"You don't know how to use it. Besides, you're holding my drink."

"I'll put it between my legs."

"Then you'll get the seat all wet. It's a rental."

"Just give me the fucking phone!"

He grimaces and hands it to me. It looks a little advanced. "How do I get on this thing?"

"You need the password."

"What is it?"

No reply. He just sits there, eyes on the road ahead.

"Are you gonna give me the damn password, or not?"

"Not."

"Then how am I supposed to read the texts?"

"It's a secret."

"A secret? What is this, you don't trust me?"

"It's mobility."

"What is?"

"The password. The password's 'mobility.'"

"Mobility? Interesting choice." I punch it in. "It says it's not right."

"Try it with a capital M."

"Got it." A little miracle. "Now what do I do?"

Lew scowls. "Give it back."

"I can do it."

"If you could do it, you'd be doing it."

"Fine, asshole, you do it!"

He turns on the overhead light, takes the phone, holds it up with his right hand, arm extended on top of the steering wheel, and clicks a few times with his thumb. Then he hands it back to me. On the screen, there's a list of text messages, with the initials "CB" next to them.

"What's C-B?"

"C is for Cam, probably," Lew says. "I don't know what the B is."

"If C's for Cam, B, that's probably his middle initial. Beauregard. Why didn't you show me these earlier?"

"I left my cell on the plane."

"What else are you keeping from me?" I start with the first message at the top and read down. "'Broken people. Utter misery trying to live. spite. children run off screaming. there is no perspective. spite me.' He's trying to say something."

"Obviously."

"Spite. It shows up twice. Spite, and then 'spite me.' What's that about?"

"I don't know."

"This is exactly why we have to be prepared."

"Stop trying to manufacture a drama, Dahd."

"It's important. It's where Foucault went."

Lew sighs and finishes his last Nugget. "Don't start with that shit."

"We can't understand these texts, but we can be prepared. Like Foucault's examination of the shepherd."

"What shepherd?"

"A shepherd is vigilant about its flock."

"Sheep?"

"No, it's about the leader who looks out for the individuals in the group."

"You mean, like all that Catholic grade school shit?"

"No, it's about how the shepherd governs."

"You can't govern hoofed animals."

"It's a metaphor, Lew. Treat each individual as it is, in its own particularity. Care for it. The shepherd will do everything possible to do that. Even at the shepherd's own personal risk."

"That sounds suspiciously like those hokey parables we got shoved down our throats at Tuna Tech."

"The shepherd's just one kind of leader Foucault talks about. Another is the wise king. In order to rule or govern well, he had to govern himself well."

Lew lights another cigarette and coughs. "Governing yourself makes no sense."

"For the ancient Greeks, governing meant caring for your soul. It involved all these practical exercises to strengthen your mind and body. Intellectual and physical exercises, exercises of soul and body. To be prepared for unexpected events."

"It sounds more like that old TV show starring Keith Carradine. *Kung Fu*. With the blind guy, his teacher who called him Grasshopper."

"The ancient Greeks weren't teaching kung fu, Lew. Also, that wasn't Keith Carradine on *Kung Fu*. That was David Carradine."

"What was Keith Carradine in?"

189

"Um, he was in the Robert Altman film, *Nashville*. And remember, he was in that weird Alan Rudolph film. He played the bizarre guy who goes missing in the American northwest."

"Oh, yeah," Lew says. "He goes rogue, becomes a vampy character."

"Yeah, he's in drag. Like David Bowie in the old days."

"That film was way over the top. What was the name of it?"

"*Trouble in Mind.*"

"Nice one, Dahd."

"The problem for the ancient Greeks was, since you can't know the future, you have to prepare. There's a price to pay. It's dealing with emotions and passions that get in the way."

"Everybody has to do that to get ahead in life."

"The Greeks weren't talking about getting ahead. It's about all the shit that can get in the way of knowing and doing the right thing. Foucault claimed that doing the right thing involved what the ancients called, 'parrhesia.'"

"You mean, Parcheesi?"

"Parrhesia. Free spokenness. It means having the courage to speak the truth to powerful people even at risk of your life."

"That doesn't sound like a very wise idea."

"It's about challenging the status quo if you think there are wrongs. It means having the courage to speak the truth to others as a way of life. That's the final turn Foucault took. In his lectures on the Cynics."

"Cynical people, speaking the truth? Makes no sense."

"The Cynics, with a capital C. They lived simply. They sought to expose the truth of who we are by their way of life. Cut out all the adornments, all the bullshit. There was one Cynic Foucault focused on. Diogenes. The Dog."

"He was a dog?"

"No, Lew, he was a dude. His father made and exchanged coins. Maybe the ancient equivalent of an investment banker."

"Interesting analogy."

"The story goes, his old man got accused of ripping people off, selling counterfeit. He got run out of town. Diogenes got exiled too, for a long time."

"Why'd Diogenes get kicked out?"

"He was probably in on the racket. Family business. Anyway, while he was in exile, Diogenes went to the Oracle for advice. Like Socrates did. The Oracle had told Socrates, 'Know thyself.' But it told Diogenes to do something very different from that."

"What'd the Oracle tell Diogenes to do?"

"Deface the currency."

"You mean like, damage coins?"

"It was a metaphor. For society."

"Damage society?"

"Not damage it. Flip it over. Stand it on its head. Challenge the norms. So, Diogenes went to Athens, the center of power and culture, and lived on the street."

"Like a homeless person?"

"He ate what he could find, begged. Slept in a barrel."

"Sounds like a downer, Dahd."

"Diogenes believed he was living the ideal of a pure life."

"Living on the street is the true life? Gimme a fucking break."

"He was trying to make a point."

"Which was what, philosophers are worthless?"

"On the contrary, he was trying to be useful, by directly challenging customs and rules that people hide behind. Like all the wars of words over differences that people engage in on the media today. Instead of recognizing the vulnerabilities we have in common."

"What, we should all be vagabonds like Diogenes, and survive by begging?"

"Foucault said Diogenes was living according to what is true."

191

"That's the true? Living on the street and hassling people?"

"The Cynics lived the true by giving up all unnecessary customs and material things, and challenging the norms that lead people astray."

"But if the focus is on living, why not live it up? Why is living in poverty true?"

"It wasn't poverty for the sake of poverty. It was about endurance."

"He could've done that in exile."

"He did what the Oracle told him to do. He got in people's faces. He confronted them in rags, challenged custom, did things people didn't normally do in public. Like urinating and shitting. Masturbating."

"That's disgusting. Is that what we're supposed to do, start beating off and screwing in the street?"

"Okay, admittedly, he was a little twisted."

"A little!" Lew exclaims. "You mean, like, so I'm walking down the street, and I round the corner, and then, oh, look, there's my neighbors, fucking on the sidewalk. What am I supposed to do, wave? Say, hey, nice to see you, lookin' good! And so's your lawn!"

"Alright, let's skip that. Diogenes was trying to get people to take off their constructed identities. Get real. Be a person."

"Be a person? It seems he was trying to get everybody to live like wild dogs."

"He was about social justice."

"Social justice? Gimme a break, Dahd. Look, if somebody wants to live on the street, and go around demanding handouts, and play make-believe that they're living a good life, go ahead. But don't go calling it social justice."

"You've got it all wrong."

"I get it, life is hard. Most people don't have it easy, regardless of race or gender or any of that. Who decided that social justice is only about certain groups?"

"Nobody says it's only about certain groups."

"That's the narrative. When other people hear about social justice, it pisses them off," Lew says. "Because nobody gives them anything, and they're struggling, too. Which is what the Republicans capitalize on."

"Yeah, so now they're the party of the lowest common denominator. Good for them."

"See, there's your bias, Rick. That's not true. They appeal to the basic idea of playing by the rules."

"The Republicans preserve the freedom to seek one's fortune and keep the revenue streams coming. That's their basic moral rule, when it comes down to it, and it's backed up by their narrow versions of Judeo-Christianity. At the expense of other versions of freedom and social justice."

"Don't give me all that shit. Social justice is code for a strategy to get advantages legislated to favor certain groups."

"Just because somebody is advocating for a fair shake doesn't mean they want to penalize someone else. People have to be able to see each other. Get past the appearance of things. See the commonality."

"There's the problem," Lew says. "Nobody talks about commonality in the media. It's all about diversity. That's not about what people have in common."

"People need the courage and humility to let down their guard before someone who's of a different race or culture. So their differences don't appear like a threat. Be a little generous with each other. Is that such a fantasy?"

"In the short run, yes."

"The problem is that people put up a cold shoulder toward each other because they're afraid."

Lew lights a cigarette. "So we gotta go up to people like Diogenes and give them a hug? I still don't understand why Foucault made a big deal about a guy who lived that way two thousand years ago."

"Foucault tried to challenge the established narratives that divide and exclude people."

"It seems like he was a sheltered academic living in his world of thought."

"Actually, Foucault was an engaged political activist, heavily involved in organizing street protests for stuff like prison reform. Got arrested a bunch of times, roughed up by police. Not your typical philosophy professor. And he ends his final lectures with Diogenes."

"Maybe he just ran out of intelligent things to say."

"Foucault was having trouble finishing his lectures, he was getting weak. He knew he was sick, sometimes he had to cut them short. Then he collapsed at home and died."

"What'd he die of?"

"AIDS. Nineteen eighty-four. That was the same year the virus was first identified, later that year, in Paris."

"Okay."

"People were dying from some unknown cause. Maybe he knew he had it. Maybe he was preparing for it by ending with Diogenes. Like he was giving up all worldly things. If only in thought."

"I wish I knew how to prepare," Lew says.

"For what?"

"An ending."

"What do you mean?"

"You asked me what my pills are for."

"Yeah?"

"I've got a growth."

"What kind of growth?"

"A tumor. On the back of my head."

"Oh, man."

"It's growing slowly."

"Has it been treated?"

"I had chemo, but it didn't work. Radiation's not an option. Because of where it's located."

"Shit."

"It's why I was in Toronto. To try a different specialist. It hasn't spread anywhere else, so far. But they can't get it to stop growing."

"Is that what the pills are for?"

"They're supposed to slow it down a little. What can I do about it? That's it."

"What do you mean, 'that's it?'"

"The prognosis is anywhere from a couple more months to maybe a year."

"God, I'm so sorry, Lew."

"Yeah. Thanks."

That's it, he won't say anymore. Not now. That's how he's always been about himself.

I try to look out the window at something, anything to see in the silence. In the darkness. Try to imagine what it's like in the light. Tumor, he said.

Out there, above the right side of the highway, unseen now behind the black, an unending ridge of snow, packed hard and dry. If the wind's strong enough, it'll shear millions of tiny granules off the edge, but it won't change the situation much.

A tumor. Shit. Lew's really sick. A year at most. Brain cancer? He didn't exactly say that. What difference does it make? Damn. What the hell? He just fucking got here.

As we cut through the air in this sleek transport, insulated from the elements, there's nothing to grasp, no grounding. No place, we're just flying through it all. An old feeling goes with that, a default program. Helpless resignation. I had it all the time when we were young, driving in circles around Detroit. Didn't understand it then. Not sure I do now.

He wants to be doing this. Maybe it's okay to hope for something good to happen, if only for a little while, once it's morning, and we're in Chicago.

Cocaine and the digital high

To reach Chicago from Michigan, you cross into Indiana on Interstate ninety-four, and pretty soon after that, the highway turns north, and you pass Gary. A hundred years ago, Gary had the biggest steel mills in the country. Gary Works. U.S. Steel. Huge employers, until the emergence of cheap foreign mills and labor. As you get closer, you pass miles and miles of scrapyards, railways, and mills that seem to be abandoned. Skeletons of the past still breaking down. Massive power lines appear intact overhead, do they still work? Industrial ponds. The whole scene looks like what's left after the *War of the Worlds*. Then all of a sudden, you're on the south side. The Detroit of Chicago. Low lying buildings for miles in every direction, like a sprawling third world city but it's not. Off in the distance, yet practically on top of you, a spectacular array of massive downtown skyscrapers living together. Gleaming. From the south side of the divide, it looks like an otherworldly kingdom. You can imagine flying vehicles coming and going, like in *The Jetsons*.

How many times, so many . . . Lew and I had made this drive in winters like this, back when Cam was at U. Chicago. All those road trips to get out of Michigan and our lives for lost weekends. In the LeMans, which

196

didn't make it this time. Chicago looks the same. The high rises and the museums and Lake Michigan. Snow on the ground. Dry winter morning sun. De facto apartheid, and black blight.

The same? Not exactly. Lew's got a tumor that sooner or later is gonna kill him and I've got all sorts of maladies that might take me first. But everything else seems the same. When we were young and fearless, Cam lived on the south side, in a huge government subsidized high rise on the edge of Hyde Park. He could qualify to live there as a student. The building was maybe thirty stories high. His place was somewhere in the twenties. It had a wall of glass facing north. The view was fantastic. You could see all of downtown Chicago. The Land of Oz.

Chicago had been a place of possibility for young suburban guys like us from southeast Michigan. It was exciting. The first big city I had been in that had a pulse. Before Chicago, I assumed all big cities were like Detroit. Nothing to do, nowhere to go, not for whites, anyway. No nightlife, except a few bars and restaurants scattered around, and you had better hope you don't have car trouble going from one to the other. I figured Detroit was the urban norm. It was a revelation to be in a city where there were a lot of people that looked like me out and about at night. Not where Cam lived. I don't remember ever seeing another person of the Caucasian persuasion there.

Cam always had cocaine. He said it was a benefit of living where he did. He could take the elevator down a few flights and buy whatever he wanted. Fearless and foolish. I never really cared for coke, but he and Lew did. After a night of barhopping on Rush Street, we'd go back to Cam's place and the two of them would do lines while I stared at the city lights with a beer and a doob and crashed. Sometimes they'd go out again, to little after-hours blues clubs nearby. It seemed a little reckless for a couple coked-out college boys to hang out late on that side of town. They shared something I couldn't penetrate. A certain adventurism.

It's about quarter to six in the morning. There's some traffic on Lakeshore but it's not crowded yet. Buses, some cars. Cabs. Sunlight's nice but I'm feelin' road trip grungy, bleary-eyed, and badly in need of a shower. Lew, Marlboro in his mouth, punches some icons on the dashboard.

"What are you doing?"

"I'm trying to use the car's GPS." He coughs. "Shit, I can't figure this out."

"Just drive, Lew, let me try to do it."

"Alright, here, take the phone."

"What do you want me to do?"

"Find out how to get to the Days Inn."

"How do I do that?"

"Shit, forget it, Rick. I'll do it."

"You don't have to be such an asshole about it."

"You need to learn these things. I don't know how you can function in today's world."

"Fine, here, take it. By the way, there's no single world, only multiple ones, perennially in flux."

He starts tapping on the phone.

"Lew, look out!"

He looks up just in time to slam the brake and avoid rear-ending a school bus.

"Jesus, Lew. It's a rental."

He crosses into the left lane to pass the bus, cutting somebody off in the process, a disheveled kid who hits his horn and extends his right arm and middle finger as long as he can while roaring around us. I glance at the bus as we pass it. Some of the kids look down at us like we're demons.

"Days Inn Lincoln Park," Lew says into the phone.

The female voice on the phone says, "Days Inn Lincoln Park. Here are your directions." Then silence.

"Where's the rest of it?" Lew asks. "Why isn't she giving me directions to the fucking Days Inn?"

"Maybe your phone hasn't had its morning coffee yet."

He peers around, gets off Lakeshore, and drives around the corner. "Where are we?"

There's a street sign. "We're on Diversey, Lew."

"Okay, good, I thought so. The Days Inn is on Diversey."

"You have reached your destination," Lew's lady blurts out.

"Where is it?" he asks. "I don't see any hotel."

"Maybe we passed it."

"Screw it, I'm just gonna park here." He lines up the car next to a parked Lexus and starts to back into a spot behind it. Looks kinda tight.

"Lew, I'm good at parallel parking."

"I know how to parallel park."

"You're too close."

"Be quiet."

"You're way too close, you're gonna take off the side mirror."

"Shut up, Rick!"

"You just hit it. Lew, stop!"

"Fuck."

"Nice going. You cracked the cover on our side mirror."

"It's just a rental. What about the Lexus?"

"The mirror's shattered and I think you may have scratched the bumper."

"Fuck this." He drives us up ahead and glides into a larger spot, shuts off the engine, and we get out.

I peer around the sky for a hotel. "I don't see it."

"There it is." Lew starts down the pavement without waiting. I follow a few steps behind. Again. Breathing his fucking smoke. At least the sidewalks are clear of snow, sort of. It's shoveled high on either side, leaving it clear enough for only one person. Or a person and a half.

"What about our bags?"

"Just leave them for now."

Fucking cold in the sun. Cold wind, ripping through me, whistling through the holes in my bones. "I still don't see it."

Lew picks up his pace, going full speed now, well ahead of me in no time, his stupid trench-coat flapping around. I can still smell his cigarette smoke. Fuck him, I'm not gonna even try to keep up. Not here, not in Chicago. A half-block later, I see it, a little yellow Days Inn sunshine sign sticking out from the second floor of a building. Looks like the whole building's only about four stories high. Must be trying to be one of those boutique hotels. Which basically means you get a tiny room.

Lew stops beneath the sign and turns around. For once, he's actually waiting for me.

"Why can't you walk faster?"

"Just go in, will you? I'm freezing."

I follow him inside. "It's too early, they're not gonna have a room ready."

"Let's check in anyway," he says. "I want breakfast."

Just inside, there's a bellhop and a valet. Really, for three floors of rooms at a Days Inn?

"Good morning, sir. Do you have a car to park?"

"How's it going, man," Lew says as the bellhop opens the inner door, and we brush past.

Brightly lit lobby. Blinding, almost. Everything's white. White leather furniture, white floor, the ceiling, the walls. The reception desk. Even the kid at the desk's wearing a white shirt, sitting behind an Apple. He looks kinda like Keir Dullea in *2001: A Space Odyssey*, only with a ponytail. What the fuck's going on in here? The whole room is like that scene where Dullea sees himself at progressively older ages, before he becomes a star-child. What was that all about? Keir Dullea. What a name. Was that the only film he made? Coulda been a stage name. Either way, his manager must've been on LSD.

The kid's slamming away on the keyboard. "Good morning," he says without looking up. Leaned forward, his face is about eight inches from the fucking monitor. Must be playing a video game.

"I have a reservation," Lew says.

"What's the name?"

"Rosenberg."

Without any break in his keystrokes, the kid gets to where he wants to go. Multi-tasking. Can't help himself. "I see a Richard Rosen."

What does that mean, kid, that you see him? Like a person's identifier on the screen is the same as the person? You haven't even looked at us.

"No, I'm not Richard Rosen. I said, Rosenberg."

"Ah yes, made it. There you are. Lewis Rosenberg. Credit card?"

He turns to face us, just long enough to take Lew's VISA. Still slamming away fast on the keyboard, he's got a look of anticipation on his face. About to reach a new level.

"There'll be two of you?"

No, kid, I'm just a hologram. "Yeah."

"Check-in's at three."

"Three?" Lew says. "We've been driving all night."

"I might have a room ready by ten, at the earliest."

"Alright. What about the breakfast?"

"Yes, our complimentary breakfast is available." He nods toward a hallway on his right. "Down that hall. I'll buzz you in."

Breakfast room. To the left, several rows of square tables and a large window facing the street. Just one person here, some guy with his back to us, eating and reading the paper. On the right, a buffet set up with the usual crap. Electric waffle iron, coffee machine, juice dispenser. Hard boiled eggs and apples, pint milk cartons and yogurt in a little fridge. Cereal dispenser,

Raisin Bran, Corn Flakes. Froot Loops. How can anybody eat Fruit Loops? Toaster and dollar-store bread. Bagels and packets of cream cheese.

"This blows, Lew. Let's go get a real breakfast."

"Don't be so negative. We're here."

Pour myself a cup of coffee and sit at a table facing the window, behind and to the side of the guy reading the *Chicago Tribune*. Looks to be a few years older than us, maybe more. He's wearing a blue Oxford shirt and dark pressed pants. Black wingtips. Bright red necktie's showing a little under the collar. Seems dressy for early morning at the Days Inn. Sips his coffee and eats in a measured way, like he's in a formal setting. Kind of an aristocratic bearing. Must be European. Distant descendent of a knight, maybe. Is that what I'm supposed to become? Full of grace and acceptance, shitty coffee, shitty food? Days Inn. Middle of winter in Chicago. Grace. I'm too far gone for grace. More like stuck. Stuck in the Inn. For the rest of my days.

Outside, people rush by, one or two in view at a time but pretty steady. Young people, bustling along, their lives in front of them, a little hyped up and I can only watch, with this dandy sitting over there. And me and my struggle with a disordered mind. Do those kids out there know how lucky they are to be hip and young and in a hurry? Where the fuck has forty years gone?

My view of the street scene and accompanying grim thoughts are interrupted by the big body of Lew and a tray loaded with food. One, two, three waffles, milk, an apple, an orange, a couple hardboiled eggs, a bagel, juice, and jelly.

"Jesus, Lew."

"What?"

"Have a meal, why don't you."

"It's free. Why don't you get something?"

"Nothing's free, you know as well as I do that it's built into the cost of the room."

"Then that's all the more reason to get something to eat, Dahd."

"I can't eat any of that shit."

"You said you wanted pancakes yesterday. Go make yourself a waffle."

"Pancakes. Not waffles."

"What's the difference?"

"I don't like the texture of waffles."

"What are you talking about, Dahd?"

"They're crusty on the outside."

"What difference does it make?"

"Too harsh on the palate."

Lew tries to slice his egg with a plastic knife. It breaks and the egg disintegrates on his plate. "Shit."

"Why do they always serve hard boiled eggs at these places?"

"Because Dahd, people eat eggs for breakfast."

"Not hard boiled. Unless you're in Germany, maybe."

"They aren't going to give people raw egg to cook themselves."

"Isn't there raw egg in the waffle mix?"

"I don't know." He's already eating away. "But you should eat, we've got a full day of work ahead of us. We gotta hit the ground running."

"Work? What do you have in mind?"

"Why do you think we're here? We're gonna go find Cam."

"I know that, Lew, but we've been up all night. I don't have a whole lot of energy."

"You heard the desk clerk, the room's not gonna be ready 'til ten."

"I told you the room wouldn't be ready when we got here."

"Quit bitching. I'm the one who drove all night."

"I'm the one whose body went through trauma. Look, my hand's still oozing from that hack's stitches."

"It's healing."

"You don't know that."

"We're here for a purpose, we can sleep later."

Purpose. Lew eats for a couple minutes like I'm not here, which is fine. Only he doesn't seem to be actually eating much. Mainly cutting it up and rearranging it with his utensils. Just a bite here and there. He abruptly wipes his mouth with a napkin and stands up.

"Let's go. Time to get mobile."

"Aren't you gonna eat the rest of your food?"

"It's awful. C'mon."

Back out on the street. Wind whipping around every corner. Goddamn Chicago's always full of fucking cold wind. Lew takes off at his Manhattan pace, staring at his phone, clicking on it, interacting with it, like he's got a metal detector and he's out to find gold. How can he do it with a tumor in the back of his head, working its way in? In my bleary grunginess, I hustle to try and keep up. Feel like shit.

"What's the address Cam gave you?"

Lew coughs. "He didn't exactly give me an address."

"What do you mean he didn't exactly give you an address?"

"He didn't give me an address."

"You told me he did! How the hell are we gonna find him?"

"I have GPS coordinates."

"GPS coordinates? That could come from anywhere."

"How would you know? You don't even have a smart phone."

"You really are on drugs, Lew."

I follow him down the block until he suddenly stops, and I crash into him. He opens a door and we're inside.

"It's a doughnut shop, Lew."

"I know that."

"Why are we in a doughnut shop?"

"Because this is where Cam was when he sent those texts."

I sigh. "A doughnut shop?"

"That's what the GPS says."

"It could be wrong."

"It's GPS. It can't be wrong."

I glance around at the ten or so people sitting at tables. "What's the point? He's obviously not here."

"Just let me do the talking." Behind the glass counter full of doughnuts, a young woman and a young man stand ready to help. College age. Maybe they're still in high school. I can't tell anymore, youth's too far away for me to know the difference.

"Welcome to Stan's," she says cheerily.

"Have you seen a guy here recently with long curly blonde hair who's about this tall?"

They look at Lew blankly. "No," the young man says.

"How old?" the young woman asks.

"In his sixties. Average build. Maybe six feet tall. He was using his phone."

"Lew, Cam isn't six feet tall, he's barely taller than me."

"What color hair?" she asks.

"Um, blonde, tinged with a little gray."

"Jesus, Lew. We don't know that his hair's still blonde. And tinged with gray. What does that even mean, tinged?"

"Shh! Let me handle this."

"He could be bald, for all we know. He could be chubby."

"Will you shut up and let me do the talking?"

"What was he wearing?" she asks.

"Maybe a winter coat, a down coat."

"What color?"

"Lew, this isn't helpful."

The young man looks at me, then at his colleague. He's probably wondering why she's bothering with this query. Women are generally way more helpful than men. Stresses men out too much, even young ones. Does he know that yet, does he have any self-knowledge?

205

"Is he a Stan's Valued Customer?" she asks.

"Um, maybe," Lew says.

She looks hopeful. "Do you know what kind of doughnuts he eats?"

Lew bends down and pokes his head around, inspecting the doughnuts.

"Um, I'm not sure. "Maybe apple fritters. Or those. Those johnny cakes."

What the fuck is a johnny cake? "Lew."

"Do you have custard? Custard filled doughnuts?"

"Yes, we have several. These are custard eclairs. And these over here."

"Yeah, he probably likes custard. Okay, I'll take a couple of those. One of each."

"You got it." She quickly puts two of the custard doughnuts in a bag. "Is that all?"

"Yeah."

"That'll be three sixty."

"Why are you buying doughnuts?"

He hands her a five. "Keep the change."

"Thank you!"

Lew takes the receipt and a pen from the counter. "If you see a guy matching the description, here's my cell number. His name's Cam. Cam Miles. He might be going by C.B."

"C.B.?"

"Lew."

"Yeah, if you see him, could you call me right away? It's very important."

She looks like she's unsure whether she can handle this responsibility. What it might entail, even for a forty percent tip. "Okay."

I follow Lew out of Stan's. Some kind of conversation those two are gonna have about us. Couple bizarre older dudes. Irregular. Shaky.

"Jesus, Lew. What's all that about C.B.? You think he's walking around with a big sign on his back and his first two initials? And what's the deal with what doughnuts he eats? Do you think that if you eat them, you'll somehow hone into his current location?"

"That would be ridiculous. There's no digits in doughnuts. I bought them because I want to eat them."

"You wouldn't have bought them if you hadn't pursued your fantasy idea that Cam bought doughnuts there."

"First of all, it's not a fantasy. We know for a fact that he really was there, he was present there, just a couple weeks ago. The GPS said so. Second, the young woman asked me what kind of doughnuts he ate."

"She was just trying to be a helpful youth. It was a "Planet Queen" suggestion. We can't expect to understand young people today."

Without slowing down, Lew takes a doughnut out of the bag. "Third, I wanted a doughnut." He takes a big bite.

"He might've gone in just to get out of the cold for a few minutes."

"It's more likely he went in there to buy a doughnut, and even if that wasn't his original intention, it doesn't mean he didn't decide to buy a doughnut. Which is approximately what happened to me. You see, Dahd, everything doesn't have to be so deliberate, we don't need to be so justly prepared to be rational, or whatever it is you've been trying to say for the last two days."

"You bought doughnuts. That has nothing to do with rationality."

"Yes, it does. I saw them, they looked good, I made the rational decision to satisfy my desire. Like you were saying about that Lockhead dude."

"Not Lockhead. Locke."

"Do you want the other one?"

Hm, do I want a doughnut? Not something I normally put in my body. Nothing remotely good for the body's in that doughnut, but I am a little hungry. "Alright."

"Good for you, Dahd. Live a little."

I take a bite. Ouch, my teeth don't like this. "Yuck." I spit it out. "I hate it."

"What's wrong with you?"

"It's stale."

"Mine isn't."

"How could yours not be stale, Lew?"

"It's not even mid-morning, they were probably just baked."

"They were probably baked yesterday."

"Then give it back to me."

"Fine, here, take it."

He takes a bite. "It's perfectly tasty."

"Enjoy, Lew."

He takes another bite. "Yours is stale." He stops at a trash bin and tries to stuff the remainder of both doughnuts and the paper bag in it. The bin's full, so he has to try and force it, with the result that the doughnuts crumble into pieces and fall on the sidewalk. Undeterred, Lew quickly lights a cigarette and resumes briskly down the block.

"What are we doing, Lew?"

He peers around. "We need to canvass the neighborhood."

"What does that mean?"

"It means we're going into every single one of these joints that's open and ask if they've seen anyone answering the description of Cam."

"We don't have a description of Cam. At least, not a reliable one."

"Will you stop putting up psychological roadblocks to our quest?"

We spent the next couple hours going up and down the block in each direction. Everything from a Starbucks to a Brazilian steakhouse to a Seven Eleven to a place that serves bibimbap tacos. Which were pretty good. After the tacos, Lew decided he'd gotten a second wind, so we extended our inquiry further still. At each stop, Lew goes through the same routine, makes the same inquiry, leaves his cell number, and asks people to be on the lookout for a ghost named Cam.

"This is a waste of time, Lew. Nobody knows who you're talking about. We don't know if he lives anywhere around here, or even if he spends any time in this vicinity."

"We know he was at Stan's Donuts."

"That coulda been just a random one-time event."

"I highly doubt it."

"If he was a regular around here somebody would've said they'd seen him. They might even know his name. Nobody has a clue."

"We just got started collecting intel. We're narrowing it down."

"We're not narrowing it down; we're not narrowing anything down. This is a huge city, even this area alone is huge. There's literally hundreds of stores and restaurants and bars and cafes around here. We'd be better off just standing on a corner and handing out flyers."

Lew stops. "That might be a good idea."

"It wasn't meant to be."

We eventually end up in a big busy café. Only there's something else going on here besides coffee with a little hot milk in it for six bucks. There's a buzz to the place, and not just coffee and phones and iPads. Some other kind of vibe. Long counter on our left, and on the wall to the right, there's a giant digital whiteboard calendar. Under the heading of December, events are listed on maybe half of the dates. Personal Investment 101. Planning your next Career Move. IRAs for Artists. Health Savings Accounts: Do you Need One? Everybody in the café is young. Under thirty, for sure. Probably under twenty-five. How the hell would I know, but they're a lot younger than us. White, black, Asian. Indian, filling the tables and couches and chairs. Some kind of music's playing, a homogenized, jazzed up reggae. On the ceiling there are abstract moving images, colorful, dark pink and purple, green and yellow, slippery shapes going in and out, squeezing and coming apart and back together again. Like a screen saver mockup of a bloodstream full of weird amoebas and lake leeches careening around, dissolving and reforming in rhythm with the music. Think I'm gonna get a little nauseated very soon.

"Can I help you?" a young woman asks from behind the counter. Short brown hair, dark herringbone suit. Looks like she grew up in one of those upscale suburbs on the north side, like Evanston or Winnetka. What's a cafe grinder doing in a business suit? Must be her first job out of college and she wants to set herself apart. Stack of glossy brochures of some kind on the counter in front of her. Further down the counter, several youngsters in black and white T-shirts take and fill orders, and a long line of people check their phones while they wait their turn. The coffee machines are all down there. What's the role of this young woman in the suit? Maybe she's the manager.

"We're just here for coffee," Lew says.

"Sure, down the counter."

As I start to follow Lew, she extends a pamphlet.

"Would you like to read our brochure?"

A little fervent, the way she's got her arm extended straight out, like an open pocketknife. "Okay."

As I reach Lew in the coffee line, I see another digital whiteboard above the coffee counter. It lists what seems like a hundred coffee and tea options. Jesus, how's anybody supposed to read that? I guess if you're young and used to reading tiny text on a tiny screen, a whiteboard's a piece of cake. Exhaustion hits me, gotta sit down, feelin' a little overwhelmed.

"Lew, I don't want coffee, I want to go to bed."

"Then just get decaf."

"It still has caffeine in it."

"Don't be such a lightweight."

"I'm gonna find a place to sit."

I walk deeper into the room. On the left against the wall there are a half dozen workstations, all occupied, and on the right, several small rooms that jut out into the main room, each with its door open. Two of the rooms are filled with young people sitting around conference tables. With their laptops, pads, and whiteboards, they look like they're having meetings of some kind. What is this place? Aren't cafes for kicking back a little? True, the Ann Arbor cafes are filled with college kids working feverishly on their laptops, but this is different. Like we're in a little Silicon Valley, Midwest outpost. What do all of the kids here know that I don't get?

On the back wall there's a set of bookshelves and a sign that says, 'Take One, Leave One.' There are software books, *R for Dummies*, and *Programming in Python*. And business pop crap. *The Twenty-First Century Half-Minute Manager, Successful Change Management,* and *Cutting Edge: New Strategies for Motivational Leadership*. No philosophy books, unless you want to count Ayn Rand, and she was full of shit. I pick up the *Cutting Edge* book, it says it's written by somebody who's a psychologist with a Ph.D. Big picture of her on the back, in a red dress, high heels and a smile. Makes me sick, that somebody would use their grad psychology degree to push motivation. Psychologist in a red dress and motivation and cutting edge. That's a problem, that's a social problem. Send her out to toil on vast Illinois cornfields to see how the other half lives. Send all the motivational hotshots there to toil and motivate each other in the sun.

I put the book back and open the brochure that the young woman in the herringbone gave me. It's got a bunch of hype about Planning Your Financial Future, with multicolored charts and thought bubbles. And on the back, in a corner in tiny print, Allstate Illinois. So that's what this is! This whole thing's a front for Allstate. It's fucking Café Allstate!

"Here, Dahd." Lew extends a cup to me.

"I said I didn't want coffee."

"It's decaf."

"There's no place to sit."

"Let's sit in here." I follow him into the empty conference room, and we sit down at the table.

"Lew, this place is a front for Allstate."

"It is?"

"Look at this brochure. It's like the ultimate Andy Warhol merger of art and commerce for the up-and-coming generation. Generation Z-Z-point-one, or whatever they call themselves."

"Excuse me." A young man wearing a white shirt and black tie stands in the doorway. "I'm sorry, do you have a reservation?"

"No," Lew says.

"I'm sorry, these rooms require a reservation."

"Then we'll reserve it."

"Um, are you part of a larger group?"

"No."

"Um, I'm sorry, the minimum group size is six."

That's three "I'm sorry" and two "um" in like, fifteen seconds. Plus, the "excuse me." Why's is he apologizing so much, unless he knows he's being an asshole?

"There's no place else to sit," Lew says.

The young man looks toward the front of the café, straining his neck, shifting his weight, like he's taking this chance occurrence to get a little workout in. Take advantage of an opportunity. "No worries. There are a couple empty seats at the window."

Little shit. We followed him toward the front. Jesus, how about a little respect for your elders? We're not going to break anything. There are a couple open stools at the counter facing the front window, and a young woman sitting on a stool between them. She's on her iPad, wearing earbuds. Her phone rests on the counter, charging up.

"Excuse me, excuse me," the young man says. She can't hear him, so he leans down and sticks his face in her line of sight. He's done this before. She takes off one of her earbuds.

"Could you move one over to accommodate these gentlemen?"

Unfazed, she gets up and moves over. That's more like it, we're gentlemen. Gents. And so, we sit. No worries. Like hell.

"All this commerce, this digital hype, makes me sick, Lew."

"I think it's kinda cool."

"You're kidding, right? It's a takeover by commerce. They're kids playing with dangerous toys."

"Laptops and pads and phones aren't dangerous," Lew says. "You want to take their toys away? What about all the things they do with their toys to make things happen?"

"Make things happen. What does that mean, exactly?"

"All these new technologies help people do things and connect and communicate."

I take a sip of my coffee and wince. Way too bitter. "Everybody's doing a lot of communicating, Lew. It doesn't mean it's any deeper than before. In fact, it's probably far more lightweight. People don't have to account for themselves."

"You're totally wrong about that. When somebody puts something offensive or nasty or inaccurate out there, people respond."

"You mean, react."

"Dahd, think about all the millions of people who can read stuff and evaluate it and discuss it who would never have seen it before the Internet. Including being able to discuss the kinds of concerns that you have about society, et cetera. Imagine that for once."

"The digital stratosphere isn't set up that way. It's set up for quick, short messages. Like twits."

"Twits?"

"Those little messages where you can have only so many characters. The twits."

"You mean tweets. They're not called that anymore."

"Whatever. We're nodes on networks, relaying little bits. With twits."

"But that's what people want to do, Dahd. You gonna make people type a minimum number of words to send a message?"

"It encourages people to think small."

"They're just messages. Lighten up. Bask in the new world. It's still in its infancy."

"Exactly. Baby-talk."

"Then give it time to grow up."

"That's what the Bolsheviks said about the Soviet Union."

"Just drink your coffee."

"It's too bitter. The Internet's an elaborate pacification mechanism. Keeps people docile and productive."

"You're so deluded, Dahd."

"People might think they're doing something with their minds but they're only using their brains."

"What's the difference?"

"It's the difference between being two-legged or four-legged. Look at these kids, tapping away, eyes glued to the screen. They might as well have their tongues hanging out like dogs. So no, I don't think there's much deep thinking about the human condition in this room right now."

"But it wouldn't be going on anyway," Lew says. "Most people aren't like that."

"Great, so we might as well keep the bar low and just make it easier to buy shit. What happens to the person?"

"What happens to the person? The person is the person."

"The person becomes known and then shaped by the Internet. And so-called 'artificial intelligence.'"

"You know what, Dahd, I really don't give a shit if these Internet behemoths have a lot of data about me. I really don't see how that's gonna make me into something I don't wanna be."

"Are you sure about that?"

"I know who I am. The Internet's not limiting me in any way."

"What I see is more capitalizing on vulnerabilities. On desires and anxieties."

"People are free to do what they want with it."

"Freedom is managed, Lew."

"That's horseshit."

"Here's an example. Doing something that requires your attention while you're driving isn't safe, right? Then we shove a cell phone in somebody's hand, and make it possible for them to type messages, and go on the Internet, and then they get behind the wheel. That so-called smart phone might as well be a live grenade."

"That's their fault, for driving and using their cell at the same time."

"That's just my point! Create a situation where you know people are going to act, and when there's human fallout, you have the individual to blame!"

"Even assuming your point, Dahd, you can't just shut down progress because of the negligence of a relative few."

"Actually, you can. These are value choices. We can question these things. Instead of uncritically believing AI chatbots just because they're easy to use and give you quick answers that look good on your screen."

"You're always harping on making things easier. AI makes things easier."

"How about using just a tenth of that brainpower and figure out how to make what everybody needs within their reach so they can take care of themselves? Then you can do all the innovating you want to make things more enjoyable for people with a lot more play money."

"All that play money creates jobs."

"Yeah, right, Lew. Minimum wage retail or scurrying around like rats in an Amazon warehouse. Or a delivery truck, being timed. Until they get replaced by drones." I stand up. "C'mon, it's after ten, let's go. I need to sleep."

215

He rises and we walk out. In front of the café, he abruptly stops to light a cigarette, and I bump into him.

"Watch where you're going."

"Then stop stopping." I try to walk next to him between the snow piles, but I can only get one foot on the sidewalk, while the other one has to walk in snow. Fucking freezing wind, burns through my cheeks. And Lew's fucking cigarette smoke.

"Dahd, whether you or I like it or not, dot-com innovation isn't gonna stop."

"Yeah, I just love how Apple and Microsoft and Google stage those multimedia spectacles in a filled auditorium to announce the latest bit of digital technology."

"That's just announcing a new product launch."

"And those insipid talks on NPR about 'big questions.' All the false drama."

Lew coughs. "I would've thought you'd like that stuff."

"Just because you're a Ph.D. in neuroscience or computer engineering or cognitive psychology doesn't mean you're remotely qualified to make grand pronouncements about where humanity is or ought to be going. They embody a culture that's seriously deluded about what human well-being means."

"What does any of this have to do with human well-being?"

"It doesn't, Lew. That's my point. Those tech companies and self-appointed thought leaders don't care for the commonplace. They're trying to get out of reality. Like all those twisted Apple people."

"What's so great about the commonplace? It's just what's already there. Boring. Commonplace can't take you anywhere."

"Where do you wanna go, Lew? Why do you have to go anywhere? These people have zero comprehension or appreciation for ordinary people and lives and needs and hardships."

"You can't pretend the world was wonderful before digital technology."

"The difference is this. The digital is easier to manipulate than the material."

"Not really. You have to know how to program, how to code, how to write algorithms. You have to be creative, have a vision, something novel that people will want."

"Vision? You're talking about a milieu that just throws shit out there to see what sticks. Never mind that it ends up making things harder. As if people are inexhaustible wells of inner resources."

"But that's what's so great about the digital, Dahd. It's practically limitless. It can't be exhausted."

"Speaking of exhausted, I can't think anymore."

"Good."

A minute later, we reached the Days Inn, and our room's ready. Third floor, room 329.

"Lew, I just remembered, I gotta get my BiPAP."

"What for?"

"So I can sleep."

"Oh, god. Alright, well, since you're going to the car, get my suitcase."

"Why can't you get it?"

"I gotta check the room out." He steps into the elevator.

"Gimme a break, Lew. You can get your own suitcase."

The elevator doors start to close, then stop and open. "Get my Twinkies, too."

Rick and Lew get in a fight

Peace, the peace of the flow, air flowing like a river through my lungs, in and out, drifting, out and in. This body, my body, floating on the river, up and down, in gentle cadence. Eyes closed, sleeping. Shine and warmth of the sun. But something doesn't feel right. Roll over, slip into the water. Eyes open, hard chlorine and baby blue of a Grosse Pointe pool all around. Wait for the body to float to the surface, that's what bodies are supposed to do, by letting go. Only mine sinks slowly, weighted down, by my gut, by the baby blue walls. Nobody, nothing else, just the baby blue. What happened to the river? Try to kick, can't get my body to rise, try to take big strokes toward the baby blue, toward the edge, to grab and find a way out. Reach, reach for it. Kick for it. But where there should be an edge to grab and save myself, nothing but endless baby blue. Can't breathe, going down, down.

Something grabs ahold of my snorkeling mask, shakes my head back and forth, pulls me roughly to the surface, and yanks it off. "Ow!"

"Get up Dahd. It's almost six."

"What'd you do that for?"

"You've been sleeping too long. You wouldn't wake up."

"Thanks a lot, Lew. My first nap since I was in kindergarten, and you rudely interrupt it."

"You were moaning." He's got his coat on. He looks like shit.

"I couldn't fucking breathe."

"How come?"

"Because you unplugged the power of my BiPAP, asshole!"

"I don't know how all your shit works. Let's go eat."

"I need to shower."

"No, you don't."

"I'm taking a shower."

"You can take a shower later, Dahd. C'mon, let's go eat. I'm starving. You got to sleep for hours."

"What've you been doing?"

"Looking for Cam."

"You mean you haven't even slept?"

"I couldn't, with the sound of that damn machine of yours. It's bad enough that we gotta share a bed."

"Lew, you've been going like thirty-six hours."

Downstairs, the kid with the ponytail's still behind the reception desk, goofing around on the Internet. Looks bored. Must've run out of Fortnite levels or lost his last game.

"Good evening, Mister Rosen."

"It's Rosenberg, man," Lew says.

"Oh, yeah. Sorry, man."

Seems they're becoming familiar with each other. I follow Lew outside and gasp in the fucking freezing wind. It's dark already.

"Jesus, Lew, it must be about five degrees. How can you stand it in that trench coat? Aren't you freezing?"

He's lit yet another Marlboro. "I just don't think about it."

"You're a weirdo. Where are we going?"

219

"The first place we come across where we can get a decent meal. I'm freezing."

We walk past a few restaurants and bars that look mostly empty. Lew stops in front of a place that's full of Celtic music blaring. Sounds like there's lots of people in there. He looks in the steamy windows, which are too high for me. A bright light above the entrance illuminates a chalkboard on the sidewalk. The Yellow Dog. An Irish Bar. Tonight's special, Shepherd's Pie, 11.95.

"Let's check this out," Lew says.

The Yellow Dog turned out to be one of those typical so-called Irish pubs, with a bunch of big sports screens showing football and European soccer games. And no stout but Guinness, which isn't really stout. Place is packed. People squeeze by each other and the music's too loud. We were able to find a table and make our way through a couple of pints of fish guts and the shepherd's pie. Well, Lew did.

"That was a pretty good meal," he says.

"It's a big plate of slop."

"It's a balanced meal."

"I hate peas. No one in the world likes peas."

"I like them."

"No, you don't, Lew. You're just saying that to disagree with me."

"If you don't like them, don't eat them. It's a free country."

"They're all mixed in with the meat and mashed potatoes and all this other shit that has no nutritional value other than empty carbs."

"Then just swallow them."

"Half of this, no, more than half of this, is just a pile of mashed potatoes."

"What did you expect, Dahd? It's an Irish dish."

"What the fuck do you know about Irish food? I can't even tell what kind of meat this is. What little there is of it."

"It's lamb."

"Figures. I hate lamb."

"Why else do you think it's called shepherd's pie?"

"Shepherds are supposed to protect the flock, Lew. Not turn it into pie. Besides, there's no pie crust. What kind of pie has no pie crust?"

"Shepherd's pie. If you're not gonna eat the rest of your food, just finish your beer, I'm gonna go pay the bill and ask that woman behind the bar if she's seen Cam."

"Jesus." I watch Lew negotiate through the crowd to the bar. Can't see the woman he's talking about with all the people in the way. Mashed potatoes and peas, I can't eat this shit. I get up, finish my beer, and make my way through the crowd toward Lew at the register.

A heavyset female bartender walks over. She's got ruddy red skin and premature gray hair tied in back. Her black T-shirt has "The Yellow Dog" in fluorescent yellow with a cartoonish dog skulking. Some sort of elaborate tattoo around her neck. What the fuck is it? Looks like a snake. A boa. She's probably ten, fifteen years younger than us, chronically overworked, burned out. Hard life.

"Thirty-eight twenty-one."

Lew hands her his VISA. Wide strap of black leather around her wrist with silver studs on it.

"I'm looking for a friend," Lew says.

She sticks the card in the machine and hands it back. "Do you want a receipt?"

"He's got long curly hair and his name 's Cam Miles."

She narrows her eyes. "That makes two of us."

"You know him? You know Cam? Cam Miles?"

"Who are you?"

"We're friends of his."

"Didn't know he had any. I haven't seen that prick in weeks. He owes me a couple months' rent. And for the big mess he left upstairs."

221

"Do you know where he lives now?" I ask.

"I have no idea. If you see him, tell him he owes me."

"Why did he leave?"

"Probably because I fired him. He's not getting his last paycheck, either."

"He works here?"

"Didn't you hear what I just said?" she snaps. "I fired him. He was drinking too much, coming around his off-hours drunk and harassing customers. Went around telling people he was gonna cut off his ears and drink the blood."

"When did you see him last?" Lew asks.

"Like I said, it's been weeks. Somebody said they seen him walk by once. What do you want with him?"

"Just wanna see if he's alright."

She kinda chuckles and looks down the bar at the other bartender, who's pouring a drink. He's got a gray stubble beard, a big gold ring through one ear, bloodshot eyes. Pirate of some kind.

"Hey Jake. These guys say they're friends of Cam's." He grimaces.

"Can we see his room?"

She pauses, then shrugs. "Yeah, why not. See what your friend did."

She mumbles something to Jake as she squeezes behind him toward the end of the bar. She has a noticeable limp. We follow her to the back of the room, past a small kitchen, then up a staircase of open wooden gray steps. Some of them have dark red specks, like the color of dried blood. She walks up slowly, leading with the same leg each step, her left leg. A set of keys on a beaded leather chain hangs from a belt loop down her right hip, and when she raises and brings that leg down, the keys rattle. She struggles a bit and has to catch her breath a couple times. Maybe she's got gout.

At the top, on each side of the stairs, there's a wooden rail and a short hallway with fading flesh-colored paint and a dark brown wooden door. Air's kinda musty, there's dust on the rails, and the entire area looks like it

222

hasn't changed since World War II. She walks around the rail on the left to the door on that side, retrieves her keys, finds the one she wants, and sticks it in the lock.

"Prepare yourselves."

She pushes the door open, walks in, and flips a light switch several times until a ceiling light goes on. Lew takes a step into the room and stops, blocking the entrance.

"Fuck," he gasps.

"Go, Lew." I try to shove him a little but he's too big. "Lew, let me in."

He takes another step into the room, just enough for me to enter. On the walls, long, broad strokes of red paint have been dragged haphazardly. Not an artist's brush, wider, like a housepaint type of brush. Lots of drippings, he had way too much paint on the brush. On the wall facing us, in large, crude block letters, BLEEDING BLEEDING EVERYWHERE. Red all over the hardwood floor, which is practically covered with pages and pages of printer paper scattered about randomly. There could be a hundred pages or more, extending into the next room, some with type, others blank. Looks like most of them are stuck to the floor from the paint. What'd he do, just go around and pour it across the room? There are some partial footprints, like he stepped in it and didn't give a shit. Some other stuff scattered about, a plastic cup, a plastic plate, pieces of broken glass, torn cardboard from a frozen meal. A newspaper on a folding chair. Otherwise, the room is empty.

"There's something wrong with him," the woman says.

I follow Lew into the next room. On a wall there, SOMEBODY GOT DONE WRONG. More paint and pages all over the floor. Next to an old metal desk, a PC is tipped over, one side missing, some of its guts strewn about, and a monitor with a busted screen. Like he got livid, knocked it down or threw it, put his foot through it. Same with the printer on the floor. Looks like he brought his foot down on it a few times. Or jumped on it. A couple paint brushes, dried out, and three empty gallon paint cans around the room, one tipped over. Another one in a corner. Kilz Barn and Fence Paint. An old couch, with a couple pieces of junk clothing. Card table, an ashtray, and a couple spent cigarettes. Cheap floor lamp, tipped to one side. There's the computer keyboard, he stomped that to death too. Lew picks up a piece of the PC.

"Looks like he destroyed the hard drive."

"It's gonna cost a lot to clean all this up," she says. "And he knew he wasn't supposed to smoke in here."

A little kitchenette. Painted across the fridge, more red. SPEECH-ACTS OF DECEIT. In the fridge, just a few things. Butter, apple juice, an old head of lettuce. Half a brown apple and an open package of Oscar Meyer Wieners. A few dirty dishes in the sink. Some bugs crawl around a spent ant trap on the counter. Not much in the cupboards, just some plates, a couple glasses, a stack of blue plastic cups. Jiffy Peanut Butter, Morton's Salt, Cap'n Crunch. Shot glass. Unopened package of Orville Redenbacher's Classic Gourmet Popcorn. No microwave. Maybe he took it. Got an image of him heaving it through a window.

"Rick."

Lew's in the bathroom. On the mirror above the sink, RIPOFF in red.

"It's Charles Manson-like," Lew says.

"Don't say that. It's paint, right? Not blood."

Lew touches it with his index finger. "It's dried paint. I think."

I walk a few steps over to the bedroom. No paper on the floor, just a little paint inside the doorway, probably from his shoes. Maybe he took them off before he entered the room. If so, it would indicate some ability to make a discerning judgment. In a little wicker trash basket, an empty fifth of cheap vodka on top of spent tissues and the box they came in. Couple of empty yogurt cups. Single mattress and box springs, a sheet, and a thin blanket. No pillow. A few pieces of clothing on the floor. I pick up a pair of jeans and reach in the pockets. Nothing. Dresser drawers are partially open, empty. Maybe there'll be pieces of somebody's body in the closet. Nothing except a few empty hangers and a pair of canvas shoes that have paint on top.

Back in the main room, Lew and the woman are standing in the middle, surrounded by Cam's red mess. Having gotten through the initial shock, I feel vibrations in the floor from the music in the bar downstairs and hear the sound coming through the open doorway. Some kind of obnoxious Irish punk.

"Do you know anyone at all who might know where he is?" Lew asks.

"He had a sometime girl, a young black woman," the woman says. "Seemed like a sweet girl, but they used to fight a lot. You could hear them from the kitchen. The cooks complained."

"Do you know her name, or where she lives?"

"Stephanie. Don't know where she lives. Real sweet girl."

"What did they fight about?" I ask.

"Don't know. Tried not to. Got worse lately. She stopped coming around, that's when he started acting crazy. He's still on the lease."

She shakes her head. "I'll leave the door unlocked, nothing worth taking here now anyway. If you find him, tell him he needs to come see me." She leaves us with the door open. The sound of her bad leg on the steps seems to keep time with the music.

Lew raises his arms wide. "What is all this shit?" He bends down and rips a piece of paper from the floor.

"You just disturbed a crime scene."

He sits down on the couch and reads to himself.

"What does it say?"

"*Evening. A large boisterous upscale restaurant in downtown Chicago. Street performers and musicians compete with beggars for the attention of people who enter and leave the restaurant. TED. 'He's just difficult, is all.'*"

"Ted?"

Lew continues. "*MADDIE. 'Do you feel he's your responsibility?' TED. 'No, I don't feel he's my responsibility. I shouldn't have mentioned his name.'*"

"Maddie? What is it you're reading?"

"It's a script of some kind. Like a stage play, or a screenplay."

I reach down and tear a portion of a page from the floor. "Lew, check this out. *Vinnie is lying on his back in a hospital bed, eyes closed, his head heavily bandaged. His eyes face the ceiling. Doctor. 'How are you feeling?' Vinnie opens his eyes and turns his head toward Doctor.*"

"Vinnie?"

I continue reading aloud. "*DOCTOR. 'You lost a lot of blood. Fortunately, your friend found you in time.'*"

Lew tears another scrap of page from the floor. "*GALLERY OWNER, looking with disdain at the tattoos covering Vinnie's body. 'I suggest you try another trade. You're not a painter.' VINNIE. 'Yeah, that's right! I'm a tradesman, asshole!'*"

"This is crazy shit, Lew."

"Maybe we could try to put it together."

"Put it together? That would take forever. There aren't even page numbers."

"I think I know what this is, Dahd. I think it's frickin' Vincent and Theo Van Gogh! Vinnie is Vincent, and Ted is his brother Theo."

"In Chicago?"

"Maybe it's about the Van Gogh brothers, only it's set in the present. In Chicago. Instead of Paris."

"Why would Cam care about the Van Goghs?"

"Don't you remember? In high school, Cam got really into Vincent Van Gogh. He was always carrying around a book of the letters Vincent wrote to Theo."

"Whatever, Lew, all I know is there's a shitload of pages stuck to red paint all over the floor. We should go back to the hotel and kick back for the night. We can deal with this shit in the morning. It's not going anywhere."

"What's your problem? You had a long nap."

"That you rudely interrupted. I still feel beat, man, and I feel like shit after that crap food. And I gotta get my pain med prescription filled somewhere."

"Stop being so health conscious all of a sudden."

"I gotta get those pain pills."

"I think we should stay here tonight."

"What for?"

"In case he shows up."

"C'mon, Lew. Cam's not gonna show up tonight."

"He might."

"There's just the one little bed."

"There's the couch."

"I'm not gonna sleep on another couch."

"Alright, Dahd. I'll sleep on the couch."

"She said he's been gone for weeks."

"We know he lived here. And he was at Stan's."

"Where?"

"Stan's Donuts."

I sigh. "You're being ridiculous."

"Maybe he's been back here, and nobody saw him."

"I don't see how that could happen, he'd have to walk right past the bar and kitchen. Can't we just leave a note, tell him where we're staying?"

"We can't take that risk."

"We'll put it on the door. And another one in his room, we could put one in every room."

"Great, go ahead, Rick. Just leave if you have to." He lights a cigarette.

"She said there's no smoking."

"I don't give a shit. There's an ashtray, and I smoke."

"How are you gonna sleep here tonight with all the noise from the bar?"

"I'll deal with it. If you gotta, go shower, then come back."

I sigh again. "Alright."

"Bring me a change of clothes. I'm gonna salvage what I can from the script and try to make sense of it all."

Salvage. Yeah, right. "I'll be back in a couple hours."

"You know, you could just shower here and help me with this."

"I'm not gonna shower here, Lew. This place is a pigpen. The tub's probably gross."

"Stop being such a wimp."

"Plus, I need to go to a laundromat."

"A laundromat? Now? What for?"

"I'm about out of clean clothes."

"You don't need to do all that tonight, Dahd. I need you here in case Cam shows up. I can't stay awake much longer, I'm gonna get delirious if I don't get some sleep."

"I told you, I'll come back in a while. Turn up the heat in the room."

I make my way down the stairs and through the still-crowded bar. Back out in the subzero air. God, I'm too much of a fucking pushover. We've been on the road all this time, and by sheer odd crazy luck, we end up finding Cam's place. It's full of shit, and Lew's gonna sit there and try to make sense of it? Just because Cam apparently wrote it, before he trashed his room, and sent Lew some cryptic texts? Maybe Lew should just be happy we stumbled upon Cam's total dump of a living space. Try to put a story together without page numbers? There's a hundred pages on the floor. Stuck there, in bloody red paint. My stomach's queasy even though I hardly touched that shitty shepherd's pie, probably all came out of a can. Paint can.

Feels like we're in a whole different context now and I'm getting worked up about it. What's bothering me? We found proof he's likely alive, real anyway, somewhere. But it's just a messed-up situation of a messed-up guy who's probably long gone. It's not a road trip anymore. It's gonna be something else. Gotta adjust, be prepared. How to do that? I didn't study the Cynics in grad school.

A little later, I finally had my long luxurious hot shower at the Days Inn. Let the water run over my wounds. And I decided to chill out and lay on the bed, free of Lew for once. On my time. Watched the Chicago news, then surfed the channels until it started stressing me out cuz there's no enlightenment, just babble. Stitches are sore. Gotta get those pain meds. Don't particularly want to go back to Cam's place, but I told Lew I would. Alright, so what do I need to take back to that dump so I can cope in reasonable comfort? A few catheters, the Surgi-Lube, Purell, the BiPAP machine, all my meds and other essentials. Will Cam's place be cold? Probably. Sneak a Days Inn blanket, and clothes for Lew. Shit, need to find a laundromat.

Need to grab the pain prescription. There's a Walgreen's down the block, maybe the pharmacy's still open. Okay, there's the little plastic bag from the hospital. Here's the instructions, and the diagnosis and visit summary. Here's the antibiotic prescription, where's the one for codeine? What the fuck? Empty the backpack, take everything else out, check all the pockets. Fuck! Where is it? Could it be in the car? No, I put the plastic bag in the backpack at the hospital. Ruse musta forgot to write the prescription. Fuck! That little shit fuckup!

Shit. Alright, can't do anything about it right now. Don't forget the BiPAP. Try to get it in the backpack with everything else but it won't zip up all the way, not with the Days Inn blanket. Don't wanna break the zipper, just leave it halfway open. On the way out of the room, I grab a pillow from the bed and shove it under my coat.

Back out in the cold toward Cam's place. On my way, I hear a dragging sound behind me. It's the BiPAP power cord. Damn that fucking little shit Ruse! He fucked me over, his incompetence, and now he's dragging along behind me, mocking my basic needs. He probably didn't write the prescription on purpose. Or maybe he wrote it and Wretched decided to fuck with me and leave it out of the bag. Either way, seems I got rused.

The Yellow Dog's still crowded, and hot. Loud. Unzip coat and the pillow falls on the floor. A few looks from a few people. Give me a break. Just pick it up and head toward the stairs. Sudden jerk stops me, somebody stepped on the BiPAP cord, get off it please. I know I'm torn and frayed, dragging a power cord around like I'm a freakin' circus monkey with a long tail. Pretty pathetic, but gimme a fucking break. What are you all doin,' acting like a pack of idiots, sitting around, drinking, shouting at each other above the fake Irish music and the sports screens, showing MMA beat-downs? Cheering a black guy and a white guy beat each other to a bloody pulp in a cage, are you kidding me? Is that what we are now?

Trudge up the creaky old stairs, under the weak light of a naked lightbulb up high, tail still dragging behind me. Maybe the plug'll get stuck under the edge of one of the steps and drag me down. Yeah, like a fish, drag me down by a hook through the lip. Ginny was right, it would be a downer to get hooked through the lip and yanked around.

Push open the door to Cam's place, mostly dark now, just the floor lamp shining on a bit of the wall. Try turning on the ceiling light, doesn't work. BLEEDING BLEEDING EVERYWHERE on the wall. Dismal. Looks like Lew tried to rip some of the paper from the floor but the pile he left on the table is mostly just a bunch of torn scraps. The whole effect is like a funhouse gone to shit. Where the fuck is Lew?

Asleep, the big ox, on Cam's mattress. Arms and legs extended over the edges, his hands on the floor. A big, undernourished ox. Like in *Animal Farm* after the pigs take over. Asshole, he said he was gonna give me the bed. At least he turned the floor lamp on for me. Gee, Lew what a gesture. Fucking cold in here, though, I told him to turn the heat up. I dump my shit on the couch and look around for the thermostat. Shit, don't they even have one? Where the fuck is it?

Sit down, try to get started. I'm supposed to read all this shit, while he sleeps? Try to fit them in a way that follows the skeleton of a story. Assuming there is one. Seems random. Why is this my responsibility? Looks like Lew did try to put it together a little bit. So it's a story about two guys, Vinnie and Ted. One's trying to be an artist of some kind, that's Vinnie. Vincent Van Gogh. Ted's Theo Van Gogh. He's got a gallery, or works at one, somewhere in contemporary Chicago. I'll walk around with the lamp, look around on the floor for something worthwhile. Gotta plug the lamp in several places to move around with it. Wish I had a flashlight. Stagger around, rip up more pieces from the floor. Hard to find anything that fits, too much can't be read cuz of all the paint, and my brain's too worn out. What am I doing here, in this dump? Sigh. Too old to be doing this shit. Don't even care about finding Cam.

Stop. There was something. Something I dropped without really reading, there was something, a few steps back. Shit, which one? A word or two, or a phrase that stood out, still there in my sensory apparatus, now only gray fill. Can't remember what I saw just a few moments ago, there's only an empty placeholder, a remnant of an impression. Okay, try to retrace my steps, like I'm playing Twister, it'll tie up your body in knots. That's not it, that's not it. No, that's not it. Jesus, what's wrong with me, something, some phrase, something important. What's wrong with my mind, that I can't remember what I'm even looking for!

Found it! This is it.

Vinnie looks out into the dark and spies a vague shape walking away. He rushes toward it with knife held high. Ted, hearing Vinnie, turns around in surprise as Vinnie leaps at him with a shout, then trips and falls hard on the pavement. TED. Do you want to kill me, is that it! VINNIE. You cannot spite me! TED. Spite you! I do not spite you! You spite me!

That's something. Enough, for tonight. A lost fly in the stream, found. Show to Lew tomorrow.

Gotta take all my meds. Open each bottle, take one out, put it on my tongue. Walk over to the kitchen, fortunately there's the unused plastic cups. Grab one, turn on the water, let it run a minute, then fill and drink. SPEECH-ACTS OF DECEIT on the fridge. What the fuck, Cam. You must've learned about speech-acts in a philosophy course at U. Chicago. The deceit part I don't get. Sigh. Alright, now, back to the couch. Unpack the BiPAP. Shit, gotta drag the couch over to the wall cuz the power cord's too short. Lie down, wear the mask, try to sleep. Sound of the machine seems to blot out the music from the bar, that's good. Try to figure things out. Why's my heart racing? Why do I feel like I'm a prelude? You spite me. Maybe he just meant, rip the paper from the floor for clues to where I am. No. Too far-fetched. Just breathe, let the machine take over. No Lew, or Cam, to interrupt the flow now.

In the morning, I awake to the sound of air hissing, like gas leaking. Head's killing me. BiPAP mask's on the floor, shit, I must've taken it off in my sleep. Explains the headache. Sit up, rip the cord from the wall, shut the damn thing off. Fucking cold in here, and my bad hand's hurting, must've slept on it. Stitches oozing a little, at least they're not busted. Fucking Ruse. There are some torn pages and scraps of the script on the blanket but most of it is still stuck on the floor, unexamined. A more or less neat pile on the table.

Remember now, kinda, I managed to put something together last night. Don't think it means much. The therapist, who was a kind of wizard, drew down the window blinds once, and told me to close my eyelids and roll my eyes toward the back of my head. Some people see something, he said. I didn't. Maybe I couldn't turn my eyeballs back far enough. Or maybe there just isn't much of anything to see back there, in the brain. What a bunch of bullshit.

Get up, check on Lew. Only he's not there. Dammit Lew, you asshole. Making my life more complicated than it needs to be. Where the fuck are you now? What I need is Advil. In the bathroom, a wet towel and tub. Lew must've showered. Let's see what's in the rusted cabinet behind the mirror with RIPOFF across it. Maalox, nail clippers, some pills in a bottle with Cam's name on it for something I never heard of. A doctor named Chen. A little medicine kit, open that up. Why would Cam have it? He clearly hasn't been thinking about his health. Maybe it came with the apartment. No Advil. Hear somebody enter.

"Dahd?"

"Where've you been?"

"I went over to the hotel for breakfast."

"I thought you didn't like it."

"I don't."

"Then why did you go back there?"

"I thought maybe they'd have something different."

"You're on drugs, Lew."

"Doesn't matter, I was too late anyway. Get dressed."

"I am dressed, I slept in my clothes to try and stay warm. Why didn't you turn up the heat for me last night?"

"I did."

"No, you didn't."

"If you were so cold, why didn't you turn it up?"

"I couldn't find the fucking thermostat in the dark. I had enough on my plate with that stupid script and this place. What time is it?"

"If you had a cell phone, you'd know what time it is."

"You know what, Lew? Fuck you."

"It's past noon."

"I've got a headache. Do you have any Advil?"

"No. Why do you have a headache?"

"Why do you think? I had to sleep on the couch, and I took my BiPAP off in my sleep."

"Why'd you do that?"

"It happens sometimes when I'm dazed and confused."

"Did you get the script worked out?"

"What are you talking about, 'did I get the script worked out.' Are we making a film?"

"Why are you being so prickly, Dahd? I just meant did you make any sense of it."

"I made a pile. Mostly with what you already had. Tried to put it in some kind of order. I wasn't gonna scour through everything on the floor."

"Okay."

I sigh. "I need some coffee. And Advil."

"Okay. Bring the script."

"Why don't you bring it?"

"Because, Dahd, I don't have a backpack."

"Fine."

"Put on your coat."

"You don't need to tell me that."

I follow Lew out of Cam's place, down the stairs with the specks of red. Now we know where those came from. Either his paint or his blood. Or both. The bar's closed, no one's around. Lew holds open the back door.

I step out. It's freezing, some new snow on the ground. "How're we gonna get back in?"

"The same way I did a few minutes ago." He props the door open a bit with a jagged splinter of plywood.

"Jesus, Lew. Is this what our journey's come down to? Having to prop open the back door of a bar with a random piece of wood? To keep barely habitable living quarters available?"

"Stop being so dramatic."

Down Diversey. Cars whiz by, people walking briskly, lots of life going on outside ours, otherwise emptiness and desolation. The smoke I have to inhale from Lew's Marlboro Light, since he's ahead of me again.

"Where are we going?"

"Stan's Donuts."

"I'm not going back to the dumb doughnut shop."

"We gotta check on whether either of those kids saw Cam."

"No, Lew. You can go do that on your own, if you think it's such a hotspot for relevant information."

"Then the Allstate Cafe."

"Alright, fine. But I gotta go to that Walgreen's down the block to get my antibiotic script filled and some Advil. I'll meet you."

"What do you want?"

"I wanna be sedated."

"Do you want a coffee?"

"Yeah, a large black coffee. And something to eat that isn't too greasy. Something dry and heavy. Like a scone."

After I got the Advil and antibiotics, I step into the Allstate. The place is busy like before, only this time Lew's managed to get us one end of a table and chairs. A coffee and a croissant.

"I said I wanted a scone."

"They don't have any."

I poke at the croissant with a fork. "I told you not to get me anything greasy. And it's too crusty."

"It's just butter, Dahd."

"I don't like butter."

"Everyone likes butter."

"Yeah, well, maybe I'm different." I down four extra-strength Advil and my antibiotic with a gulp of coffee. "And I'm not gonna be able to stay here very long."

"Why is that?"

"Why do you think? Because of all the mindless keyboard tapping we're surrounded by."

"Stop bitching already. Let's see what you put together last night."

I reach into my backpack and take out the torn pages and scraps. "Like I said, I tried to put it in some kind of order, but I was too burned out."

Lew puts out his hand. "Just give it to me. I'm not going to critique your script editing. We're looking for clues to Cam."

"More like confusion." He tries to take the pages from my hand but I won't let him. "Wait, Lew. It might be better if we read it out loud."

"Why would we want to do that?"

"To hear it at the same time. We could take on the roles."

"You mean, you wanna read it like we're the characters?"

"Yeah. I wanna be Vinnie."

"Sure, Dahd. Except everybody in here would think we're a couple of absolute morons."

"I'm just kidding. But none of these kids gives a flying fuck about us. And maybe we are morons."

"Just give it to me."

"Fine."

He starts reading through it a little too quickly. Too impatient. I wait and watch for him to get to the "spite me" page.

"That's the spite me part."

"I know, Dahd, I can read." A couple minutes later, and he's done.

"That was fast."

"I was just skimming it. I need to read it again, more slowly."

"Give me a break." I have to sit there, for I don't know how long, while Lew goes through each torn page. With nothing better to do, I pick up the croissant and tear it in half. Start to chew on one piece. Too buttery. I'm about ready to get up and walk around the cafe, to investigate what other creepiness Allstate's up to in here. Finally, he's done, and pushes the pile across the table to me.

"I'm gonna go have a cigarette."

As I go through the pile, it's even less coherent than I thought last night. Miscellaneous scenes that don't seem to fit any of the others, and characters that appear just once or twice. Can't tell what's important and what's not. And there's a lot of it back in Cam's place, still stuck to the floor.

A few minutes later, Lew's back. "Okay, are you done?"

"No."

"Well, hurry up."

"You just read it through twice, Lew. Be patient for once."

"You're getting butter all over it."

"That's your fault. I told you to get me a scone."

"You could've wiped your fingers off on a napkin."

"What do you care? You've already read this shit."

Lew drinks his coffee and eats his croissant while I try to work my way through the script. "Okay, Lew. Ted's this young guy who's conflicted, right? He likes the art scene and being around rich people who like to buy art. And Vinnie's some kind of art student."

"Vinnie's a student at the Art Institute of Chicago," Lew says. "He hates it, gets belligerent with some other students. And with the teachers. He doesn't wanna learn technique. At some point, I guess he drops out and gets tattoos covering his whole body. Like *The Illustrated Man*. And he becomes a sort of street performance artist. He crashes gallery showings and hassles patrons. Ted gets in Vinnie's face for being a derelict."

"And Vinnie's always broke. He gets kicked out by his girlfriend. He shows up at Ted's place to crash sometimes. I think he's living there, more or less."

"Yeah, Vinnie sleeps during the day and goes out at night looking in dumpsters for junk that he drags to Ted's place. He calls it 'found art.' Ted thinks it's a bunch of crap and keeps tossing it in the street and they argue about it."

I like the way this is going. Let Lew do most of the talking, he seems kinda enthused, and less work for me.

Lew finishes devouring his croissant. "At some point, Vinnie leaves Chicago with another guy. Some other artist who's also on the fringe. They talk about art as they hitchhike south. End up someplace in the south where they get in a bar fight with a bunch of skinhead neo-Nazi types, and they all get arrested. Ted shows up with a lawyer who manages to get Vinnie off, but Ted has his lawyer get Vinnie committed to a mental hospital. Vinnie sneaks out and ends up on some farm owned by a crazed doctor with a meth habit."

"I think the doctor's supposed to be a veterinarian, Lew. He's got all these animals that wander around the farm. They're more like pets, a llama and a giant tortoise and a few flamingos. Some dogs and cats. And a monkey."

"And some hoofed animals."

"The vet's kinda like Doctor Dudelittle."

"Doolittle."

"That's what I said, Lew. Dolittle."

"You said Dudelittle."

"No, I didn't."

"Yes, you did, Dahd."

"Anyway, it seems that Vinnie lives with this vet dude as kind of a farmhand, although it doesn't seem like much farming is going on. And the vet doesn't seem to have any clients."

"Like, none. It seems like he lets the fields go fallow."

"Fallow?"

"Yeah, fallow. It's a farming term, Dahd, you know, when you let your farm go to hell and collect oodles of cash from the fucking government. Vinnie finds a bunch of paint in the barn and starts painting the animals in abstraction. And there's this big guy."

"What big guy?"

"The guy who goes out in the fields with Vinnie. Gerard," Lew says. "I think the vet brought him in to help Vinnie whenever he freaked out. There was the scene where Gerard held Vinnie when he had a fit."

"What was that show, when we were kids, with the giant and the giraffe? And the castle."

"*The Friendly Giant*?"

"Yeah, good recall, Lew. Wasn't Gerard the name of the big giraffe? You know, the giraffe that visited the Friendly Giant in his castle. Stuck his head in the window."

"No, it was Jerome."

"Yeah. Jerome the Giraffe. Very good recall, Lew. They didn't really do much on that show, did they?"

"They just kinda hung out. The only props were those little pieces of toy furniture that the Friendly Giant used to rearrange at the end of every show. Pretty grim."

"Let's get back to Cam's stupid story. What happens to Ted?"

"He wants to buy the gallery where he works," Lew says. "It's his uncle's. But somebody else gets it, another guy he works with, and Ted loses it one night and trashes the place. He damages a lot of paintings and other art pieces, sculptures. Then he holes up in his apartment and starts a downward spiral. Shooting himself up with heroin."

"Vinnie makes his way back to Chicago," I add. "One night, he attacks Ted with a knife, only Ted knocks him to the ground. And Vinnie says, 'you can't spite me,' and Ted replies, 'I don't spite you; you spite me!' Then Vinnie threatens to go down to the river and jump off the bridge."

"Did you find anything about him jumping off the bridge?"

"No."

"We don't even know if he jumps off the bridge?"

"Sorry, Lew. I wasn't about to spend all night ripping up more off the floor just to find out if Vinnie jumps into the Chicago River. Besides, what we just went through isn't even half of what was on the floor."

"What's all this got to do with Cam?"

"I think the whole thing, it's about society being on the edge. Like a struggling artist who's living on the margins."

239

"Where are you getting that?"

"*Fin de siècle*. End of the century, end of an age. Van Gogh croaked near the end of the nineteenth century. And we're at the end of an age, the Baby Boomer age."

"Oh, shut up, Rick. That's ridiculous, to try and draw some grand parallel."

"It's not a grand parallel. But I don't get why the Ted and Vinnie characters are drawn to each other in the first place."

"They're brothers. People are drawn together for all sorts of reasons."

"Maybe that's what we need to figure out. Like, maybe the Vinnie character is really Cam."

"That's ridiculous."

"Seriously, Lew. We know Cam wrote it, and we know he's been living like a madman."

"Oh, shut up," Lew barks. "This is like all the shit you've been talking about the last couple days. All your Foucault shit, and race and politics and making things easier and your shit about the Internet. Now you're trying to relate this shit to fucking Baby Boomers."

"What are you all pissed off about? All I said was maybe Vinnie is Cam."

"Just stop it, will you? Stop with all your crap. How about, people who complain just need to get their shit together?"

"Easy for you to say."

"Oh yeah? I've worked my ass off. What have you done, screwing around in Ann Arbor all these years?"

"You were the one who dragged me on this trip."

"To find Cam. That's all. Not to hear all your griping about politics."

"Yeah, well, maybe you're a closet right-wing reactionary."

"Fuck you, Rick."

"Cam sent those texts to you. Not to me."

"So?"

"You said it yourself; he was reaching out. To you. Why you?"

"I don't know, Rick, he somehow had my number."

"Then you had other communications with him, before this?"

"No."

"What's the 'spite me' about?"

"How the hell should I know!" He abruptly stands up.

"Where are you going?"

"I gotta get the fuck away from you awhile. I'm gonna go look for Cam some more."

"You're not gonna find him, Lew."

"Not by wasting time with your imaginary bullshit. If I hadn't asked, we wouldn't even have found his apartment."

"Yeah, and he's a nut job and he's long gone. Maybe you're wasting time, thinking you can find him. Maybe you're the one who's full of shit."

"Fuck you." He stalks out of the café. I watch him stop on the sidewalk and quickly light a cigarette. His hand holding the lighter is shaking a little. A moment later, he's gone.

Bad ganja

After Lew left, I sat there for a while, a little startled about our verbal volley and his abrupt departure. What happened? We've been together nonstop after hardly seeing each other for thirty years. Shit, we were bound to get on each other's nerves. Maybe even overdue for it. Where could I reach for some kind of compensation? The greasy croissant. I dunked it in lukewarm coffee and scarfed it down like a starving dog.

Cam's stupid script. Or rather, mere fragments. I stuffed it in the backpack and headed out of the Allstate Cafe. Walked around in the cold for what seemed like hours, thinking some more about how Lew left. Spite me. Did I touch a nerve? Is he getting frustrated at the prospect that Cam might not be found? Poked my head in a few little art galleries I happened upon, imagining that Cam might emerge. Eventually I had a cheap sushi roll someplace and sat down at the Subway next door. Drank Diet Coke 'til dusk. Let the sickly-sweet rush through my blood down to fingertips and toes.

Something's changed. Maybe it's time for a reckoning of some kind. Time to split? Do I tell Lew, hey, bro, it's been real, we tried but I'm burned out, gonna head back? I could take the train. Back to guitar ghetto, like a little Bilbo, and resign myself to the only direction left in my remaining years. Driving in circles. The semester starts in a few days anyway. On my way out of Subway, I dumped the script in the trash and wandered back toward Cam's place, hoping Lew'd be there. Gotta tell him, get it over with. Time to go home. Can I really desert him? He's seriously sick. My old friend.

He's not here. Must be canvassing way beyond Lincoln Park, north or west or wherever. Always on the move, can't sit still. Go back to Europe, Lew. There's nothing more to be done. All I can do is wait in this dead place with all this shit on the floor and the walls. After all these years, waiting for him to return. Still. In the river, if I lost my last fly, I had to wait for him to wade back upstream. He always tied flies faster than I could, he never ran out on the water. There's nothing left to do in a river if you can't engage it. Here in Cam's place, it's a different kind of animal, there's nothing moving, it's more like human waste. As if Cam wanted to exceed material limitations but the confinement of the walls held him back. So, he staged a bloody riot.

It's dark outside when Lew finally shows up. With a brown paper grocery bag and a small plastic one.

"Where've you been?"

"Looking for Cam." He seems kinda upbeat. Odd. Like he's got a happy, intimate secret. Not sure I want any of it.

"Any luck?"

"I covered some new ground. A couple people may've seen him. And some guy in a bar said he's heard the name."

"Really?"

"Yeah."

Gotta bite my tongue. Lew, you're deluded. You've been getting a wonderful workout, but people in a bar will say anything. "What's in the bag?"

243

He pulls out a six-pack. "I got you some stout."

"Hey, thanks. Founders Imperial, that's pretty good." Although brewed in the red part of Michigan, by believers in the so-called Founders, no doubt. Or they just figured it was a good moniker to sell beer. Probably both.

He sits down and lights a cigarette. "Dahd. Sorry I bolted earlier."

"That's cool. I coulda been better."

He opens a couple of the bottles and hands me one.

"It's cold," I say.

"Of course, it is. I don't buy warm beer."

"Stout's better at room temperature."

"How would you know?"

"I read it on the Internet."

"Do you believe everything you read on the Internet? I bought you stout. Don't be an asshole. And I don't appreciate being called a closet right-wing reactionary."

"I'm sorry, Lew. I don't think you're a reactionary. I just think you're more right-wing than you think you are."

"Yeah, well, you're not as on top of things as you think you are."

"I don't know fucking anything anymore." Do I tell him now, I think it's time I head home? "What's in the other bag?"

"I bought some brownies."

"Brownies? What for?"

"Just a snack." He takes one out and unwraps the tinfoil. It's a mini brownie. "Here, have one. We deserve a little treat."

"It's pretty dinky." Pop it in my mouth. "Pretty fudgy."

Lew eats one, hands me another. We sit there, drinking our beer, eating little brownies. Brownies and stout, and a couple older adult idiots.

Let him down gently. Create a new context. "What do we do now?"

"Finish the brownies."

"I mean about Cam."

"Just gotta keep looking," he says. "It might take a while."

"I don't know, Lew. I can't do this much longer."

"Just relax and be patient for once."

"Me be patient, are you kidding me? I think I've been very patient."

"Just wait for it."

"Wait for what? What are you talking about?"

"For the drugs to take effect."

"What drugs?"

"The brownies. They have pot in them."

"They're pot brownies?"

"Yeah."

"Why didn't you tell me?"

"I just did."

"You mean, I just ate pot brownies?"

"You did, Dahd."

"Where the fuck did you get pot brownies? Some dispensary?"

"No. From Stew."

"Who the fuck's Stew?"

"The kid behind the desk at the Days Inn."

"What're they giving out pot brownies to hotel guests now?"

"I bought them from him."

"What's the desk clerk at Days Inn doing selling pot brownies on the job?"

"Not my problem."

"How on earth did you even think to ask that kid if he had pot brownies for sale?"

"He's got a ponytail. It was just kinda spontaneous."

"How much did they cost?"

"Ten bucks."

"For all of them?"

"No, you idiot. Apiece."

"Ten dollars apiece! That's a rip-off!"

"He said it's real high-quality stuff."

"What's the point in eating pot brownies?"

"I thought it might loosen up some neurons. Get them to fire off more, for new ideas about how to find Cam. Better sniffs."

"Sniffs? That's great, Lew. We're in our fucking sixties, and I just ate four pot brownies."

"I counted five."

"Five? I've had five?"

"I bought ten, there's two left, and I've had three."

"I can't believe you did this. Pot brownies."

"Actually, they're hash, I think."

"Shit, Lew, I don't wanna be stoned."

"Desperate circumstances call for drastic responses. Quit bitching and just drink your beer." He hands me another beer.

"It should be at room temperature."

Lew goes into the next room with his beer and cigarette. "What is it with all this shit on the wall? 'Bleeding, bleeding everywhere?'"

I look at the words on the wall across from me; 'SOMEBODY GOT DONE WRONG.' "You know, Lew, you're a real asshole."

Lew walks back into the room. His body is moving in strange ways. "What'd you say, Dahd?"

Whoa. Drug just kicked in, big-time. "Something about you being an asshole."

"No, something else."

"That's pretty good, Lew." I'm suddenly very aware that I have lips and can move them in lots of ways.

"What's pretty good?"

"How you can twist your body in the wind."

"I'm not twisting my body."

"Yes, you are. You're twisting your whole torso. Like one of those big inflatable figures at used car lots, you know, jerking around in the wind. You're going way slower, though. Like what's his name, Rubber Man." Jaw's feelin' loose, really loose. Like it's gonna fall right off.

"You're hallucinating."

"No, you are, and your body's moving like that rubber guy."

"Gumby?"

"Not Gumby. I mean, I mean the guy from the Fantastic Four. Who could elongate his body, remember? Stretch it like a mile long. Like Silly Putty, only in an instant. Like snapping your fingers." I try to snap my right thumb and middle finger, the form looks good but no snap, none I can hear. It just stretches my stitches. Are they coming undone? No pain.

"Why are you doing that?"

"I'm trying to make a sound. It doesn't work. That's a rip-off."

"You're stoned, Dahd."

"What kind of animal can unhinge its jaws?"

"You mean, snakes? Like a boa?"

"No, lizards. Like the Lizard King."

"Stop."

"Can you give me sanctuary?"

"Stop."

"Or Felix the Cat. With his bag of tricks, it had spots on it that kind of shimmered in different tones of gray. Right? They shimmered."

Lew blows smoke rings toward the ceiling like he did in the old days, when he'd light up after multiple bong hits. "I don't remember."

He always maintained on drugs better than I did. "Lew, don't you remember how all those spots on Felix's magic bag shimmered, or glimmered? That show was in black and white and different modes of gray." Although it coulda been in color, we only had a black and white TV, when I was a little lad. Just a little lad, I was. I wanna think that magic bag was made in black and white, that's what I want to think right now. "That was a hallucinogenic show. What was the name of the bad guy?"

"What?"

"The bad guy. On *Felix the Cat*. The wonderful, wonderful cat. What was the bad guy's name?"

Lew blows another smoke ring. "The Professor."

"No, not him. The other entity. The garbage can that talked with its lid."

"Um, Master Cylinder."

"Yeah, nice recall, Lew! Very nice. Master Cylinder. Master Cylinder. Truly hallucinogenic show. And then there was *Tom Terrific*. Didn't really like that kid. I gotta piss." Stumble to the can, fast, too fast, slam the door shut, and crash my hip against the sink.

"Are you alright?"

"I'm cool." Reach for a catheter, pick up the Purell from the edge of the sink and squirt some on my fingertips. No, that's not the right order, too late now. Rip open the catheter package, it's loud and violent. Okay, now squirt some Surgi-Lube on my hand. Yeah, I had the right order after all, I know what I'm doing. Spread it out on the catheter, ever so evenly, back and forth, like an artisan would. Like a master artist, like Master Cylinder.

This doesn't have to be such a lonely enterprise. "I can do it, Lew! I can stick the catheter in properly even when I'm stoned! No problem!"

Listen for a response above the sound of urine slowly cascading on water. Nothing. I will sing. I look down at the toilet. Think of a song. What's appropriate, given the circumstances? Grateful Dead's "Ripple." How does it go? I should know it by heart. Fuck. "Hey Lew! How does 'Ripple' go?" Somethin' about magical waters. "Lew!" Nothing. Just the sound of urine, making ripples in the water. Maybe it's too loud for me to hear him. "Hey, Lew, do you remember the time we dropped acid and walked naked through the Ann Arbor Art Fair?"

Finally tapped out of pee. How'd the bottle of stout get on the floor, musta left it there. Didn't even knock it over. Interesting. Let's reach down for the stout, take a step and swoop it up like Lew did with the Twinkies on the shoulder of the highway. You can do it, like a shortstop, one motion. Give it a try. Only a bottle's not a baseball, nor a double pack of Twinkies. Bottle goes flying up in the air, clunks the ceiling, falls, and explodes on the floor as my left shoulder crashes against the edge of the sink and I fall on my face. "Ow." Don't feel a thing. That's interesting. I said ow without pain, like Pavlov's Dog.

Fuck. Cheap glass, some tiny bits, beer everywhere. Can't lick it up like Iggy would, my tongue doesn't have calluses. It'd get shredded like Cam's script. Better pick it all up. No way can I do this lying here on my elbows, gotta sit up. Or at least, get on my knees. Alright, move your body, I know, I know, it's hard. Lots of work, and glass everywhere, can't avoid it, too hard, it's cutting me up. Teeny tiny pieces, not like when I worked on a Grosse Pointe garbage truck, over there by the Detroit border. People would leave old glass panes out with their trash. Even storm windows. Couldn't get away with that in the heart of Grosse Pointe. A few people would leave bottles of cold beer for us, but the driver would always take it all for himself. Entitled dickhead right-wing unionist.

Fuck this, I've already got one wound, don't need to go back to doctor what's her name. Doctor Stoned. She was pretty Irish, probably thought I'm an idiot. Underdeveloped for my age. On the road like Willie Nelson, yeah, he's a pothead.

"Hey, Lew!" Still no answer. Didn't he hear the crash and fall? Reach up for the doorknob and the edge of the sink, pull myself up. Ow. Something does hurt, or maybe it's my imagination. Push the door open, oh, you gotta turn the knob and pull.

"Lew?" Wander around this shithole, where the fuck is he? Ouch my shoulder's hurting now, and my right cheek. Hallway door's wide open. Shit, he split. Asshole! Stumble out there. Loud Celtic music from below, it hadn't registered 'til now, so it must be I'm really stoned. Lew probably got the munchies and he's down there eating shepherd's pie. Gross mash, his face in it, out like a light.

The stairs. Can't do that, no way. Too risky, too steep a drop, chute of fast water, they're only half-steps, I could fall between those boulders. Might break my neck and die right down there, in the whirlpool at the bottom. Gotta be careful or you'll get bowled right over by the current. Lickety-split the ice-cold rush fills your waders, and you gasp, as you're off, down the river 'til nothing's left of you but bones. Blood all sucked out by invasive sea lampreys, skin and loose organ meat and entrails gored by lots of baby fish, ripping at your carcass, selfish brutal little aggressors, desperate to eat.

Alright, get a grip, turn around, man. Stagger back in Cam's place and safety, face first into the couch, knees hit the floor, ouch. Hear, feel heart pound, and blood flow. Body breaking down, feel every inch of it, all the maladies at once, heavy breathing rush and all inner systems turned up high, dig-dig-digging my face into the cushion, of the davenport. Wipe it off, try to get straight, wipe it all off, all the maladies.

Don't feel so good, better get back to the toilet. Get up, off the davenport, don't even try to stand up, the river's blown out. Stay low, down on all fours, crawl to the bathroom. Here comes Mister Bill's dog, Spot! Ruff! Crawl, like in the olden days, like when a few of our ancestors managed, somehow, to crawl, or slither, out of the water, through the soft sand, and reach high ground. There's an achievement for you. Way bigger than that "one giant leap for mankind" crap, when we landed on the little galactic ball composed of the kind of gray ash shit that accumulates at the bottom of your charcoal grill. The Moon. Big deal. It's not even that far away.

Gonna puke. Just hold the toilet bowl, hold it with both hands like Doctor Stoned held mine, nice and firm and gentle, too, the one bloody oozing hand how'd it get there and the other one, the top of the thumb's cut, what the fuck did I do now? Shit. New blood, dark red, dripping down the bowl into the water, real red streaks. Cam's red paint? No, that's blood. Rest your chin right there on the edge of the bowl, so when you have to heave, you're prepared. Like a little puppy, feels kinda good cold. Be happy you're really not a dog, cuz you'd be drinking out of the bowl, ruff ruff. It's okay and alright to stay here on the edge with the stain of piss and fecal matter, it's comfortable and besides, your autoimmune system's already shot.

C'mon, puke! I guess it didn't take a lot of higher order thinking for those ancient fish to make it out of the water, just a crazy notion and the will to see it through. Without one bit of technology or know-how. Although they coulda been pretty intelligent. Maybe they were just real limited in terms of their vocal cords and range of motion. Look, Mom, no thumbs, even, but they made it out anyway. Perhaps some kinda ancient nasty fish will come right up in the toilet water, that'd be cool.

Ohhh, vomit, finally, get it out, let it flow, all that bad ganja and stout and brownie mix, the Diet Coke too, yeah, it's a drug. Get it all out, all the shit spinning around the brain, all this shit about society, that's what Lew said. Yeah, well, there's a long history of homo sapiens getting all giddy about possibilities and potentialities. All the overdetermination and overdrive, led by the nation that presumptuous people call America.

Flush, flush, flush it all down. All the maladies. I got through the West Nile disease but the doctors weren't ready for the time I went into, whatchamacallit? Septic shock. I couldn't see anything, just hear them recite numbers, up and down, up and down, then down, down, sounded like they were losing control and I thought, well, so this is it, this is how it goes, clinical death, no epiphany. They're feeble at the wrong time and I'm the only lowdown calm one in the room on account of the morphine and wide spectrum something or other, mix it all together and it made me go blind.

What could I do there in the dark other than focus on the one thing? Get primed for the mind to float up to the ceiling, join all the dead philosophers, and see how disillusioned they are about the state of humanity, since they'd know maybe. Yeah, they were up there with a few saints, everybody in white terrycloth robes and cute little sandals. Hovering, they never have to get up, get dressed, and go to work, they get to just hang out and drink black coffee and smoke all they want and watch TV. Bastards. I never made it that far, somethin' sharp jabbed me in the gut. Coulda woulda probably was Ginny tellin' me, "where the fuck do you think you're going, asshole!" She punched me! I'm fucking blind, trying to float upward, and she punches me! But she's right, women know better than men about responsibility to others. Especially right before Christmas, the kids' presents were already purchased, and she doesn't know where I left the receipts.

Alright, alright, Ginn, lighten up. I'm comin' back. That was it, my one shining moment, I see that now thanks to Lew's bad ganja, fighting off the loss of gravity, willing myself back down with desperate breast-stroke kicks in thin air. I swear I heard a single voice coming from up there on the ceiling, though everybody's lips moved like on *Clutch Cargo*. Coulda been the Voice of the God-Child. It said somethin' about, "who came up with the loony idea that you're supposed to worship a deity, that's really fucked up, like you're still a bunch of pagans or something. And FYI, all the stories in the Holy Books were devised to appeal to primitives, so put them all away and deal with your own shit like frickin' adults." I replied, by telepathy, "I've often wondered about that myself, so there's something You and I have in common." There was no response, which was probably a good thing. This all happened after the doctors put me on a combination of Haldol and lithium so maybe I was hallucinating. Huh. Then they hooked me up to a machine and tied me down for good and I got the ventilator blues.

Ohhh, fuck, here comes more puke. Ohhh. All those maladies, nobody could make sense of them, not even the weirdo infectious disease guy from Russia. It's like Foucault said, when the early curiosity hounds cut through the surface of the skin to see what's underneath, they found a disparate collection of arbitrary shapes, sizes, textures, and colors in random locations. Systems, each having its own economy of bodily functions, accidents with no underlying unity, looping, and nothing to hold it all together except a bag of skin, precluding any possibility of a resolution with anything outside us. Whereas before, before they cut into the gut and called it anatomy, before they realized that discontinuities in languages happened due to random unpredictable shifts in the movements of the masses, before biology and economics and then psychology and sociology and finally psychiatry and cultural anthropology, before the idea that you could safely study literature, before there's even something called literature in the modern sense, which is itself questionable, if you follow Foucault. Before all of that there had been an order, modeled on those silent entities that grow out of the ground and mature in like patterns, in other words, something grounded. Now we're technologies, relay points well beyond artificial limbs and organs, soon we'll have digital implants so the software can read our thoughts and initiate intentions in the world. At that point we'll no longer be people. We'll be an evolved form, like in those kids' video games. The next level.

Ohhh. Feel like death. Lew, where the fuck are you? You can't just go and buy shit from a stranger named Stewie, not these days, it's way stronger than what we had. America doesn't like thought, just talk, and Chicago's all right angles, and ohhh, more vomit. Get it out! Twisted misguided pursuit of knowledge and freedom and social control in the name of the self-made man, get it out, all that sophisticated vulgarity, all the alibis, yeah. The reasonable man standard. Wipe chin, wipe mouth with bloody hand. Wipe it on my sore right cheek. Ouch. All the conceit. Poor innards, Lew, what did you expect of me, my body never did like drugs a whole lot. Best part was waking up with a clear head. That walk we took on acid at the Art Fair, we didn't quite make it to State Street before we freaked out and ran back through the Diag to the LeMans. Local rabbi was handing out invites to the Chabad House, he always asked if I was Jewish, never asked Lew. That time, I could swear, as we ran by, he leaned in to see if I was circumcised.

Back in the day, another day hot as hell, poking papers on the side of the highway for three-fifty an hour, coulda been less. On a prehistoric government plan called Career Education and Training Act, or something like that. Are you kidding me, training for a career poking papers on the side of the fucking Ford Freeway so somebody could count you up in a report to make it look like something in Detroit's actually changed for the better? What an Act. If you were lucky you got to go out once in a while with the Dog Crew to pick up carcasses in the road that fell apart in your hands like that collie did. Horrible stench. Once in a while, one or another of the black guys would look up from poking litter and scan the horizon. Like, this is the reality I'm faced with, this wasteland, what am I possibly gonna do with it? Find a way to make money that's within reach. Not that different from the rural white kids wandering around little shit fall apart towns and trailers with tiny gardens for food like tomatoes and some flowers. Not all that different, not really, except on the surface.

Flush. There's no reason for it, no good reason for all the serious glee and preening that goes on every day from one end of the National Mall to the other by you elected Georgie Porgies, so stop pretending when you're really rationalizing the terms of why one person's got it all and the other's in the toilets. Just because of the order of words. And who controls the programming. At the elementary school Mom taught at, there was no gym, no lunchroom, no playground. Too dangerous to take the kids outside, one of them lost a brother in the drug den across the street. When it got really hot, she'd take them down to the basement for a little relief. No light down there, no chairs. All they could do was stand in the dark and breathe. A funeral director told me he learned to embalm in Chicago on the nameless bodies that were brought in every day or so on trucks from Cook County Hospital. It shouldn't matter, the particular placement of bodies in time and space, that's just for animals in the wild, that's not who we're supposed to be. It doesn't square, none of it, with the message of the schoolteacher nuns.

None of it squares, Cam, thinking you could rise above all these things without bad bruises building up and eventually subverting your big plans. It's pretty damn apparent that things have not quite worked out the way you wanted by whatever crazed formula you followed. Nobody's supposed to be living like this, not you, gone off to Chicago on scholarship. While the scientists endlessly produce superficial empirical snot and take equity in tech spinoffs financed on the public dime, and the quality of public discourse remains lightweight. That which can be seen rather than thought. The therapist, who was a kind of apologist, asked, why does it have to be fair? It was a rhetorical question. You know, Cam, U. Chicago's where all those right wing anarcho-economists taught, how did they manage to theorize around the poverty that surrounds the university walls? Shit, haven't they ever read anything important?

S'cuse me for a moment, head's pounding like a piledriver and the body may have to heave again. Only this time, I really am out, what did we call it? Dry heave. Ohhh. How'd my ear end up down in the toilet bowl, the left ear, the compromised one, it's down there. Or is it the other one? Can't tell for sure. I do feel, I know, that I'm here, resting on one ear in the toilet. I think. Ohhh. Socrates famously said, "The unexamined life isn't worth living." Most Americans would probably say that was just his personal problem. The real Western madness is form over substance, like the way certain values soak up ostensibly free brains and make us willing participants in our own subjugation. Like this, in my own filth, in the madness of this method. What would the commercial news media do, if viewers stopped being roused by so-called "thought leaders" who pander to prejudices? What would happen if everybody recognized that their beliefs about how to live are entirely the product of their own particular circumstances? What if people got out of the mud and actually listened to each other's practical concerns, respecting individual differences? If people sought common ground or compromise for the sake of living in peace?

Fuck, how'd I get pieces of glass in my back, guess that's why it's itchy. Cam, you weren't thinking straight when you spread your blood all over the walls. I get it, you had to throw yourself into it and I really did try to make sense, I did. But "spite me," what the fuck are you talking about, and where's the rip-off? The West's exhausted, I know that. The artist Robert Rauschenberg knew it a long time ago, when he took an Italian art critic's advice and heaved all his work into a deep dark river. The Arno, I believe. Imagine it's pretty dirty and long gone now. "What's the point?" I kept asking all the way here. All this driving, driving blind, is that what intellect is for?

Smoke, in my lungs, open my eyes, how is smoke in my BiPAP, what the fuck? Couch, daylight. Must be a fire! Rip off the mask. No. Lew's sitting in the other room in front of a window, looking out, smoking. Sunlight streams in, revealing stain on the glass. Old dirt. Why doesn't Lew look at me, he must've heard the loud hiss of air just now, before the machine shut off. An illusion, is this a different stage of stoned? Where's my shirt? What's the deal with my thumb? Wrapped up in white, triple normal size. Gotta be an illusion. What the fuck? I thought we did that already, Stone took it off, oh, that's the other hand.

Just watch Lew a minute, a peaceful respite, he's not moving for once. Tumor's a microscopic inchworm, intentional, single-minded and persistent. Like a bullet grinding its way in. No use, can't wait any more, need to get out of my head, connect with the outside world.

"Lew."

"Hey." Quietly.

"What happened to you last night?"

"The question is, what happened to you?"

Sit up. Lew's voice is different, low register. Somber-like. Something's off-kilter, not normal. Am I still stoned? Stand up. Whoa. "Why'd you take off, Lew?"

"Thought I'd give it one last try."

Last try. "When did you get back?"

"I don't know. Late. My cell lost power at some point."

"You were out in the cold all that time?"

"I went in and out of many warm places, Dahd." He's still staring out the window.

"Warm places."

"Got in a little trouble."

"What happened?"

"Up around Wrigleyville, somewhere up there, I was in an alley, peeing against a dumpster and these cops must've been cruising. Pulled up with their light flashing."

"Really?"

"Really. Made me pay them two hundred bucks each to avoid all night in a holding cell."

"You're kidding me. You shoulda had a catheter with you, it coulda provided a plausible excuse."

"Didn't have much money on me after I bought the brownies. Who carries cash these days."

Why doesn't he look at me? Why's he just staring out the window and blowing smoke? Why the low monotone?

"What'd you do?"

"They drove me around 'til we found an ATM I could use."

"You're kidding me."

"Stop saying that. I'm not kidding you. Okay, Rick?"

Ouch. "What happened after that?"

"They drove me back here."

"At least they gave you a ride home."

"I don't have a home."

"Uh."

"You were passed out in the bathroom. You managed to gash your thumb; I assume it was from the broken beer bottle. Blood all over. You've got a nasty bruise on your face."

"I kinda remember. Puking a few times."

"Somebody might've thought you were trying to kill yourself."

"Hm. That's interesting. I don't think so."

"I cleaned you up a little with a washcloth."

"Thanks."

"The side of your head smelled, what'd you do, stick you head in the toilet after you peed and puked?"

"Ah, that coulda happened." What did you expect, Lew, giving me bad ganja?

"Thought you'd be better off on the couch. Don't you remember me putting your mask on? Your eyes were half-open."

"No."

"Your catheter shit is all over the floor in there. What'd you do, faint while you were peeing?"

"Maybe. Where's my shirt?"

"On the floor somewhere. It had all these little pieces of glass stuck in it. And puke."

Try to feel around my back, look for new blood on my hand. "Was my back bleeding?"

"A little. Scratched up pretty bad. The stitches on your other hand were oozing a bit."

"What was the deal with that hash?"

"Coulda been synthetic or something. I puked too."

"Or a bad brownie mix. Maybe your young friend Stewie sprinkled angel dust in it. You oughta go back to the Days Inn and demand a refund from him."

"Why bother."

"You could blackmail him. Threaten to tell management he's dealing at work."

"But then I'd be making life harder for him, wouldn't I? You keep saying, make life easier for people."

"Uh."

"We're not gonna find Cam. He's gone." Lew lights another cigarette, takes a drag and exhales smoke that floats up against the dirty window and seems to stick there. "I looked everywhere last night. He's nowhere around here, he's probably far from here. He could've even left Chicago for all I know."

"You don't think he's gonna come back?"

"That woman downstairs, she said it's been weeks."

"Yeah. We're probably not gonna find him."

"I thought he was reaching out."

"Maybe he was."

"I was too late."

"How were you supposed to be here any sooner? You weren't even in the country."

"I got here as soon as I could. I had appointments with specialists on two continents."

"You did your best, Lew."

"I wish I knew that he's okay."

"Me too."

"There's something I want to tell you." He's still not looking at me, why? "I was trying to repair something."

"Repair?"

"We were together."

"Who?"

"Me and Cam. We had a thing."

"What do you mean?"

"I mean, just what I said."

A thing. My throat's gone dry, stiff like somebody's jammed a wide flat stick, the kind you gotta use to stir up house paint, straight down my throat, trapping air inside against my eardrums. Can't breathe, get out. Get the fuck out. I turn around, grab my coat, and walk right out.

Down the stairs, out the back door, bare-chested into the cold, no catheters. Not going back for them. Fuck. Heavy breath, lungs going hard, heart pounds. Light's too bright. A thing. More than a fling. They had a thing, you heard him. Great well fuck. He coulda told me before. Pissed, yeah, real pissed, yeah, I can't think straight. Why would he have told me, what woulda been the point?

Still, taken for a ride these last couple days, after all the years. So, they had a thing. Lew and Cam, and I'm the guy who didn't know. Slow learner. Piss on them. Put your coat and gloves on, it's freezing, the dried blood one with the holes and the other one, I can't get it over the wounded thumb. Fuck you guys. All those late-night disappearances. The fishing trips, those visits here to see Cam, the alleged blues clubs. Hell, maybe even at Club Maya, yeah probably, all kinds of places to hide there, the walls hold memories, yeah you two going after monster trout. Don't know what this is, can't think, too many chemicals firing at once.

Fuck you, Lew. Just sitting up there. Fuck you. Keep walking, all I can do, go south, adrenalin uptick, past people, lots of them, shopping, walking dogs, pushing strollers. Trying to repair something. Fuck. What about our relationship? Maybe I'm pissed at being left out though I don't think I woulda wanted in. Old sawmill pathway, the two of them, standing there, fly rods in hand, grinning in the sun. Yeah, great, fishing vests and nothing else. Somebody had to hold the camera. Somebody had to be on the margin. Is that what this is? Me along for the ride? Just a passenger, hold the camera, otherwise anonymous? Spite me. Who left who? Or some other thing. Who knows, they do, I can't, couldn't get it all off the floor. Lew knew what the story was about. Of course, he did. Fuck you both. Trains overhead, cold's gotten between the innards of my coat and bare skin, I wasn't prepared, not for this rip-off. Just walk, stop thinking, just walk. Straight, easy to do that in this city, in the Midwest. Down, down. Get away, fast. South. Like Vinnie, like Cam.

Why couldn't he tell me before we got here? I don't give a shit what they did. Do I? Not now. Maybe he couldn't 'til now. His plan. Maybe he had to see Cam first, see what's going on with him, before he could tell me. Maybe they would've never told me. Big deal, it's not about me, it's about him. But then why include me? For what? What do I care, I've got a home. All these people just living, everybody's trying to deal, trying to get by. All right, all right, Lew and Cam, Cam and Lew, fine. Gold Coast, whoopee. I don't give a shit. Do I? Then why am I so pissed off? We were just kids.

Head toward the dirty river, toward the bridge. Trying to kill myself, bullshit. Fuck you, Lew. That's you in the river. You and Cam. On the street, people in suits, mostly white men still, and younger than me, with drawn expressions. Fervent. Foot soldiers, trying to get from point A to point B, or B to C, which amounts to the same thing. Thing is, most Americans just want the security of making it to point A, while the others want to take precedence, justified by a loaded idea of progress and the self-made man. What's really at stake behind the exhortations to do your very best? Suffering doesn't pay except on the way up, where it's idealized, whereas real suffering, out of gas on the side of the road, is never legitimized, never really dealt with, except on the edges, by underpaid social workers. People just drive by.

Walk 'til I can't anymore, legs killing me, don't know why, what's the use. All these fucking miles. Lean against some monolithic building, sheer charcoal gray, smooth as ice. How do they do that, all the effort to make it shine and repel scratches? All that thought and planning and organization and money and brute force applied to matter and digits. Imagine if we put that kind of effort into making it easier for everybody. Look at that security guard on the other side, on the lookout. At a subsistence salary, looking right at me. How about making security mean what it should? Where's the public sphere, where everyone gets a voice, untainted by presumptions? The therapist, who was a kind of social critic, said there's a lot of countries freer than the U.S., although he didn't elaborate what he meant by "freer." That's a problem, that terms like freedom and democracy and equality are never defined, just spouted off as props and code words and weaponized. America's always about rebellion from authority, from the get-go. On the other hand, we're more open to ideas than anybody else on the planet. Less bound by the past.

Gotta go back, nowhere else to go. Don't know how to get to the train for Ann Arbor and don't feel like asking anybody. Risk sounding stupid, saying something nobody'll understand. Gotta go back to Lew, I've got no one else here and he's wasted alone. He said he has no home, that's something. I'll get a cab, because I don't know how to use Uber, even if I had the means. Turn around, raise my hand, the one with the big thumb sticking out like a hard-on, the one Lew wrapped in white too many times. I've never been very good at getting anyone's attention. Too cautious, afraid to go through the yellow light. Maybe it'll help get me noticed, this thumb.

Shit, there goes one, right by me. Alright, now I'll wave, stand out, get off the curb, in the street, if I get hit, so be it.

Here comes another one, he sees me, he's pulling over. Number twenty-eight or nine and something.

I slid in behind the driver. Is it a he? Can't tell. Yeah, it is, gotta be. Comfy, these yellow cabs, with the vinyl upholstery. The kind you can wipe easily, wipe up messes like too much tartar sauce. Or fish guts. Do I still smell like puke? Glance at the mirror, eyes meet the driver's for a second, or would have but for the tint of his shades. I quickly dart mine away, don't mean to pry.

"Just take me up toward Diversey. Please."

Silence. He didn't want to ask. He's got something else on his mind. Does the driver ever think of what needs changing, or does he just want what he's due? It's his domain, I'm just another piece of meat. His own dominium, everybody's gotta have one. I'll look outside at all the pedestrians hurrying along the storefronts and the signs. Nothing there. God, I need a fix of freezing cold Diet Coke.

Look again at the driver from behind, maybe he's one of my kind, all I can see is too much hair under his funny hat. Salt-and-pepper. Could be a lot younger. Maybe he's one of those classic cab drivers, the ones who've checked out for one reason or another, educated or not, they've gone into anonymity. He will be obsolete soon, then what will he do? That hat, like a baseball cap except there's flaps on each side that hang over the sides of his head. Not like Larry's hat back in Michigan, with the furry flaps for winter. This one's more like those desert hats. Meant for summer, meant to reflect white light. Maybe he's from the South. The Florida Keys. What brought him here, why's he wearing it in the winter cold? It doesn't go with the weather, or his dirty mottled mop.

That's far enough, time to get out of this thing. At least it's calmed me down some. Enough to say some kind of goodbye to Lew.

"You can stop here."

Meter says fourteen ten. Hand him a twenty.

"Keep the change." Good deed done, one more moment with a stranger over safely, real paper currency given, nothing's been defaced and I'm out. Close the door gently, don't need to slam it, just let it go, normally.

As he turns toward me. "Thanks, Ace."

Shot. Is that what he said, he said it and I'm shot, no other words, shot, not like the other one, still the shock to the body's the same. Down the nerves and across at once, nothing to do about it, can't be prepared for shock. Cuts you down and too late, the door's closed, couldn't have reversed the laws of Newtonian mechanics, took a step too soon, ice in the waders, river's blown out and the cab's already down the rapids. Ace! That's what he said, no doubt! Air-hunger sick. Bend over. Somewhere deep inside the intestine hisses, angry about the bruise disrupted. What about that cab, it's got a number, but I can barely see it, too much structure blocking my vision.

Fuck! Don't just stand there, move your ass! Run! Maybe it'll stop at a light! A bit of a jog only, can't run with this fucking fake hip. People stare, never mind, do a kind of jog-lurch between them, swinging my arms.

"Excuse me!" Mouth opens to heave in air, come on, move, but keep your eyes ahead, don't drift, stay focused! Where is it, too many bodies in the way, can't see worth shit.

"Excuse me!" There it is! A yellow cab anyway, I think, move, don't lose sight of it again or you're lost for good, maybe you can catch up, if he just follows the river. Please, stay in the fucking river, Cam! There, the light turned red, it's stopped up there! Move!

"Excuse me." Shit, gotta cross here to catch up, fucking traffic, hell if I'm gonna wait, gonna just cut across, fuck you, shit, almost hit me asshole! Light up ahead's changed, gotta get up there, where is it, keep going, there's one up there, is it the right one?

"Sorry!" Fuck, can't see, too many goddamn people! Another light up there, just turned green, can't keep this up, beat, watch it disappear, it must've turned. Driven away with the current. If that was even it.

Don't see any yellow anywhere. It's gone. Fuck! Keep walking, walk fast as if there's still purpose, it's the best that can be done now, what was the fucking number, twenty-nine something, twenty-nine or twenty-eight, four numbers, keep walking, heaving, too hard. Chest pounding. Fuck, gotta stop, stop, hands on knees, concrete down there same as always, catch your breath. Spit. Sweat everywhere, over eyelids, salt in there and wet down my neck, all over my chest, back, keep going, maybe he's up there.

Can't do it. Snot is dripping down my nose. Too late, far-off fantasy, he's gone. Who else says Ace? People brush by, soothes a little like a cold stream can, nobody stops, can't speak. Straighten up, walk slow now cuz it doesn't matter anymore. Unzip coat, cold air, let it in, feels right, like a trout stream. Is that why he turned, is that where he's heading? To the river?

Nerves still on fire, gotta sit somewhere. Calm down someplace, think this through, weigh options, radical doubt, some call that weak. Did he still have ears? Couldn't tell with that dumb hat. Was that why he was wearing it in the winter? No ears left? Or maybe, no lobes, just bloodied and bandaged up. I wasn't prepared. You can read about it, study it, but then you've gotta go do it and I've never been very good at that. Need to sit, clear my mind.

There's a fucking Starbucks, kitty-corner. Of course, it is. Cross the street, still weak legged from the ice-cold shock. Step inside the fish tank, young people tapping away, intensely focused, on the move, or so they think. Haven't lived long enough to be jaded. Nobody looks up, they shouldn't. Sit at a counter along one window, next to a young woman on her iPad, my feet can't touch the ground. Was it him? Of course, it was, who else says Ace?

Look at all these kids, and Cam, driving a cab they'll never take, preparing to take a leap. They got their Uber and bitcoin, no need to carry cash for another, no reason to say a word. What do they know, these kids, of another side? What do I know of it, really? Calm down and think. It was Cam. Shit. Take off the sweaty blood-stained glove. Don't have to keep breathing hard anymore, calm down, way out of shape, growing old. Just breathe.

Scan the café at all these daughters and sons, well-dressed all, I'm the only slob here. No worries, that kid at the Allstate said. Can they know the other side, when they can so easily immerse their minds in continuous feedback? Soon their smart phones will run on solar and really be limitless. They'll only have to direct their thoughts through the software and tell it what they want. To log on, gain access, achieve. Attain desired outcome measured in wealth generated and managed. Whatever's left are just troubles of the mind. Cam. Had to be.

The young woman glances at my wounded hands there on the counter, the merest of glances, then back to the safety of the screen. Like snapping your fingers, just a glimmer. Too messy, she's thinking, something's wrong. I wish he wasn't sitting next to me. Nasty bruise on his face. Smells like puke. How could she understand if I can't find the right words and put them in the right order? It takes two and she's got other things to do here, locked onto her little looking glass mirror. In false transcendence. No, these kids aren't trying to transcend anything, they're engaged, like Lew said. Engaged in the moment, everyone, using, connecting, for a purpose. One big drug den.

Despite my misgivings, these kids have fewer hang-ups about differences than people like me do. Less bound by the past. Or maybe that's just what we see in the computer-aided imagery on the screens. Not sure they know the difference. We're still children at knowing how to govern ourselves, that's what Kant said a couple hundred years ago. When you have toys that get upgraded every few moments, you don't have to grow up. Do they know what's right? These kids are in motion. Fluid. Maybe that's it, somehow. Instead of the black and white way of doing things. Don't leave us behind.

Time to go. Out in the cold again, another door closed, this one with a whoosh. Light's too bright. White light, white heat. Zip your coat up you idiot. Start walking again, down and out toward the Days Inn. Back to this old life with an old friend. I never could keep up with him, only now he's disabled, maybe I can help. Like a friend's supposed to do. If the Diet Coke doesn't kill me first. And you know what, Cam? You don't get Lew. He's mine now. My reparation. Fuckit, maybe I won't even tell him about you. Rock's always about somebody got done wrong. We all did it.

Mourad, Jr.

Lew and me, we're at the tail end of the Boomers where there's just exhaustion and reproduction of the status quo. Tired but not ready to go home. We could follow the Hunter S. Thompson maxim and keep moving. Maybe all the way to Montana on a pygmy pony. It's mostly red but I hear there's a couple college towns not far from the big streams. I could teach my classes next semester online. If the kids complain, I'll tell them to get with the technology.

Yeah. Have flyrod, will travel. Shit, those buttheads Larry and Jerry have our rods. No matter, we'll get new gear. Maybe find someplace to hunker down for the winter that provides shelter from the storm. Learn to tie the right flies while we wait 'til the spring snowmelt has run. Or we could go all the way to the high Sierras for California cutthroat. If it's still inhabitable. There's supposed to be a little town named Weed out there on the Oregon border. We could look for Ollie, he's out there somewhere, probably still promoting rock, selling drugs. Or even Johnnie Wall, another ghost, maybe he's still alive, I hope so. What else is there, besides old friends? Call it white flight. Ginny will understand. Maybe I can eventually come home a fulfilled man. No, that's not realistic at this point. How about just a little more together? Probably not.

I gotta tell Lew about Cam. Not now. That's what we'd always done, it's what we had to do. We had to fuck with each other, fuck each other over, to cope and preserve ourselves. It'll be my soft parade, to keep a secret 'til we get out of the Midwest. When he finds out, Lew'll be pissed off at me for a while because sometimes I make it harder than it needs to be, but he'll get over it—once we step in the river.

We'll get back in the water. River going where it will without people in the way, elbowing and jostling and fighting and killing to be first in line without really knowing why. Water defying expectations, except when people dam it up. Better to make things easier, go for more flowing riffs. The way the water moves, it's never the same ripple.

The other thing with rivers, and all that's around them, the watershed, and what's overhead, and everything in those spaces underneath the edges, each little crevice, is maybe a kind of fluidity. Nothing's black and white. Just lots of tans and grays. What was once a caddis fly, now a couple of leaves and some thistle sewn together. Until it's split apart again to become some kinda sustenance for an invertebrate, or part of a nest for a bank swallow. Or fur for some other creature, a bear, or a beaver, or a homo sapiens that leaves tracks in the wet, unbounded by the civil state.

If I slip in a strange river, and Lew's gone down before me and my waders fill up with freezing cold water, after that initial gasp, maybe then it'll be time to go with the flow. If the river says no, and I get washed up wasted near the edge, I'll try to crawl then walk again. Maybe I can hold on long enough to sacrifice what's left, somewhere soft in the sand.

No, no sense in ever going with the flow. Too easy. Doesn't really matter anyway, cuz I already know what I'm gonna get. Sisyphus, with a fish.

Roger Mourad, Jr., PhD, JD, worked as an attorney and in higher education research for many years. His degrees were earned at the University of Michigan in Ann Arbor. He has authored numerous papers that have been published in international academic journals of social and political thought. When he's not writing or reading, he might be fly fishing, playing in the dirt with native plants, breeding tropical fish, or playing his guitars. *Road Trip to the Future* is his first novel.

Roger Murrad, LL.D., J.D. worked as an attorney and in higher education research for many years. His degrees were earned at the University of Michigan in Ann Arbor. He has authored numerous papers that have been published on international, national, and local and political thoughts. When he is not writing or writing, he might be in the studio playing in the city with other planets, breeding tropical fish or playing his guitar. Rose Tom of the Future is his first novel.

www.ingramcontent.com/pod-product-compliance
Lightning Source LLC
Chambersburg PA
CBHW011214120626
46545CB00008B/2982